ENDORSEMENTS

Ed Quibell is a man who has held onto and honoured God's Word over a lifetime. Because his 'weekly word' flows from that place of lived-out truth, it carries life - I have often found it is just the 'bite' I need for my own day!

Marti Green, Co-founder (along with Lynn Green) of YWAM England

Ed is one of my heroes of the faith and I have always been a huge fan of his 'Morning Thoughts.' His deeply insightful reflections from scripture, as well as his provoking questions and insights, have often been timely exhortations in my own walk with Jesus. I'm very grateful that now his writings are finally in book form. I can't wait to use 'Have a Good Day' as part of my daily time with the Lord. Thanks, Eddie!

Jim Brown, friend and mentor

Ed's thoughts have inspired, comforted and challenged his friends for over twenty years. They hit the mark with unerring regularity and precision. This body of work deserves a wider audience who can benefit from this remarkable treasury of wisdom.

Rt. Hon Lord Michael Bates

It is a privilege and a joy to commend Ed's book - a collection of his daily devotional thoughts that have enriched me over many years. His thoughts are nuggets of gold that have been fashioned in the furnace of suffering and loss when, in 1989, he was struck down with cancer. His thoughts are distilled in the secret place, where God's Word has nourished and strengthened him to continue to trust God daily. Psalm 84: 4-6 sums up Ed's journey: 'Blessed are those whose strength is in you, whose hearts are set on pilgrimage. As they pass through the valley of Baka (a place of weeping), they make it a place of springs'. We drink from the waters he has discovered.

The Revd Canon John Hughes

Receiving a 'Morning Thought' from Ed felt like a healthy shot in the arm each morning: thoroughly biblical, challenging yet graceful, humble and real, and with a light touch and twinkle of fun. This combination reflects the man and servant of the Lord that Ed is. His integrity and love for Jesus are an inspiration to so many. Despite enduring deep suffering, his passion for God and His Kingdom shine brightly. It is a joy to commend this book, which I pray will prove a real treasure to your heart.

Revd James di Castiglione, Rector, Parish of Chanctonbury, West Sussex

Ed played a significant part in me becoming a Christian while at University. Since then he has been a faithful friend who has continued to walk with Jesus even in the face of growing health issues in his life. Every time I read his 'Morning Thought', or speak to him, I am so encouraged by his honesty and desire to live for Jesus. Thanks, Ed, you are a legend.

Revd Ollie Clegg, Rector, St Mungo's Church, Edinburgh, Scotland

I have known many leaders across the world, but few of the calibre of Ed Quibell. Ed has walked along one of the most difficult roads that a human could ever walk, yet he has shone as one of the brightest lights that I have ever seen! I know that as you read 'Have a Good Day' you will experience exactly what I have over the past years from Ed's emails to me... the pure and simple empowering voice of your Father. I know that you will experience each day, a fresh encounter with His love and His praise over you. May Ed's walk and his writing unlock the triumph of our resurrected Jesus inside of you, so you can change your world!

Dave Harvey, Director, Bethel Leaders Network, Redding, California

WELCOMING GOD INTO
EVERYDAY LIFE

HAVE

A

GOOD

DAY

ED QUIBELL

First Published in Great Britain 2022

Copyright © Ed Quibell 2022

Independently published

ISBN: 9798777062550

Edited by Philly Pearson-Miles with Sophie Meldrum

Cover Design and Typesetting by Matt Collison

This book is dedicated to my wife and daughter.

Michelle, thank you for being such a faithful companion on my journey to get here.

Emily, you are our best breakthrough.

I thank God that together we are Team Quibell.

A big thank you to the team that have helped make this possible: Michelle Quibell, Thomasin Quibell, Philly Pearson-Miles, Sophie Meldrum, Matt Collison and Saskia Peill

If you would like to receive Ed's weekly morning thought, email: edsmorningthought@gmail.com

HAVE A GOOD DAY

'My grace is sufficient for you, for my power is made perfect in weakness.' (2 Corinthians 12: 9)

"Ed, you have a rare form of cancer and there is a 50/50 chance of survival."

This was the devastating news my dad delivered to me on Good Friday, 24 March 1989. I was just 18 years old, still at school and about to sit my A-Levels. I was fighting fit, playing sport at national level, full of youthful energy and cockiness, and life was good.

The discovery of cancer came following a routine procedure to remove my adenoids. I began intensive radiotherapy treatment and - miraculously - was given the all-clear five years later. However, the long-term effect of the radiotherapy took its toll long after the cancer had gone, and has caused irreversible damage to my cranial brainstem nerve cells which control hearing, swallow, speech and hormones. These all began to deteriorate over the next 19 years.

In 2008, having just got married and taken on my first appointment as a vicar, my body began to decline at an alarming rate. I was suddenly hit with sickness and weakness. Thirteen years on, my saliva and pituitary glands have stopped functioning; my tongue muscles, jaw, neck and shoulders only allow very restricted movement; I can no longer hear or speak clearly; and I am fed through a gastric tube directly into my stomach.

As a family, we now lead a life of medical appointments, equipment to help me breath, and medication to deal with infection levels. I have known days spent sick and weak in bed, occasional blue light trips to hospital by ambulance, and many nights praying that I will make it through to morning.

Although it would seem at times like our dreams have been dashed and fear often tries to crouch at our door, as a family we are blessed with great joy and hold on with hope for our future. I have known - and continue to know - the faithful grace of God, whose power - unhindered by my physical weakness - surges through me, making all things good and perfect.

Have a Good Day reveals how God's Word has not only sustained me over these last 32 years, but also has kept my faith alive and active. Although my body, my ability to communicate clearly and my identity have been stripped away, God's Word has never let me down. At times, it has given me hope when I was falling apart, or inspired me to walk closely with Father God, despite the difficult circumstances I found myself in. God's Word has reassured me that He is my loving Father and that He never leaves me. In everything I have faced and in every situation I have found myself in, He has constantly been speaking to me through His Word, which, when prioritised and lived out, enables each one of us to 'Have a Good Day', whatever our circumstances.

I first started writing what became known as 'Ed's Morning Thought' in 2000. Since then, these 'thoughts', along with a few verses of scripture which have caught my attention and spoken to me, have been shared with friends, nearly every week via email.

As you read this devotional book, I hope you will catch a glimpse of just how awesome and real Father God is, and experience how relevant His Word is for every situation you face - the good, the bad and the ugly. As Jesus said in Luke's gospel, 'Heaven and earth will pass away, but my words will never pass away.' (Luke 21: 33)

God's Word brings truth and revelation to those reading it. It is 'alive and active...sharper than any double-edged sword.' (Hebrews 4: 12)

When the outlook is bleak, when the light is fading, when troubles are brewing, and circumstances are out of control, it is God's Word that remains steady, true, and life-changing.

Love Ed

April 2022

WELCOMING GOD INTO
EVERYDAY LIFE

LET'S PRAISE GOD!

'But I will sing of your strength, in the morning I will sing of your love, for you are my fortress, my refuge in times of trouble. O my Strength, I sing praise to you. You O God are my fortress, my loving God.' (Psalm 59: 16-17)

We have a wonderful Father who is there for us and protecting us. He has the strength to carry us through.

God loves His children and He loves the sound of our voices praising Him - whatever we may sound like to others!

I have never been able to sing in tune and now I can't sing out loud because my vocal cords are damaged. However, my wife Michelle is a very talented singer and she says that one of her favourite sounds is the one that I make praising God. She loves how I do it in my own way, refusing to be held back by sickness, refusing to be intimidated by others looking on. It is a sound that brings her great joy!

Take some time to praise Him today, to tell Him how much you are thankful for His love for you. Will you praise Him?

When you do, it is amazing how He steps in and meets us where we are.

Abba Father, you are amazing, you are all I need. Hear my praise today. I am so thankful for all you have done and will continue to do for me. Amen.

HAMMER IN YOUR STAKE

'I've pitched my tent in the land of hope.' (Acts 2: 26b, MSG)

A few years ago during a prayer ministry time at the end of a church service, my wife Michelle was given this verse. The woman praying for her shared how, despite all the many complex and painful trials she had faced, she had determined to drive her stake down to pitch her tent firmly in 'the land of hope'.

We were so impacted by this verse that we took it onboard and resolved to do the same: to camp out 'in the land of hope', whatever may come. Many times since then, seemingly hopeless circumstances have raged against us, but we have endeavoured not to let go of hope. At those moments, we have sought to climb inside the covering of Father's tent and bed down with Him.

As we begin this New Year, I encourage you to take a moment to think about what land your tent is pitched in. Is it a land of hope, or does your landscape loom with fear, anxiety or hopelessness?

Why not make this coming year one of hope in God? Resolve to drive your stake down deep into His goodness, and camp out in His faithfulness and love. If you do, what a year it will be!

Father, I choose a new way to live this coming year. Teach me how to live fully in your promises, pitching my tent in your truth. Amen.

HOW TO LIVE A JOY-FILLED LIFE

'You have made known to me the path of life; you will fill me with joy in your presence, with eternal pleasures at your right hand.' (Psalm 16: 11)

Here in this one verse we discover a simple truth: being in the presence of God will bring you joy. You don't have to do anything; you don't have to buy anything; you don't have to win anything.

These days, I am more convinced than ever that joy is one of the key elements to having a good life. Michelle and I have learned that choosing to be joyful releases strength physically, mentally and emotionally. Joy has helped us to escape from many slimy pits of self-pity and fear. Joy is such a good antidote to the dark world we live in.

I am growing in this wonderful adventure of being in His presence throughout each day, increasingly aware of His presence in all I do.

As you spend time in His presence, it will make such a difference to your life and the situations you are dealing with.

Make a simple start and build it up. God is waiting to fill you with joy. Go for it!

Father, I desire to have a joy-filled life. May my time in your presence today fill me with the joy of heaven. Amen.

LET THESE TRUTHS DRENCH YOU

'He called you out of darkness to experience his marvellous light, and now he claims you as his very own. He did this so that you would broadcast his glorious wonders throughout the world. For at one time you were not God's people, but now you are. At one time you knew nothing of God's mercy, because you hadn't received it yet, but now you are drenched with it!' (1 Peter 2: 9b-10, TPT)

There are such wonderful truths in these verses for all of us to be thankful for, but also to believe fully that these words are truth and to live them out each day.

At one time, we were in darkness; at one time, we were not children of Father God; at one time, we did not even understand the magnitude of God's mercy. Wow - what a difference Jesus has made! What an opportunity we have to live in the truth of who we are - children of the living God! What an opportunity to be set free from darkness and live in the light, in such joy and freedom, to be a receiver of God's mercy, knowing that we are loved and forgiven!

So today, simply enjoy these truths, breathe them in, believe them and you will indeed be a wonderful broadcaster of His glory.

Jesus, thank you so much that you died on the cross for me so that I can enjoy a new life - a life that is so remarkable and breathtaking. Amen.

DON'T GO ANYWHERE WITHOUT GOD

'And he said to him, "If your presence will not go, do not carry us up from here. For how shall it be known that I have found favour in your sight, I and your people, unless you go with us? In this way, we shall be distinct, I and your people, from every people on the face of the earth." The Lord said to Moses, "I will do the very thing that you have asked; for you have found favour in my sight, and I know you by name."' (Exodus 33: 15-17, NRSV)

We are called to be distinguishable, to stand out, and to be different. Moses refused to go into the Promised Land unless the Lord's presence went with the Israelites. It was His presence that set them apart from any other people on earth at that time. God did listen, He agreed, fulfilled His word, and went with them, and they settled in the Promised Land.

I am more convinced than ever that being in the presence of God and walking with God is key to everyday life. Inviting Him into every situation we find ourselves in, is the key to living life in all its fullness.

One of the things I do to help me is simply to stop at moments throughout the day, still my body and breathe slowly. Then I silence all my thoughts, so that I am just with the Father. It's amazing what a difference it makes to me and to my everyday life!

We have the remarkable opportunity to carry the presence of God, not only within us, but also upon us. Let's not just be 'normal'. We are called to be different. His presence can change the atmosphere around us. His presence can shift the impossible, and His presence can bring freedom to you and to others.

Father, I choose not to be 'normal' today. I will carry your presence into every situation that I am in. Thank you that you will be with me and we will expand your Kingdom today. Amen.

THE KEY TO LIFE IS SEEKING HIS PRESENCE

'The Lord would speak to Moses face to face, as a man speaks with his friend. Then Moses would return to the camp, but his young assistant Joshua son of Nun did not leave the tent.' (Exodus 33: 11)

The Lord made Himself known to Moses in the tent... His presence was there. However, seeing the impact of God on Moses, Joshua would remain in the tent; he chose to stay. The word 'would' suggests this was an ongoing choice. When Moses left, Joshua chose to stay and savour the privilege and opportunity to grow his own intimate journey with the Lord.

It is interesting to consider and connect this knowledge with how Joshua had the trust and courage needed to conquer Canaan for the Israelites at such a young age. I wonder if he understood how important this was. Not leaving the tent as Moses did, shaped his life, and enabled him to serve God as a young leader with such courage. How did he grasp that understanding, that to be in the presence of God was the right choice, even when he was the only one there?

It is when we choose to be alone in God's presence, being still, that we can hear Him speaking to us as our friend; in doing this, we can find the courage to serve Him and face the demands of the day ahead.

Are you seeking God's presence? Do you make time to connect with God, so that God can be glorified in and through you? Is that not the true purpose of our lives?

Father, I want to know you more intimately than I do now, so that I may bring glory to you in all that I do. Amen.

GIVE SOMETHING AWAY TODAY

'A cheerful look brings joy to the heart, and good news
gives health to the bones.' (Proverbs 15: 30)

'A cheerful look' and 'good news' are powerful tools in our hands today. This verse shows us that these aren't soft and fluffy things, but rather they have the power to change hearts and heal bodies.

Do you really believe that? Do you understand the impact your very countenance has on those around you? Do you have revelation of the healing power that shared testimonies of good news can bring? All around us people are living with heavy hearts and weakening bodies, but we can be the answer! Overflowing with the Holy Spirit, we can bring transformation to people's lives.

So our challenge today is: can we look beyond ourselves and be the 'cheerful look' and 'good news' to someone else today? Let's get practical and bold and think of ways to do this, however big or small. Hold onto the truth that by doing this, we will be bringing joy, wholeness and supernatural health as we release the Kingdom into someone's life.

Be led by the Spirit and don't hold back from sharing testimonies. Think about it: be creative and have fun!

Father, show me how I can share good news and give away joy that will transform someone's life today. Amen.

FOCUS ON HIM

'O God you are my God, eagerly I seek you; my soul thirsts for you. My flesh also faints for you, as in a dry and thirsty land where there is no water. So would I gaze upon you in the holy place that I might behold your power and your glory. Your loving-kindness is better than life itself and so my lips shall praise you.' (Psalm 63: 1-4, NRSV)

What a wonderful set of verses! They are rich and powerful; a great reminder to seek Him, to desire Him and to see His glory.

Often we look for something to feed our hearts, minds and souls. The Psalmist says that God's love is greater than anything else that the world offers. Indeed, verse 4 declares: 'it is better than life itself'. Only His 'loving-kindness' can truly satisfy us and allow us to experience life in all its fullness.

As we fix our eyes on Him, we begin to experience His loving-kindness which 'is better than life itself'. As we do so, He reveals to us His power and glory.

Focus fully on Him today. Try not to find substitutes for His love. Avoid the temptation to run away and hide from His love whilst looking for something else to fill your needs and desires. Embrace the Father's love - it is endless and available for us to enjoy. Be reassured, He promises that you will be satisfied.

Lord, you are the source of life. You have everything that I need in order to live a full and healthy life. May my eyes behold your glory today and praise be on my lips. Amen.

GOD HAS THE BEST PLANS

*'In his heart a man plans his course, but the Lord
determines his steps.' (Proverbs 16: 9)*

Do you ever get frustrated when the things you plan take longer than you
want them to?

One of my heroes in life has been William Wilberforce, a man who
committed his life to abolish the slave trade within the British Empire and
the world. It took him 34 years to achieve that goal and he died three days
after the bill to abolish the slave trade was passed. It's an amazing story. It
was a long and hard road with lots of disappointments and setbacks. Yet
in every setback, in every obstacle that he and his friends faced, God was
guiding their steps and they achieved the impossible.

Today, I pray that you will know that God is with you, that you can keep
walking forward in faith, knowing that those steps that God has planned
for you to take, will lead you in the right direction and you will reach your
goal.

So hold on, persevere, have hope and don't lose heart. There is light ahead
of you; your heart will rejoice, and you will see that God is and has always
been with you. It may not be in the way you expected or in the time-frame
you hoped for, but He will determine your steps.

***Father, help me to continue to trust you even if I can't see the way ahead
of me. I know you will show me the right steps to take so that everything
in the end will be accomplished for your glory. Amen.***

HIS WORD NEVER FAILS

'For no word from God will ever fail.' (Luke 1: 37)

These words were the last words that the Angel Gabriel said to Mary before he left her: "No word from God will ever fail".

I had not seen this translation before from the NIV, but it jumped out at me as I read it and got me thinking, do I really believe that God's Word will never fail? Yes, I love reading His Word, but do I really believe it to be true and powerful, or is it just words that fill my mind?

Smith Wigglesworth, one of the great apostles of faith wrote this: 'It is one thing to handle the Word of God; it is another thing to believe what God says.' [1] As one of my resolutions for this coming year, I have decided to grow deeper in believing that God's Word is more than just words on paper, but to live out daily that His words are actually real and they are powerful. I want to step up to another level and see God's Word in action.

Therefore, can I encourage you to take those steps and also believe God's Word for your life, your family, your work and your ministry? If each of us really believes that His Word never fails, it will be a transformational year.

Father, may my thoughts and my faith be founded on your Word. This year I choose to stand on the truths in Scripture. Amen.

NEVER STOP LOOKING FOR JESUS

*'Once the crowd realised that neither Jesus nor his
disciples were there, they got into the boats and went
to Capernaum in search of Jesus.' (John 6: 24)*

The people had a hunger for Jesus. There was an exciting buzz in the
air. They wanted to be with Him and see what He would do for them.
Jesus had just performed an amazing miracle: he had fed 5000 men
the previous day and they wanted more (vs. 14-15), so the crowds went
searching for him. (The boat business must have made a good profit
that day!)

Today, the danger is that we spend more time searching the world wide
web for answers to our situations than going directly to the One who
created us! More time is spent trying to feed our desires with things that
cannot ultimately satisfy.

Is there still a desire within you for more of Jesus? Will you go searching
for Him today? Or are other things clamouring for your attention? Don't let
today pass you by. Seek Jesus and be changed by an encounter with Him.

*Jesus, I will never give up searching for you. You, and you alone have
the answers I need. Amen.*

ALWAYS SEE THE BEST

'Pray for us. We are sure that we have a clear conscience and desire to live honourably in every way.' (Hebrews 13: 18)

Bill Johnson, Senior Pastor of Bethel Church, Redding, California gives a great definition of what it means to honour someone: 'to celebrate who the person is and not stumble over who they are not'. I am sure that in those days under Roman rule, it would have been so easy to see the bad in people and in situations, and very difficult to live honourably. But the writer of Hebrews wanted to be different, wanted to do the opposite: to live with a Kingdom-mindset, and to counter the prevailing culture. That is why he asked to be prayed for, as this could not be done through hard work alone!

Today, choose to see the gold and the good in people and not the bad. Choose to live honourably and make someone feel valued and loved for who they are. It will bless them, and you never know, your kind word or action may spark something in them that may well change them.

So go for it!

Jesus, you saw the good in your disciples. You saw their potential and you asked them to follow you. Help me today to see the good in others and draw that out in word and deed. Amen.

WARRIOR GOD

'Sing to the Lord a new song, his praise from the end of the earth! Let the sea roar and all that fills it, the coastlands and their inhabitants. Let the desert and its towns lift up their voice, the villages that Kedar inhabits; let the inhabitants of Sela sing for joy, let them shout from the tops of the mountains. Let them give glory to the Lord, and declare his praise in the coastlands.The Lord goes forth like a soldier, like a warrior he stirs up his fury; he cries out, he shouts aloud, he shows himself mighty against his foes.' (Isaiah 42: 10-13, NRSV)

God is a mighty warrior who will triumph over His enemies. He is on your side.

Maybe you have been facing a big issue or have an impossible situation in your life and just don't know how to pray anymore. Isaiah encourages us to worship, to sing, to praise and raise our voice to God, who is a mighty warrior, full of zeal.

Maybe if you have not done so before, instead of praying, why not have a time of worship: singing, rejoicing and even shouting His praise. See how this stirs up His zeal and how the Lord will rise up, march out and fight for you.

God loves it when His children worship Him. Go for it!

Father, thank you that you will step in for me and fight on my behalf today. Amen.

GIVE THANKS TO THE LORD

'Speak to one another with psalms, hymns and spiritual songs. Sing and make music in your heart to the Lord, always giving thanks to God the Father for everything in the name of our Lord Jesus Christ.' (Ephesians 5: 19-20)

Paul, the author of Ephesians, reminds us of a simple, yet profound truth - that we should give thanks to God for everything.

I was encouraged by a friend to learn to give thanks to Father God every morning for at least 10 minutes. Whether it be the big or small things of life (for example health, family and friends, finances, possessions, work, home etc), I have found that thanking Him daily, both in times of peace and in times of crisis, has made such a difference in my walk with Him.

In the battle to conceive our daughter, my wife Michelle and I endured many years of fertility treatment. During one particular cycle of treatment, I found Michelle speaking out thanks and recalling God's faithfulness over her life. When I questioned her, she said that she had just discovered that the treatment hadn't worked and the only option when faced with such a wave of pain and hopelessness was to give thanks to God.

So, if you have not done so for a while, take some time today and give thanks to God for everything, however small it might be. Whether in laughter or through tears, He loves to hear our praise and thanks for all He has done and all He has given us. By doing this, any burdens, worries, stress, hopelessness and many other things, are defeated as our heart and focus come back to God.

It's such a good way to start the day.

Father, hear my sincere thanks for all you have done for me. May my praise and worship be a blessing to you this day. Amen.

LIGHT AND TRUTH

'Send forth your light and truth, let them guide me; let them bring me to your holy mountain, to the place where you dwell. Then I will go to the altar of God, to God, my joy and my delight. I will praise you with the harp, O God, my God.' (Psalm 43: 3-4)

Here are two wonderful words to grab hold of and add to our thoughts today: Light and Truth.

The Psalmist paints a wonderful picture of what these two words can do: they lead us into the dwelling place of God and can help us be in His presence with more clarity and confidence - 'I will go to the altar'; 'I will have great joy and delight'. Being in His presence is the essential part of our spiritual life. He is the source of all we need.

Both Light and Truth help us to move forward with greater freedom. The Light shows us the way out of the darkness, whilst Truth leads us to greater freedom from the lies and troubles of this world.

Let His Light and Truth overwhelm you today and see what a difference they will make in your life.

Ask the Lord to send forth His Light and Truth for you to enjoy.

Father, thank you for these wonderful words: Light and Truth. I ask today that I may be guided by them and enjoy a new lease of life in your presence. Amen.

OPEN MY EYES TO SEE AS YOU SEE

'Be perfect, therefore, as your heavenly
Father is perfect.' (Matthew 5: 48)

How amazing is The Sermon on the Mount! Halfway through it, Jesus says, 'be perfect, therefore, as your heavenly Father is perfect'. As a disciple of Jesus, this is a tough command to live out today.

The well-known author Oswald Chambers writes this: 'being a disciple means deliberately identifying yourself with God's interests in other people'.[2]

So how can we be perfect like our Father? When you meet someone today, make a conscious effort to see them as God sees them, rather than through your own eyes, with your own thoughts, feelings and interests. God's perfect interests in a person may well be very different to yours.

Lord, I know that I am only made perfect in you, therefore, please help me today to be more like you in all that I do and say. Amen.

NO FISHING ALLOWED!

'You will again have compassion on us; you will tread our sins underfoot and hurl all our iniquities into the depths of the sea.' (Micah 7: 19)

What freedom it brings to our lives to know how God, in His great love and compassion, handles our sin: He 'treads it underfoot and hurls it into the depths of the sea'. What a powerful image and what powerful truth!

When we come to the throne of grace and repent, we are forgiven. In fact, it says in Hebrews that God 'will remember our sins no more' (Hebrews 8: 12).

There is a well known quote from Christian author Corrie Ten Boom that elaborates on this verse: 'When God forgives He forgets. He buries our sins in the sea and puts a sign on the bank saying, "No Fishing Allowed".' [3]

I am a keen fly-fisherman and only wish that my hours on the riverbank would equal the time I spend fishing around in the murky waters of regret.

Today, I encourage you to take the truth of this verse and stop fishing! Instead, dive into the waters of grace - live daily and hourly in grace. Keep short accounts with God, be quick to repent and then move forward in freedom.

Our hearts will be lighter and our lives more joy-filled when we live fully free from past regrets and instead live with grace in the present.

Father, today I choose to lay down my 'fishing rod' and to step into grace. I trust you with my past mistakes, and trust that you will restore and mend. Thank you that I am forgiven. Amen.

IT'S TIME TO SEE JESUS MOVE IN YOUR LIFE

'When the wine was gone, Jesus' mother said to him, "They have no more wine." "Dear woman, why do you involve me?" Jesus replied. My time has not yet come. His mother said to the servants, "do whatever he tells you to do."' (John 2: 3-5)

Mary saw, heard and knew everything that her son Jesus was capable of. That is why she said to Him, "They have no more wine." She believed that Jesus would do something to save the wedding feast. Nothing was impossible for Him. And that's why she said to the servants, "Do whatever He tells you to do." Mary knew Jesus, knew where He came from and who He was. She believed in Him.

Do not forget this truth today: nothing is impossible for Jesus.

Are you in a tight situation? Do you need a supernatural breakthrough at home, at work or even personally within your own heart? Raise your belief in Jesus and, like Mary, be specific with your request. It is time for Him to step in and help you now. He is more than capable.

Jesus, I want to believe in you for more today. I know you are willing and able to do miracles in my life. Amen.

DON'T GO WITH THE FLOW

'And let us consider how we may spur one another on towards love and good deeds... but let us encourage one another.' (Hebrews 10: 24-25)

Today's society tends to do the opposite of 'encouraging one another'. There seems to be a focus on bad-mouthing one another, pulling people down and trampling over their feelings. We need to be different to the world around us, even though we are called to be 'in the world but not of the world' (See John 17:1; 14–15).

One of the principles I use in life is this: "Don't say anything to someone else unless you can say it to their face." Just imagine if everyone did that, it would stop the spread of gossip and certainly make life much easier.

So let's impact the world around us. Let's encourage everyone we meet today. Let's spur them on towards what is right and noble. Let's be kind, honest, speak the truth, and share feelings with friends, family and colleagues face to face.

Holy Spirit, will you guide me today, so that my words, my actions and my thoughts may be pleasing to you. Amen.

WILL THE REAL ME PLEASE STAND UP

'Then Saul dressed David in his own tunic. He put a coat of armour on him and a bronze helmet on his head. David fastened on his sword over the tunic and tried walking around because he was not used to them. "I cannot go in these," he said to Saul, "because I am not used to them," so he took them off.' (1 Samuel 17: 38-40)

David the shepherd boy knew his identity. He knew who he was and where his strength came from. It was not the armour that would protect him, but God. It was not in the sword, but in the sling.

Are people, circumstances, past mistakes or words spoken about you, hampering you from being who you are created to be? Is it time to strip these off and stand up as who you really are?

A good place to start today is to remember your true identity: you are a child of the living God, you are good enough for Him and He loves you.

Father, today I will stand up in the truth that I am your child. I am your precious friend and you are with me. I will not be influenced by my past mistakes; I am a new creation. Amen.

GOD LOVES IT WHEN WE ACKNOWLEDGE HIM

'When Jacob awoke from his sleep, he thought, "Surely the Lord is in this place, and I was not aware of it."' (Genesis 28: 16)

I love this verse of scripture, it's such a powerful truth.

Jacob woke from his sleep and although he knew that God was there, somehow he hadn't recognised Him. Perhaps he was tired from a long day so just set up camp and went to bed.

I know that feeling. I have done that loads of times, just crashed out and haven't even acknowledged God's presence with me. But God wants us to acknowledge His presence and recognise that He is with us wherever we are. He loves to answer our requests and draw near.

Chuck Parry, Director of Bethel Healing Rooms, Redding, California often says that to begin walking in the supernatural, the first step is to simply recognise that 'He is already here'. This is a simple truth that needs to be remembered every day: God is with us, He is Emmanuel.

Wherever you go today, ask God to reveal Himself to you so you can be aware of His presence with you, and if He is with you, there is nothing you can't do.

Father, today I don't want to miss out on your presence. I will acknowledge that you are with me and that you will bless me and be by my side. Amen.

TAKE THAT STEP FORWARD

'They go from strength to strength, till each
appears before God in Zion.' (Psalm 84: 7)

We can so easily become stagnant and settle for just getting by, but the Psalmist encourages us in this verse to step forward, because when we do, we find our strength in God and not in ourselves.

In His strength, we can build His Kingdom on earth; in His strength, we will reach our goal; in His strength, we can have supernatural encounters; and in His strength, life can be lived as it should be.

Are you moving forward? Are you growing stronger and stronger in your walk with God?

Today, why not check and see if there is an area of your life that is not moving forward and not going 'from strength to strength'.

Father, give me the strength to take that step forward today. I need to move on and become stronger in who I am and who you made me to be. Amen.

IT'S TIME FOR SOME NEW WINE

'Neither do men pour new wine into old wineskins. If they do, the skins will burst, the wine will run out and the wineskins will be ruined. No, they pour new wine into new wineskins and both are preserved.' (Matthew 9: 17)

Is it time for a new wineskin and new wine in your life? Make this year, a year of fresh breakthroughs. All we have to do is allow Jesus to pour His new wine into us.

Why do we find this so hard? We can so easily remain in our old 'wineskin'; in our restricted attitudes, be set in our ways, bound by our own perspectives of life and stuck in our own thinking; but we miss out on the new wine that Jesus wants us to have.

God wants to do something new in your life. Will you let Him pour His new wine into you and expand and enlarge your vision?

Lord, please remove any old wine and old wineskins from my life. May I have a new wineskin and some refreshing wine today. I want to change so that I can walk in your ways. Amen.

IS IT TIME TO STAND OUT?

*'The plan seemed good to Pharaoh and all his officials.
So Pharaoh asked them, "Can we find anyone like this
man, one in whom is the spirit of God?... there is no-one
so discerning and wise as you."' (Genesis 41: 37-39)*

I am sure you know the story of Joseph: favourite son, sold into slavery, thrown into prison, forgotten and then called in front of Pharaoh to interpret his dreams. What did Pharaoh see that day? He saw a man on whom the Spirit of God rested, a man who was discerning and wise.

Joseph had not allowed his circumstances to overwhelm him and define him, but instead he chose to keep upright and humble, and the Lord God blessed him. When his hour came, Joseph stood out and was different.

How will people see you today?

Today, ask for God's Spirit to rest upon you, then people will see the real you - alive in Jesus! I encourage you to take some time to connect with your Father who loves you very much, and ask to be refreshed in the Holy Spirit.

Father, only you can make a difference in my life. Today, I ask you to refresh me in your Holy Spirit so that you shine through me and that others may see you in me. Amen.

YOU CAN DO IT

'The angel of the Lord appeared to him and said to him, "The Lord is with you, you mighty warrior." Gideon answered him, "But sir, if the Lord is with us, why then has all this happened to us? And where are all his wonderful deeds that our ancestors recounted to us, saying, 'Did not the Lord bring us up from Egypt?' But now the Lord has cast us off, and given us into the hand of Midian." Then the Lord turned to him and said, "Go in this might of yours and deliver Israel from the hand of Midian; I hereby commission you." He responded, "But sir, how can I deliver Israel? My clan is the weakest in Manasseh, and I am the least in my family."' (Judges 6: 12-15, NRSV)

I don't know about you, but I can easily forget who I am and fall into the trap of thinking that I am no good at this, or can't do that, or that nothing works for me...

Gideon didn't think much of himself either: 'I am the least in my family'. He had pretty low self-esteem, but God saw his gifts and talents. God always sees the best in us and knows our gifts and our potential. In Him, you are a mighty warrior, fully armed and equipped to face the enemy or any challenge that comes your way.

Today, remind yourself of who you are - a child of the living God, loved, valued and equipped by Him. Embrace this truth and believe who He says you really are.

Father, help me believe that in you I can do it - I can make a difference, I can be this and do that. Thank you, Father, that you believe in me. Amen.

FAITH IN ACTION

'When Jesus heard this, he was astonished and said to those following him, "I tell you the truth, I have not found anyone in Israel with such great faith."' (Matthew 8: 10)

I remember being in a playground with my daughter, pushing her on the swing. There was another lady there doing the same. I noticed she had a cotton bung in her ear, so I asked her what was wrong. She said she had a really bad infection and was in quite a lot of pain. I stepped out in faith and asked if I could pray for her. I simply said, "In Jesus' name, infection go." Shortly afterwards, my daughter and I left the playground and went home.

Three days later a friend came up to me and said, "Did you pray for a lady in the playground the other day? Well, she was healed instantly!" Wow! I was astonished! And we celebrated, and praised and thanked God.

Will Jesus be astonished by your faith today?

Father, help me today to walk in faith and believe more than I can see right now. Jesus, thank you that you inspire me to go forward in faith in you, and I look forward to seeing what you will do through me. Amen.

SEEING PEOPLE FOR WHO THEY ARE

'When Simon Peter saw this, he fell at Jesus' knees and said, "Go away from me, Lord; I am a sinful man!" ... Then Jesus said to Simon, "Don't be afraid; from now on you will catch men."' (Luke 5: 8; 10b)

Jesus is remarkable. Sitting in the boat with Peter, He deals with him with such compassion and grace. He builds him up and reveals his destiny: "you will catch men". There is no criticism, no judgement, just compassion, grace, love and words of truth.

How many of us would do the same if a similar situation arose in front of us? If someone fell on their knees and confessed their sins to us, how would we respond? I think our natural response might be to get them to repent, or even highlight further where they are getting things wrong. Or maybe we might even be slightly wary of them, seeing them as a bit 'messed up'. Would you want them to join your ministry?

Jesus' response is so different to that. Instead, He comforts and reassures Peter and brings to life the gold that lies within him. The impact on Peter and all his companions was profound. That day they left their fishing business and followed Jesus (v. 11).

Today, let's see people through the eyes of Jesus; see their potential, affirm them and release them into their destiny.

Lord, open the eyes of my heart to see people as you see them. Amen.

FELLOWSHIP IS A PRECIOUS GIFT TO ENJOY

'We proclaim to you what we have seen and heard, so that you also may have fellowship with us. And our fellowship is with the Father and with his Son, Jesus Christ.' (1 John 1: 3)

At the heart of fellowship is intimacy, honesty, commitment, love and time together. It is so important that we spend time with the Father, just as Jesus did, in order to develop deep intimate spiritual communion with Him.

God's desire is to have fellowship with you, and His Son Jesus desires the same.

Would you be confident to say that today, your fellowship with the Father and with the Son is good? Why not spend time with the Father and with Jesus today so that you may strengthen your fellowship with them.

Father, thank you that I don't walk alone because you are with me today. May I be more aware of your presence and your love for me. Amen.

TIME TO TRUST GOD

'O Lord Almighty, blessed is the man who trusts in you.' (Psalm 84: 12)

Blessed is the man or woman who trusts in God.

Wow, I don't know about you, but I love to be blessed by God! This verse implies that as we trust Him, He blesses us.

Are you going to trust God today? Are you in a season of your life where things are not going as planned - financial hardship, relationship unease, unemployment looming or health issues? Trust means you can simply say, "God, will you sort this out for me? Please take over."

Will you put your trust in Him today? He is waiting to bless you.

Father, I will trust you to step in and help me today. Amen.

DON'T LOSE YOUR FOCUS

'When you have eaten and are satisfied, praise the Lord your God for the good land he has given you. Be careful that you don't forget the Lord your God.' (Deuteronomy 8: 10-11)

Does God truly satisfy you? Is He all you need in life, or do you seek comfort elsewhere?

For 40 years, Israel had been in the desert, and every day God had provided manna for them in the morning. But that was about to change as they entered the Promised Land. They were entering into a good land, which would bless them more than anything they had known in the desert... but they were warned not to forget God. Why?

How easy it is to forget God when all things are going our way! We must keep our focus on God all the time because only He can satisfy us.

How do you feel when you perceive that provisions and blessings don't come your way? Are you still satisfied? Does He fully satisfy your needs today, or do you need something else to help you?

Today, why not spend some time remembering and thanking God for providing all your needs.

Lord, thank you for meeting all my needs. I choose to focus on you to help me move forward in the journey you have for me. Amen.

NOT ON YOUR OWN

*'He came to his hometown and began to teach the people in their
synagogue, so that they were astounded and said, "Where did
this man get this wisdom and these deeds of power? Is not this
the carpenter's son? Is not his mother called Mary? And are not
his brothers James and Joseph and Simon and Judas? And are
not all his sisters with us? Where then did this man get all this?"
And they took offence at him.' (Matthew 13: 54-57a, NRSV)*

Something had changed in Jesus and people couldn't quite understand how their local lad had changed so much and they were a bit upset by it! It says, 'they took offence at him'.

Some people don't like change. What had happened to Jesus? What had brought about that change? What had enabled Him to operate with miraculous powers or to have greater wisdom than most? He had been anointed by the Holy Spirit (Matthew 3: 16) and moved and worked in the power of the Holy Spirit.

During my time at university, I was able to share my faith with many of my peers and, through God's grace, I saw many come to choose Jesus for themselves. However for me, this was a season when I was very passionate about the Word, but had very little understanding of the Holy Spirit. Having graduated, I moved to London and started to meet people who understood how to move and work in the power of the Spirit. This had a huge impact on my life and set my course for the next 30 years.

So today, are you moving and working with the help of the Holy Spirit in your life? Be sure to be asking for help from Him. It will radically change your life.

Father, I need more of your presence and power in my life today. Holy Spirit, I ask you to fill me afresh today so that I can do all that you ask me to do. Amen.

KEEP WAITING... GOD WILL STEP IN

'I am like a deaf man, who cannot hear, like a mute who cannot open his mouth; I have become like a man who does not hear, whose mouth can offer no reply. I wait for you, O Lord; you will answer, O Lord my God.' (Psalm 38: 13-15)

I think these verses sum me up pretty well! This is why I love reading the scriptures because they continue to speak to me directly. (I encourage you to keep reading them, particularly if you have lapsed a bit in that area of your spiritual journey). God wants to speak to us through His Word. It is His primary way of communicating with us.

Despite all David's troubles, he knew deep down that God would answer his prayers. He had mastered waiting and trusting in Father God. So if you are facing a tough time in life right now, or finding it hard to hear what God is saying to you, be confident that God will answer your prayers. He has heard you and He will act. He is a good, good Father.

Keep waiting in faith.

Father, may you open my ears to hear you speaking to me. I choose to wait in peace and confidence, knowing that you will answer me and that you will come and help me. Amen.

NEVER, NEVER GIVE UP

'Even to your old age and grey hairs I am he, I am he who will sustain you. I have made you and I will carry you; I will sustain you and I will rescue you.' (Isaiah 46: 4)

I think I have a few grey hairs these days... but what a wonderful word from Father God!

Recently, Michelle and I have been involved in giving more hands-on care to my Dad in the autumn of his years. This has been such a blessing and a privilege, though challenging at times. What has impacted us both the most, is that although my Dad has become physically weak and dependent on others to help him, the thing that remains is his love for Jesus. His faith and relationship with God is like a sparkling jewel, sustained and strong when everything else has been stripped away. God is sustaining him, even to old age!

God promises that He will sustain you. He will carry you and He will rescue you. These are powerful words and promises to take hold of and believe in. We don't have to face today's struggles on our own.

Ask Father God to fulfil these promises for you today. You are not alone, He is with you. He will give you strength and hope to live a full life.

Father, thank you that you promise to sustain me, to carry me and to rescue me. I know you will not leave me alone and that you are with me throughout this day. Amen.

YOU ARE MORE VALUABLE

'Look at the birds of the air; they do not sow or reap or store away in barns, and yet your heavenly Father feeds them. Are you not much more valuable than they?' (Matthew 6: 26)

This one verse is so important for us to really believe and understand deep down in our consciousness. To help with this, I look across our garden each morning and see the birds eating away at the food I have put out for them, and every time I do, I say to myself, "Ed, are you not much more valuable than those birds? God will take care of you."

Since I have started this daily ritual, I have seen this truth increase and become more real for me and I believe in it more than I did before. I am enjoying discovering more deeply, how valuable I am to God, fully taking on board that He will care for me. To encourage me further, I have had some timely answers to specific prayers, and through these I have felt more valuable in God's eyes than I have done for a long time.

So now, when a lie comes into my mind or a tough situation arises, I am ready for it, knowing that I am important and loved by Him and so the lies seem to bounce off me more quickly than they did before.

I encourage you again, to seek to believe God's Word more than you have done before. Perhaps take this verse and start believing it. You are so much more valuable to God than you think you are right now.

Father, thank you that I am more valuable to you than the birds in the air. Today I choose to believe this and know that you will care for me. Amen.

DO NOT TAKE YOUR EYES OFF THE LORD

'Manasseh was twelve years old when he began to reign; he reigned fifty-five years in Jerusalem. His mother's name was Hephzibah. He did what was evil in the sight of the Lord, following the abominable practises of the nations that the Lord drove out before the people of Israel. For he rebuilt the high places that his father Hezekiah had destroyed; he erected altars for Baal, made a sacred pole, as King Ahab of Israel had done, worshipped all the host of heaven, and served them. He built altars in the house of the Lord, of which the Lord had said, "In Jerusalem I will put my name." He built altars for all the host of heaven in the two courts of the house of the Lord. He made his son pass through fire; he practised soothsaying and augury, and dealt with mediums and with wizards. He did much evil in the sight of the Lord, provoking him to anger.' (2 Kings 21: 1-6, NRSV)

Manasseh did evil in the eyes of the Lord.

Perhaps many of us would be confident to say that we are not doing evil things and evil practices in the eyes of the Lord. But as I have read this passage a few times, it has encouraged me to sit still and search my heart and mind. Am I putting up subtle idols in my life? Am I consulting or reaching for other things before I turn to God? Am I worshipping or doing things or thinking things that are not good and not pleasing to the Lord God Almighty? Am I provoking Him to anger?

Take some time today to make sure you are right in the eyes of the Lord. Is your life and lifestyle good and pleasing to Him?

Father, search my heart and mind and keep them pure, so that my life may reflect you and your glory. Amen.

KEEP POSITIVE

'Enlarge the place of your tent, stretch your tent curtains wide, do not hold back; lengthen your cords, strengthen your stakes.' (Isaiah 54: 2)

Our walk with God is all about growing and moving forward. As someone once said, 'Always keep positive and moving forward.' Today, our reading encourages us to enlarge, to stretch wide, to lengthen and to 'strengthen your stakes'.

Is it time for a change in your life, your work situation or family life? Perhaps you are approaching a new season?

Don't hold back from taking that step of faith that is needed for God to move and bless you. Once you take that step, He will be faithful. He will 'enlarge your tent'. He will bless you.

Father, give me faith today to make that bold step to go forward and to trust you. Amen.

MAKE THE KINGDOM REAL TODAY

*'When Jesus had called the Twelve together, he gave
them power and authority to drive out all demons and
to cure diseases, and he sent them out to proclaim the
kingdom of God and to heal the sick.' (Luke 9: 1-2)*

I love this scripture. Jesus gave His disciples the power and authority to advance His Kingdom on earth. Jesus was saying, 'go and show people what my Kingdom is like'.

Jesus is saying the same thing to us and we too have His power and authority.

How will you be showing God's Kingdom in your life today? Will you step out and pray for someone who needs help or healing? Will you share a prophetic word of encouragement with someone? Will you bless someone with extravagant grace?

Let's be demonstrating God's Kingdom on earth today.

Jesus, thank you for giving me the same power and authority as the disciples had. May I live for you and take every opportunity to expand your Kingdom today. Amen.

SEEK THE LORD'S WISDOM

'The shepherds are senseless and do not enquire of the Lord; so they do not prosper and all their flock is scattered.' (Jeremiah 10: 21)

This simple truth is so often forgotten: we fail to communicate with God on every level.

The great leaders in the Old Testament and even Jesus The Great Shepherd were human beings, who only did what the Father showed them to do (see John 5: 19). They all 'enquired of the Lord'.

Today, I encourage you to enquire of the Lord, asking Him what He thinks; what His views are; what is the way forward for you; and what His plans are for your life. Let Him be more involved in your daily life and in the decisions that need to be made. Often, when we fail to do this, we make choices that can lead us out of peace and cause complications which were never intended for us.

Let's be sure that we enquire of the Lord, confident that He has the best plans for us.

Lord, I need you to give me directions in every area of my life. Today, may I seek your advice and may I hear your wisdom and make the right choices. Amen.

ALWAYS BE THANKING GOD

'Give thanks to the Lord, for he is good; his love endures forever.' (Psalm 118: 1)

Psalm 118 is a wonderful reminder of the importance of learning to give thanks to God. If you take up an attitude of thankfulness every day and find things to be thankful for, it is amazing how troubles, worries and everything else that life throws your way seem insignificant. The Psalmist seems to understand this and throughout the Psalm (well worth a read), he gives thanks to God, despite the tough situation he is going through.

Michelle and I have found this so helpful in times when life has become challenging. When my health has taken a turn for the worse, we have turned our concerns into praise and thanksgiving to God. It makes such a difference.

So today, do spend some time thanking God that He is good and for everything that He has given you. From the rising of the sun to the setting of the sun, be praising and thanking God.

Father, thank you that you are good and your love endures forever. May I always be thanking you for everything you have done for me. Amen.

YOU ARE SPECIAL

'You will be a crown of splendour in the Lord's hand, a
royal diadem in the hand of your God.' (Isaiah 62: 3)

I love this verse and the truth within. It gives an amazing picture of how God sees you.

A crown of splendour and a royal diadem were symbols of beauty, wealth and importance. God delights in you and you are special and valuable to Him. The way that God sees you is that you are simply stunning!

Today, allow this truth to sink deep into your heart. The more we are secure in who we are in God's eyes, the more freedom we will enjoy for ourselves, and in turn we will have a greater impact on others.

Father, help me today to believe that I am special and loved by you today. Amen.

BE A LIGHT FOR PEOPLE TODAY

'Arise, shine, for your light has come, and the glory of the Lord rises upon you. See, darkness covers the earth and thick darkness is over the peoples but the Lord rises upon you and his glory appears over you. Nations will come to your light and kings to the brightness of your dawn.' (Isaiah 60: 1-2)

I imagine each of us would have our own idea about what 'darkness' it is that covers the earth.

I heard recently that people are more in debt than they were in 2008, before the financial crash. At the time of writing, we are in a year of Covid-related lockdown and experiencing the huge consequences of that on our nation and on the world.

Whatever your view is, it seems that darkness really is covering the earth. There is only one answer for us: we must turn to God.

Today, we need to allow the Lord's glory to rise upon us so that we can be a light in this dark world. As we allow His glory to arise and shine in us, the darkness will retreat and people will be drawn to Jesus.

Be a light today in this dark world and allow God's glory to be upon you.

Father, today I want to be a light in this dark world. I want to point people to you, for you have the answers to everything. May I carry your glory with me today. Amen.

LET'S MOVE TOWARDS FORGIVENESS

'Then Peter came to Jesus and asked, "Lord, how many times shall I forgive my brother when he sins against me? Up to seven times?" Jesus answered, "I tell you, not seven times but seventy-seven times."' (Matthew 18: 21-22)

Forgiveness is such an important part of our walk with Jesus and in these verses He encourages us to forgive. The opposite - unforgiveness - is such a powerful weapon which the enemy uses against us. If we do not pursue forgiveness and instead live in unforgiveness towards someone, we become trapped in hurt, anger and bitterness. Unforgiveness can lead to such destruction of oneself and others. It is much better to seek to forgive than to sit back and live in unforgiveness.

I remember praying for someone who had suffered with a back problem for 15 years. As we prayed, I had a sense that this person needed to forgive someone. We gently prayed this through and they forgave someone who had hurt them over 15 years before. Once she had done that, we prayed again and her back was immediately healed.

Is there someone you need to forgive today? Seek God's help, move into forgiveness, and enjoy the freedom that it brings. As you forgive, remember before God, to engage with your feelings about how that person made you feel. At the heart of forgiveness is letting go and trusting the situation to Father God, because He is the perfect judge, not you.

Let's not live in unforgiveness. It is so damaging for us and that is why Jesus put such emphasis on the need to forgive. It is so key to living life in all its fullness.

Jesus, thank you that you have forgiven me. Please help me take bold steps towards forgiveness of those who have hurt me. Amen.

IS IT TIME TO DREAM A BIT MORE?

'While they were going out, a man who was demon-possessed and could not talk was brought to Jesus. And when the demon was driven out, the man who had been mute spoke. The crowd was amazed and said, "Nothing like this has ever been seen in Israel."' (Matthew 9: 32-33)

Jesus did amazing supernatural miracles during His time on earth and He continues to do the same today. Miracles, healing and restoration are all part of God's Kingdom.

But what I want to draw your attention to is what the crowd said: "nothing like this has ever been seen in Israel."

Why not take some time today to dream about what you would like Jesus to do, or what you would like to be involved in, so that people could say about you, or your family, or your ministry, or your church, or your work, that "nothing like this has ever been seen in xxx".

Jesus is real and Jesus will work with you so that His Kingdom will grow.

Start dreaming and have fun!

Father, today I want to step out and believe in you for more. I have all I need to do even greater things for your Kingdom today. May I dream with you and see your Kingdom come. Amen.

THERE IS SOMEONE OUT THERE WHO NEEDS YOU TODAY

'Jesus stopped and called them. "What do you want me to do for you?" he asked.' (Matthew 20: 32)

In the busyness of His day and surrounded by a large crowd of followers, Jesus stopped and took an interest in two blind people who were calling out to him. They needed help and Jesus was willing to stop and help. All too often I think I am too busy to stop and help, or I am preoccupied with my own plans and so miss someone who is in need of help.

Today, let's look beyond ourselves and see if there is anyone out there who is calling out for help and who we need to stop for. Think about the question that Jesus asked them: "What do you want me to do for you?" It is the same question that we could ask them. That person may well be willing to engage with you, open their hearts and share their specific need.

Let's be looking and listening today to find out who it is that Jesus wants us to stop and interact with.

Jesus, today may I walk like you and be willing to stop and interact with the person who needs to meet with you today. Amen.

IT IS TIME FOR A MIRACLE

"But so that we may not offend them, go to the lake and throw out your line. Take the first fish you catch; open its mouth and you will find a four drachma coin. Take it and give it to them for my tax and yours." (Matthew 17: 27)

The tax collectors were after Peter and Jesus, wanting to make sure they were paying their dues. (That sounds familiar!) They were faced with a problem: what should they do? Peter would have had to go out and fish all day long and then sell the fish to pay their taxes. But not so with Jesus. There was another way, a different solution, a divine intervention. Jesus instructed Peter, "Go and catch one fish and take the coin from its mouth and pay the tax". (I have been fishing for over 40 years but have never found any coins in the mouths of any of my fish!)

Jesus may have a solution to your situation right now; listen to what He has to say to you. He may well have divine provision or insight that will change your situation.

Don't be slogging away at life in your own strength - God wants to help you like He helped Peter.

Father, you are the God of amazing miracles and nothing is beyond your capacity to provide. So today will you release the storerooms in heaven for me. Amen.

IT'S TIME TO PROCLAIM

'I will not die but live and will proclaim what the Lord has done.' (Psalm 118: 17)

We are not sure who the author of Psalm 118 is, but the underlying message is one of being delivered and winning a tremendous victory over the enemies of Israel. The Psalmist encourages Israel at this time to celebrate and give thanks to the Lord for this victory.

We can also live in victory today, because Jesus has won a great battle for us on the cross 2000 years ago. And not just for us, but for all of humankind. So we must learn to proclaim all that the Lord has done for us while we are alive. It is a good thing to give thanks privately to God because gratitude can transform our lives. However, we are also encouraged to proclaim with words and deeds what God has done for us.

So let's start today and make this a year of proclamation, telling others about everything that God has done for us and reminding others what Jesus has done for them.

Don't keep it a secret - tell others your story as well as your breakthroughs.

Father, give me the courage to proclaim more about who you are and what Jesus has done for the whole world. Amen.

TAKE THAT STEP OF FAITH

'"Lord, if it's you," Peter replied, "tell me to come to you on the water. "Come", he said. Then Peter got down out of the boat, walked on the water and came towards Jesus.' (Matthew 14: 28-29)

It was the middle of the night and the disciples thought they had just seen a ghost, but Jesus called out to them and said, "Take courage! It is I. Don't be afraid" (v. 27). At that moment Peter clearly thought that it would be a great time and a great place to trust Jesus a bit more! I do love Peter - He reminds me of myself: spontaneous, brave and often saying things when I don't really know what they mean! "Tell me to come to you on the water, Jesus." The other disciples must have turned and looked at each other, thinking, 'oh no, what's he doing now? He's put his foot in it again!'

But Jesus said to him, "Come" Peter stepped out of the boat and went to join Jesus on the water. That must have been a whole new level of faith for him and for the rest of the disciples!

I have recently read the life story of Hudson Taylor, the man who took the gospel of Jesus to China back in the 1860s. It is an amazing story of faith. When he was 20, he wrote this in his diary: 'I felt that I could not go to China without having still further developed and tested my power to rest upon His faithfulness.' [4]

Like Peter, and like Hudson Taylor, take that step of faith so you can see the impossible happen and your faith in God will be even stronger.

Father, where do I need to trust you in a new way today? Where do I need to step out to allow you to do what only you can do? I want to step out and believe in you for more. Amen.

DON'T MISS YOUR SLOT

'At daybreak, Jesus went out to a solitary place. The people were looking for him and when they came to where he was, they tried to keep him from leaving them. But he said, "I must preach the good news of the Kingdom of God to the other towns also, because this is why I was sent." And he kept on preaching in the synagogues of Judea.' (Luke 4: 42-44)

The ministry of Jesus was kicking off. He was healing the sick, casting out demons and everyone was amazed and astonished by what He was doing. News about Him was spreading very fast. Jesus was going viral! He had His purpose and He was determined to keep focused, despite the pressure from the people to stay with them. He was in demand and was busy.

Is that a bit like your life today? I believe the key for Jesus to keep on track was to get time alone with His Father. He would go to a solitary place to be with Him. He would not allow a busy schedule to stop Him from having time with His Father.

Today, try to find that time with the Father for yourself, space to connect with Him, recharge your batteries and gain insight, wisdom and encouragement from Him. It will help you keep focused. It does not have to be a long slot, but just enough to be alone and lock eyes with Him and know you are His beloved child.

Father, I want to connect with you, alone, just you and me, so that I can know that I am loved and cherished by you. Amen.

JESUS IS FULL OF HEAVEN

'When he saw Jesus, he fell with his face to the ground and begged him, "Lord if you are willing, you can make me clean." Jesus reached out his hand and touched the man, "I am willing," he said. "Be clean!" Immediately the leprosy left him.' (Luke 5: 12-13)

I just love Jesus! He was willing to cross boundaries and bring help to people who needed it. This is a powerful story that helps us to understand the fullness of life that Jesus carried.

Jewish law believed that touching a leper made you unclean. However, it would seem that Jesus was so full of life and goodness that the moment He touched the leper, the reverse happened. Jesus was unaffected but the leper was made whole and clean and the sickness had to go immediately from his body. Life came in and death had to leave.

Today, Jesus is willing to touch your life. He carries fullness of life; His joy is greater than any despair we face; His peace is greater than any anxiety or worry; and His love is stronger than any hatred.

Will you be willing to fall down on your knees to encounter Jesus today? He is willing to touch you if you ask Him.

Jesus, thank you that you have the power to work miracles. I ask you to touch me afresh today with your fullness of life in every area of my life. Amen.

JESUS IS MAKING A DIFFERENCE TODAY

'When he said this, all his opponents were humiliated, but the people were delighted with all the wonderful things he was doing.' (Luke 13: 17)

Jesus was on the move and making headlines.

What headlines are you hearing each day, week in week out? Sadly, most of the time when we turn on the TV or radio or go on social media, there is bad news or stories of lives broken by circumstances, and we rarely get to hear good news.

I am very privileged to be living in a community where every day and every week people are sharing stories of what Jesus is doing. I am constantly hearing testimonies of how amazing Jesus is, and how He is transforming people's lives, doing miracles of physical healing as well as setting people free from lifelong struggles. He truly is alive and doing wonderful things! It is a delight to know Him and see Him at work.

Are you delighted in what Jesus is doing around you? Why not give thanks to Jesus today for all He has done for you and what He is doing in your family, your church and your community.

Dare to ask Him to do more, so that others can be as delighted as you are.

Jesus, you are so amazing and I am so thankful for all you have done for me. Amen.

HOW IS YOUR ASSIGNMENT GOING?

*'What, after all, is Apollos? And what is Paul? Only
servants, through whom you came to believe - as the Lord
has assigned to each his task.' (1 Corinthians 3: 5)*

You are a new creation in Christ, you have a new spirit inside you and each one of us is on an assignment for Christ today.

Paul and Apollos both completed brilliant assignments and that is why you and I are full of faith today!

Do you know what your assignment is? Ask the Lord what He wants you to do. Listen and obey. We each have a specific task to complete that will enable the Kingdom of God to be seen on earth by others today.

So let's be active and keep advancing in our faith so that others will come to believe in Jesus as their Saviour.

Lord, I want to hear you guiding me today so that I am walking forward in what you have called me to do on earth. Amen.

YOU ARE HIS BELOVED

'I will get up and go to my father, and I will say to him, "Father, I have sinned against heaven and before you; I am no longer worthy to be called your son; treat me like one of your hired hands." So he set off and went to his father... Then the son said to him, "Father, I have sinned against heaven and before you; I am no longer worthy to be called your son." But the father said to his slaves, "Quickly, bring out a robe—the best one—and put it on him; put a ring on his finger and sandals on his feet."' (Luke 15: 18-19; 21-23, NRSV)

Do you know who you really are?

Jesus came to reveal the Father. This parable gives us a glimpse of what Father God is really like.

What strikes me about this story is that the son had lost his identity and felt he was nothing more than a hired hand. He wanted to let his father know this was how he felt, but his father never even let him finish his sentence - he never let him declare that over himself. Instead he stopped him mid-sentence and told his servants to fetch the best robe, get the family ring and the finest pair of sandals. Those items were all symbols of Jewish identity. The father was giving his son back his true identity, whilst his son was wanting to identify himself as a hired man. Through his actions, the Father was saying, "I love you, you are part of this family and you always will be, never mind what you have done."

Do you know today that you are God's child - His son, His daughter - deeply loved and cared for?

Take a moment and let it sink in.

Father, thank you that you love me, that I am your child. May I know this deep in my heart today so that I can be all you made me to be. Amen.

THE LORD WILL ACT

'May the favour of the Lord our God rest upon us; establish the work of our hands for us.' (Psalm 90: 17)

Have you ever thought of what God's favour might be? It might be too big for us to comprehend, but recently I have started to ask for more of God's favour in my life. It keeps my prayers simple and helps me steer away from a 'to-do' list for God. It has been amazing to see Him answer my simple prayers.

Recently our car needed a service and the bill was a bit more than we thought it would be, so I simply prayed, 'Father, will your favour be upon us and help us with this bill'. Guess what? The next day a cheque arrived out of the blue and we were able to pay for the service!

I encourage you to begin to ask for God's favour in your life. If you do that every day, I know that He will be faithful in answering.

Watch and see how the Lord's favour comes to you.

Father, thank you that you are so generous and that nothing is too big or too small for you to help with. May your favour rest upon me and my household today. Amen.

MAKE THE MOST OF YOUR INHERITANCE NOW

'Jesus continued: "There was a man who had two sons. The younger one said to his father, "Father, give me my share of the estate", so he divided his property between them.' (Luke 15: 11-12)

Back again to the story about the father and his younger son. It is key to remember that through this story, Jesus is revealing the characteristics of His heavenly Father to the world. What the younger son asked his father was outrageous and self-focused. Essentially, he was saying 'give me my inheritance now'. The father was wealthy and had a large estate. He could have said no, but he agreed and the son went off with his share of the money.

Author Mark Stibbe sums it up very well in his book on this story, he writes this: 'the younger son is basically saying, dad I want you dead so I can have my share of the inheritance now - can you hurry up and die'.⁵ But the father gave his son his inheritance there and then. He was an amazing and generous dad - just like our Father in heaven.

Do you know that you have an inheritance to enjoy now? Do you know that the riches of heaven are available now? The storerooms of heaven are full and Father God wants us to ask Him for them. Obviously not with the attitude of the younger son, but with thanksgiving and praise.

Don't wait until you die to enjoy your spiritual inheritance, make the most of it now and see how Father God not only provides for you, but also may you discover how vast and incredible the Fathers' storerooms are.

Whatever you need today, God has it.

Father, thank you that you are gracious and loving and you want to bless me today with the abundance of heaven. Amen.

THERE IS SO MUCH MORE FOR YOU

'This, the first of his miraculous signs Jesus performed
in Cana of Galilee. He thus revealed his glory and
his disciples put their faith in him.' (John 2: 11)

The disciples believed in Jesus and were about to embark on their greatest journey ever. For the next three years, they would see the impossible and be completely amazed as Jesus brought the Kingdom of God to earth. They would see the dead rise, the sick healed, the eyes of the blind open, and many more miraculous signs.

We are His disciples today. How is your belief in Jesus today? When was the last time you put your faith in Him and trusted Him?

Keep going, keep believing, and keep being expectant that you will indeed see the miraculous, and 'the goodness of God in the land of the living' (Psalm 27: 13).

Don't give up, but always hold on to the hope that there is more than you can see today.

Lord Jesus, thank you for your earthly ministry and for what you did
on earth so many years ago. Thank you, Jesus, that you continue to do
amazing miracles today. May I trust you more than I have done before,
so that I can see your Kingdom come on earth today. Amen.

CONTINUE TO LISTEN

'But when he, the Spirit of Truth, comes, he will guide you into all truth. He will not speak on his own; he will speak only what he hears, and he will tell you what is yet to come.' (John 16: 13)

Throughout scripture, God tells certain people what is yet to come. For instance, He warned Noah of the flood and told him to build a boat. He told Moses that he would free His people from Egypt and that Moses would have to ask Pharaoh's permission to do this, but that God had hardened Pharaoh's heart. He showed King David the battle plans for the fight against his enemies on numerous occasions. Then when Jesus came on earth, He only did what His Father told him to do (see John 5: 19-20). What an impact Jesus had on the people He met!

Are you a good listener? I believe the Spirit of Truth has something to say today for your life, your family, your work, and your ministry. There is something yet to come, so don't miss out.

Listen to the Spirit. God is always speaking through His Spirit.

Spirit of Truth, will you guide me today, and show me what I need to know and hear, so that I can be walking as Jesus walked. Amen.

WILL YOU LET HIM IN?

'Here I am! I stand at the door and knock. If anyone hears my voice and opens the door, I will come in and eat with him, and he with me.' (Revelation 3: 20)

In his painting depicting this verse, the artist Holman Hunt shows Jesus standing at a big oak door knocking, but the handle on the door is missing. Only we can open the door from the inside to let Jesus in.

Billy Graham, one of the greatest preachers of the last century, died at the age of 99. You may well have your own personal story of how Billy Graham impacted your life - I know that I do. He inspired me to dream of speaking in front of thousands - if not tens of thousands of people - delivering a powerful message of the gospel. He was a role model in the way that he lived his life and shared the good news of Jesus Christ to millions of people. He was always encouraging people to open the door of their hearts to Jesus and let Him in.

I know that I did this back in the summer of 1984. What a great day! Can you remember when you let Jesus into your heart and into your life?

Let's not forget that Jesus is still knocking on the door of people's hearts, still wanting to come in and eat. So let's take that bold step and either invite Jesus in, or encourage someone else to do so.

Jesus, thank you that you have come into my heart and have changed my life. Today, may I give someone an opportunity to invite you into their heart. Amen.

BE AWARE OF THE DEVIL

'Then Satan entered Judas, called Iscariot, one of the Twelve. And Judas went to the chief priests and the officers of the temple guards and discussed with them how he might betray Jesus.' (Luke 22: 3)

We see in this verse what Satan is capable of doing. In another piece of scripture, he is described as 'a roaring lion' prowling around, looking to cause trouble (1 Peter 5: 8). We must be on our guard and not allow him to enter our thoughts, our minds and our hearts. We must be careful not to hand power over to him. Judas was taken in and deceived, which ultimately led to his death.

Recently, I was caught up in a mental struggle and sensed that I had to make a choice: either to entertain and give power to those thoughts, or to say no, and step into God's presence and seek His truth. I chose the latter and immediately felt the peace I needed.

How aware are you of the power that you can give Satan over your life, through a thought, or believing a lie, or because of a broken relationship, a misunderstanding or hardship? Be on guard. When we are not at peace in an area of our life, it is always good to seek the Lord and ask Him to show us what the cause is.

God's truth is stronger – choose to partner with Him.

Father, thank you that Jesus died and rose again and that the power of the enemy is defeated. Help me to walk in a victory-mindset and not allow the enemy a foothold in my life. Amen.

STAND FIRM

Therefore my dear brothers, stand firm. Let nothing move you. Always give yourselves fully to the work of the Lord because you know that your labour in the Lord is not in vain.' (1 Corinthians 15: 58)

Is your relationship with God on solid foundations or is it a bit shaky?

Paul encourages us to stand firm and not to be moved or shaken. Trials come and go but we are to stand firm, and not cave in or give up.

Keep going, keep pressing in for more, and keep focused on what God has called you to do. You will reap a reward, and breakthrough will come... maybe not now, but it will come.

So stand firm in who you are: a child of the Living God.

Lord, I need your strength today. I need to stand firm, so that I can do all that you have asked me to do. Amen.

SHARE AND TELL ALL

'O give thanks to the Lord, call on his name, make known his deeds among the peoples. Sing to him, sing praises to him; tell of all his wonderful works. Glory in his holy name; let the hearts of those who seek the Lord rejoice. Seek the Lord and his strength, seek his presence continually.' (Psalm 105: 1-4, NRSV)

Recently I had the joy of spending time with two other couples who Michelle and I have journeyed through life with for a number of years. Lockdown due to Covid-19 meant that we were not able to get together for over a year. During our time of sharing our hearts and our lives, it dawned on me that we were living out these verses from Psalm 105: yes, we could give thanks to God; yes, we could share how He has done great things amongst us; yes, we did rejoice and we did find God's strength as we sought Him together. Also, each one of us were facing some tough challenges ahead, so I decided to make a declaration that the next time we met together, we would give thanks to God and tell each other of all His wonderful acts in our lives and family.

May I encourage you today, to take hold of these verses and, with a friend or family member, share, rejoice and believe God for even more wonderful acts to happen in your life. Let us believe in Him for more than we can see now.

Don't give up, but instead seek Him and He will give you the strength that you need.

Father, you love doing wonderful acts. I declare that I, as well as my family and friends, will be witnesses to these in the days and months to come. Amen.

HIS WAYS LEAD TO REST

'For forty years I was angry with that generation; I said, "They are a people whose hearts go astray, and they have not known my ways." So I declared an oath in my anger, "They shall never enter my rest."' (Psalm 95: 10-11)

We are constantly reminded in the Old Testament how the Israelites not only failed to listen to God, but had proud and stubborn hearts and would not follow God's ways. This often brought them into conflict with God, who not only got angry with them, but would allow things to happen to them because of their attitude towards Him.

Here in these verses we see that this generation would not enter the Promised Land: 'they shall not enter my rest'. Wow... those are tough words...!

Are you confident that you are walking in God's ways today? Are you spending time listening to what Father God has to say to you, or is your heart hardened to His voice? If your heart is hardened to God's voice and to His ways, then you need to do something about it or you will not find true rest. One thing I have found helpful is to stop being so busy. Busyness is a great threat to any human being; it can so easily take our focus off God's ways and take us on paths that either lead to nowhere or to a restless place.

Father, help me to slow down, so that I may know your ways and know your voice calling me forward. Amen.

ON YOUR KNEES

'"Even now" declares the Lord, "return to me with all your heart, with fasting and weeping and mourning." Rend your heart and not your garments. Return to the Lord your God for He is gracious and compassionate, slow to anger and abounding in love and He relents from sending calamity.' (Joel 2: 12-13)

God's desire is to be in a relationship with His children. He wants us back and He wants us to enjoy all that He has for us. These verses paint a wonderful picture of God's heart for His children: it is just full of love, grace and compassion! We can so easily have a wrong image of God as being perhaps distanced, out of touch, or non-relational, to name a few. But here in these verses we see just how big His heart is and that His desire is for us to be with Him.

The prophet Joel uses the word 'rend' when referring to your heart, 'rend your heart' - to me that suggests a time on our knees, seeking Him in an act of total surrender. If we do this, the eyes of our heart will begin to open to see just how good God really is.

So seek Him today and do not be afraid to come to Him. Search your heart to see if there is anything not right or if there is something you are holding on to. Your heart is so precious to God.

Father, I will return to you today. I bring my heart to you, knowing that I need to change, knowing that I am in need of your forgiveness, love and mercy. Amen.

TAKE YOUR ANNUAL MOT

'"Your wickedness will punish you; your backsliding will rebuke you. Consider then and realise how evil and bitter it is for you when you forsake the Lord your God and have no awe of me," declares the Lord, the Lord Almighty.' (Jeremiah 2: 19)

This is a challenging verse from the prophet Jeremiah. It is calling us to get right with God, and a reminder that we need to be cleansed and cleaned up so that we are good to go.

Every year I get a reminder from my local garage that it is time for my car to have its annual MOT. I book a slot and then leave my car there for the day. Normally it passes and I pick it up later. However, there is often a small glitch or something that needs replacing and changing.

I find that I need to have a 'spiritual MOT'. I try to see where I am falling behind or where I have slipped up, or where I need cleansing. I simply ask the Lord to show me where I might be backsliding, or to show me if there is some bitterness or evil in my heart or mind that I have picked up but not dealt with. I might not be as pure and holy as I think I am! One of the toughest questions I ask myself is: "Are there things in my life that make God slightly smaller than me?"

When was your last spiritual MOT? Do you think you would pass today? Remember, He is forgiving and full of love and knows you better than you know yourself.

Father, I give you permission today, to show me where I have fallen, where I have not walked in your ways. Search my heart, Lord, and remove any evil and bitter thoughts. Amen.

IT'S TIME TO TALK ABOUT JESUS

'Then, leaving her water jar, the woman went back to the town and said to the people, "Come, see a man who told me everything that I've ever done. Could this be the Messiah?" They came out of the town and made their way towards him.' (John 4: 28-30)

What a great day for that Samaritan woman! Not only did she discover the Messiah, but also, she must have felt loved and valued for the first time in ages. No wonder she was full of joy as she went back to the town and shared the good news with everyone!

Notice she seemed to have a hunger for the Messiah. I think that hunger is still found in people today. For instance, during the Covid-19 pandemic, our church decided to do some door-knocking to see how people were doing. We were really surprised how people were so open to Jesus and the gospel, as if He was working in their lives before we even talked!

Today, you may be with people who need to discover Jesus. Be thinking and praying: "How can I share Jesus with them today?" It might just be a simple smile or a small act of kindness that opens up their heart to Jesus. Or perhaps a direct question: "Do you know Jesus Christ personally?"

Jesus, thank you that you are working today in the lives of people. Help me to be bold and step out and show people who you really are. Amen.

HELP ME SEE THEM

'Then Levi gave a great banquet for him in his house; and there was a large crowd of tax collectors and others sitting at the table with them. The Pharisees and their scribes were complaining to his disciples, saying, "Why do you eat and drink with tax collectors and sinners?" Jesus answered, "Those who are well have no need of a physician, but those who are sick; I have come to call not the righteous but sinners to repentance."' (Luke 5: 29-32, NRSV)

The Pharisees and others like them just could not see God at work through Jesus. They just couldn't understand why Jesus would hang out with the 'worst' people of society - in their view, it just was not right. They were blinded and stuck in their ways of thinking and were restricted by their attitudes and traditions. So instead of loving people they were quick to judge. That's called 'religious pride': 'my way is right and your way is not'.

However, Jesus was showing them what was on God's heart. He was revealing what was really important to His Father and how He desired to heal the sick, bring restoration to 'sinners' and bring them into His Kingdom.

Today, continue to ask God to show you His way, His thinking, His attitude towards people in the situations that you are facing. Get His perspective on things; see people and situations as God sees them, not as the world sees them.

Father, may I think like you today. May I see people as you see them. Amen.

ARE YOU UP FOR A CHALLENGE?

'The Lord said to Moses, "Speak to the entire assembly of Israel and say to them: 'Be holy because I, the Lord your God, am holy."' (Leviticus 19: 1-2)

Would other people say that you are a 'holy' person?

I think being holy is one of the most challenging calls that God puts on our lives. Holiness is our goal.

It is God's desire that we be holy like Him. It is a wonderful challenge! God would not have said that if He did not believe that we could be holy like Him. The more we connect with God, the more we will reflect Him and who He is. He is holy. He lives within us, so as you pursue Him, you will become more like Him. The best place to start, I have found, is to believe.

Today, simply believe that you are His beloved child and you are loved by Him. It is the best step towards holiness.

Father, thank you that you are indeed holy and that your desire is for me to be like you. Help me believe and know today that I am loved by you. Amen.

GOD'S WORD IS A POWERFUL WEAPON

'So is my word that goes out from my mouth: It will not
return to me empty, but will accomplish what I desire and
achieve the purpose for which I sent it.' (Isaiah 55: 11)

I don't know where I would be today if it wasn't for God's Word. I reckon I would be lost, confused and certainly not in a good place. Since I started writing these daily thoughts back in 2000, each week God's Word has been directing me and fulfilling its purpose in my life. I think just writing this book is a testimony of that.

Take some time today to think back and reflect on the scriptures that have spoken to you most in your life. See how they have achieved their purpose in your life. Maybe even speak them out and declare them again over yourself and your family and friends.

Give thanks to God, for His Word is still speaking today and achieving its purpose.

Father, thank you so much that your Word has given me hope and the
strength to carry on. It is not empty but full of truth and life. Amen.

JESUS KNOWS THE BEST PLACE FOR YOU

'The Lord is my shepherd, I shall not be in want.' (Psalm 23: 1)

This is a great reminder for us today: Jesus is our Shepherd.

He is the Good Shepherd who will always be with you, and will always lead you to green pastures and to waters that will refresh your soul. He will never leave you nor abandon you, even when everything is falling apart around you. He promises to lead you 'through the valley of the shadow of death' (v. 4). You will never be in want if Jesus is your Shepherd. All you have to do is listen to His voice and He will guide you to the place that you need to go.

So today, give thanks to Jesus, the Great Shepherd and allow Him to lead you to the still quiet waters that refresh your soul.

Jesus, you are with me today; you will lead me to the place that I need to go. May I follow you and learn to put my trust in you today. Amen.

LET'S WALK IN CLOSENESS WITH FATHER GOD

'Jesus gave them this answer: "I tell you, the Son can do nothing by Himself; he can do only what he sees His Father doing, because whatever the Father does the Son also does. For the Father loves the Son and shows Him all He does. Yes, to your amazement he will show him even greater things than these."' (John 5: 19-20)

Here, Jesus gives us a great model on how to live our Christian life on earth. It is a simple reminder that Jesus did not work alone, and that He was very close to His Father. He was interdependent and not independent in His walk with God.

Are you walking independently from God or is your walk interdependent with Him? I think many of us would be tempted to say, "yes I am interdependent with God." But can you honestly say that you are seeing greater works of God's Kingdom than Jesus in your life and ministry?

Maybe take some time today to check that God is in every area of your life and that the two of you are working together, so that you will see 'even greater things'.

He is waiting to tell you what to do.

Father, please show me where I am being independent in my life. Help me to see where I am not listening to you guiding me, or showing me what I should be doing. I want to see more of your Kingdom on earth today. Amen.

DON'T SHY AWAY FROM TAKING THAT STEP

*'Therefore, if you are offering your gift at the altar and there
remember that your brother or sister has something against you;
leave your gift there in front of the altar. First go and be reconciled
to them; then come and offer your gift.' (Matthew 5: 23-24)*

Here is a simple but profound truth today. We must make sure that we are reconciled with our brothers and sisters.

I remember when I was at university and I was praying with a group of people and suddenly a thought came to my mind: "You are not in a good place with your friend; go and find him and reconcile". So I did just that. I found my friend, (who was not in a good place with me!). We had to talk. I had to say sorry and seek his forgiveness and we were reconciled. He has now been one of my closest friends for over 30 years. We walk side by side.

Take that step today and ask the Holy Spirit to search your heart to see if there is anyone you need to be reconciled to. If so, take steps to ensure that everything is done the way God desires it. The consequences if you do this could be amazing, and equally if you don't do it, things could get out of hand.

Take that step towards reconciliation.

Father, is there anyone I need to reconcile with? Give me the courage and strength to take the right steps towards reconciling with them. Amen.

IS JESUS ON BOARD YOUR BOAT?

'When evening came, his disciples went down to the sea, got into a boat, and started across the sea to Capernaum. It was now dark, and Jesus had not yet come to them. The sea became rough because a strong wind was blowing. When they had rowed about three or four miles, they saw Jesus walking on the sea and coming near the boat, and they were terrified. But he said to them, "It is I; do not be afraid." Then they wanted to take him into the boat, and immediately the boat reached the land toward which they were going.' (John 6:16-21, NRSV)

'Don't be afraid'. What wonderful words to hear today!

Are you facing a tough situation in life right now, or is there a storm brewing ahead? Don't be frightened by it. Instead, welcome Jesus into the situation and let Him take over; let Him calm the wind and waves; let Him bring you the peace and guidance you need.

I love the word 'immediately' used here; it is as if things changed miraculously with Jesus on board and they suddenly arrived on the other shore without delay. It will be the same for us when we let Him climb on board.

Today, don't sail through life in your own strength, instead learn to rely on the supernatural presence of the Holy Spirit.

So welcome Jesus on board and watch what happens. It is so much better to have Jesus in your boat with you than to try and go it alone.

Jesus, you calm the storms of life. I invite you to calm my storm, and climb on board and change the situation today. Amen.

FORWARDS OR BACKWARDS

*'For when I brought your forefathers out of Egypt and spoke to
them, I did not just give them commands about burnt offerings and
sacrifices, but I gave them this command: obey me, and I will be your
God and you will be my people. Walk in all the ways I command you,
that it may go well with you. But they did not listen or pay attention;
instead, they followed the stubborn inclinations of their evil hearts.
They went backwards and not forwards.' (Jeremiah 7: 22-24)*

This is a good word from the prophet Jeremiah. There are a few thoughts
to ponder on today, and some questions to ask ourselves as we seek to
connect with Father God.

Is there an area in your life that is not in obedience to the Lord or where
God is not Lord? Are you walking well in your life today? Are you going
forward in your faith journey? Are you giving yourself time to listen to
God and what He has to say? He is always speaking to us; we just need to
tune in and hear what He is saying.

Choose to be going forward today.

*Father, I don't want to be stubborn or to have any evil in my heart. Lord,
will you guide me and cleanse me from anything that is not good, so
that I can move forward into all you have for me today. Amen.*

WHAT CAN YOU DO?

'The greatest among you will be your servant. For those who exalt himself will be humbled, and those who humble himself will be exalted.' (Matthew 23: 11-12)

Over the years, Michelle and I have been the grateful recipients of people serving us and going beyond themselves to bless us: people who chose to place our needs over their own. Whether it's been the friend who arrived at hospital when I was suddenly admitted, to make sure Michelle had enough change for parking; or the person who snuck into our house to clean whilst Michelle underwent fertility treatment; or the gifts left on our doorstep when we had received bad news; or invitations for dinner so that we have felt included, even though I can no longer eat; or patient friends who have sat with me at a noisy party and engaged with me in a conversation, despite the hearing obstacles to overcome, rather than being drawn into the easier ones to be had in the room. Small and big ways that have blessed us beyond words and ministered deeply into our hearts.

Today, why not seek the best way forward. Is there an opportunity to serve someone today, an opportunity to go the extra mile, an opportunity to bring a blessing to someone else? Is there an opportunity to promote someone above you and let them shine?

God will exalt you in His way and in His time. It is better to be humble than to exalt yourself.

Lord, help me lift others up before me so that I may be exalted by you. Amen.

SIMPLY BELIEVE

'Then they asked Him, "What must we do to do the works
God requires?" Jesus answered "The work of God is this:
to believe in the one he has sent."' (John 6: 28-29)

This is a simple truth for us today, but why do we find it so hard to live it out?

I don't know about you, but I can so easily slip into the mindset of doing things for Jesus: I must do this, I must do that, I must go here - which may well be necessary at times, but they can start to dominate you, and it soon becomes about striving and not believing. If we really believe Jesus' words and live them out, surely life will become stress-free and much easier!

I remember a friend, who once received a large bill from a company. She took one look at it and said to Jesus, "This is yours", and stuck it to the ceiling of her kitchen! True to His word, God honoured her belief in Him, and money came in to cover the bill.

Believe 100% in Jesus today. Bring Him into everything and see the Kingdom of God grow through you and around you. A day of not doing anything but believing - it sounds like a perfect day!

Jesus, I want to believe in you more than I have ever done so before. In you and with you, I can move any mountain and change any situation that I find myself in. Help me today to believe in you. Amen.

MAKE GOD YOUR FOCUS AND PRIORITY

'Whom have I in heaven but you? And earth has nothing I desire besides you.' (Psalm 73: 25)

If you stop and think about this verse for a few seconds, it becomes one of the most challenging verses in the bible.

Recently, I was listening to a sermon online and the preacher asked this question: "Do you spend more time thinking about God than you do about money?"

Our goal in this earthly life that we live, must be to focus our thoughts, dreams and desires on God. Nothing on earth is better than having an intimate relationship with Father God.

Do your utmost to set your heart and mind on knowing God, not only as a Father, but also for who He is and what He can do through you. If we fix our focus there, then His Kingdom will naturally expand and grow through us on earth.

That is something to desire more than anything else.

Lord, search my heart and show me today if there is anything that I am putting before you, or anything that is bigger or better than you that needs to leave my heart and mind. I want to know you more. Amen.

ARE YOU PREPARED?

'But he said to me, "My grace is sufficient for you, for my power is made perfect in weakness."' (2 Corinthians 12: 9)

I find myself constantly going back to this verse in scripture that Paul wrote to the early Christians. I still do not think I have totally understood its meaning and power yet, but each time the Lord reminds me of this verse, I am drawn into a deeper understanding of it.

Many of us will be weak at some stage of our lives and will encounter hardship or suffering. It is part of life. Jesus said, "In this world you will have trouble" (John 16: 33). But the challenge we face is to make sure that we are ready and prepared when the troubles come, so that when they do, God's power can be seen to be the perfect remedy in our weakness. Without His power, (and I must say grace, as I have found out on numerous occasions), I so easily slip down the road of self-pity, negativity and doom and gloom. I need to learn to live in His grace and live in the understanding that God's power is so much more than anything I face; that in my weakness, His plan and purposes will still prevail and His name will receive glory and honour.

So today, can I encourage you to enter into the fullness of God's grace for you, and believe that whatever your weakness is, God's power will prevail and be shown to others through you.

Father, thank you that your power is all I need and your grace is sufficient for me. May I honour your name in the trials of life. Amen.

WALK IN THE SPIRIT

*'Jesus, full of the Holy Spirit, returned from the Jordan
and was led by the Spirit in the desert.' (Luke 4: 1)*

Jesus had just received a wonderful blessing from His Father at His
baptism: "This is my son whom I love; with you I am well pleased"
(Luke 3: 22).

Wow, Jesus' identity was revealed, so no wonder He was full of the Spirit!
He was on fire!

But our challenge today is this: are we being led by the Spirit?

Jesus was led into the desert by the Spirit. A tough place and a tough
assignment, but He got through it and overcame it.

Does your life reflect that experience?

Make sure today that you hear those same words from the Father to you.
You are His child and He is smiling on you and is full of joy. Keep asking
the Spirit to lead you into the places He wants you to go. If you do, you
will be able to face whatever comes your way in a better and stronger way.

*Holy Spirit, I give you permission today to lead me forward. I want to be
guided by you and know your presence. Amen.*

WHAT A COMBINATION

'Jesus returned to Galilee in the power of the Spirit, and news about Him spread through the whole countryside. He was teaching in their synagogues, and everyone praised Him.' (Luke 4: 14)

Yesterday we read that Jesus was led by the Spirit and now He has the power of the Spirit. He's gone turbo!

That is a good combination to have. The Spirit's presence was so important to Jesus. He needed Him. He could not do the ministry that God asked Him to do without the Spirit.

I encourage you today and for every day, to simply release the Spirit's presence into your life. He's got unlimited resources and is looking for willing children of God to be open to Him.

It's time to see more of the supernatural power of the Holy Spirit in your life and in the world.

Father, may people begin to praise you everywhere! May your name and fame spread out through me. I need a fresh anointing of the Holy Spirit. Come alive in me today. Amen.

YOU HAVE ALL YOU NEED

'And I will ask the Father, and he will give you another
Counsellor to be with you forever – the Spirit of truth. The
world cannot accept him, because it neither sees him nor
knows him. But you know him, for he lives with you and will be
in you. I will not leave you as orphans.' (John 14: 16-18b)

———————————————

There are two wonderful truths that Jesus speaks to us today.

The first is that we have the Spirit of truth within us. He will guide and direct us which makes us different to everyone else around us.

A friend once shared this story with me: A rail worker was approached by another colleague, who said to him, "You are different to everyone else. I have been watching you, you don't swear, you don't drink, and you always see good in others. What is it you have that I don't?" His simple answer was this: "I have the Spirit of the living God in me".

The second truth is that Jesus does not leave us as orphans. We are not alone; we are heirs and children of the Most High God. Jesus' desire is for us to know the presence of the Spirit within us, and to know that we are His children, adopted into His family, and that we are not alone.

Today, celebrate the presence of the Spirit in your life. Give thanks that you get to display His goodness and that you are a son or daughter of the Most High God.

Father, thank you that I am your child and that the Spirit lives in me.
Help me to know this today and to live a life that reflects it as well.
Amen.

HE IS THE BEST TEACHER

'But the Counsellor, the Holy Spirit, whom the Father will send in my name, will teach you all things and will remind you of everything I have said to you.' (John 14: 26)

Why not take some time today to reflect and think back to all that the Spirit has said to you in your life and give thanks? Be reminded of the scriptures that have jumped out at you; of the words of encouragement that have made you who you are today; the prophetic words that have been spoken into your life and given you confirmation that you are heading in the right direction.

Give thanks for all these wonderful treasures that make you who you are. The Holy Spirit is real and active and is the best Teacher to have, and He will give you all you need to know, to live life to the full.

So today, plug in and enjoy all that He has to say to you.

Holy Spirit, will you be my Teacher. Help me to be a good student and listen to what you are saying and help me to obey you. Amen.

IS IT TIME FOR MORE FRUIT?

'So I say, live by the Spirit, and you will not gratify the desires of the sinful nature. ...But the fruit of the Spirit is love, joy, peace, forbearance, kindness, goodness, faithfulness, gentleness and self-control. Against such things there is no law.' (Galatians 5: 16; 22-23)

Which one of these fruits needs to be more active in your life today?

I went through a season of asking for the fruits of kindness and gentleness to be more active in my life, particularly during that season of lockdown during the Covid-19 pandemic, when we all lived together under the same roof, all day every day for nearly a year. I think without them I would have not enjoyed that season as much as I did. These fruits can really make a huge difference in our lives in how we react and respond to people and situations.

Today, there may be an opportunity for you to display one of these fruits to someone.

Be praying that the fruits of the Spirit may be powerful tools as you show someone some more love, or more joy or more kindness etc.

Holy Spirit, thank you so much for these amazing fruits. I ask that you help me grow and develop these in my life. I ask for, in particular... Amen.

LET US SING

'So I have looked upon you in the sanctuary, beholding your power and glory. Because your steadfast love is better than life, my lips will praise you. So I will bless you as long as I live; I will lift up my hands and call on your name. My soul is satisfied as with a rich feast, and my mouth praises you with joyful lips.' (Psalm 63: 2-5, NRSV)

I think God loves it when we spend time praising Him and, as we do, it blesses us as well.

David, the author of this Psalm, had seen the power and glory of God. He had been in the sanctuary of the Lord God Almighty. He had every reason to glorify God with his lips. Wow, that must have been something special!

Have you seen the power and glory of God yet? Faith is all about believing in the unseen.

Today we have the privilege of sitting with Jesus in heavenly realms, in the inner sanctuary, the holy of holies. So let's be in awe of that and let's praise God and glorify Him! If we do this, it will make such a difference to us and we will be satisfied and not left empty or lonely and we will know the love of Father God more deeply.

Father, thank you for who you are, and thank you so much that I can sit with Jesus and celebrate and give thanks for all that you have done for me. Amen.

THERE IS MORE

*'So Naomi returned from Moab accompanied by Ruth the
Moabitess, her daughter-in-law, arriving in Bethlehem
as the barley harvest was beginning.' (Ruth 1: 22)*

Ruth had left Moab with her mother-in-law. Behind her lay the death of her husband, her wider family, her culture and her identity. Ahead of her she faced living out her days as a childless widow. By leaving and going with Naomi, Ruth was in effect laying down all chances of a new life and a new family. Yet Ruth chose to do it.

Earlier in the chapter, in one of the most famous scriptures in the bible, Ruth said, "Where you go, I will go... your God [shall be] my God" (v. 16). Ruth had chosen to follow God whatever the cost.

Here comes the goodness of the God we serve: Ruth arrived as the barley harvest is beginning, and though she didn't know it yet, she was about to walk from death and despair into life and fruitfulness, and ultimately into full restoration through marriage and motherhood.

This story fills me with such hope. The Father's plan is for us to live in a constant cycle of restoration and fruitfulness, and we can do this because we carry the very life of heaven within us.

I encourage you today to choose God. Whatever your present struggles, whatever the painful details of your past, choose Him. As we do, we get life, and we get to reap blessings, and we get to move forward into all He has prepared for us.

Lord, I choose you again today. I choose to believe that ahead of me lies plans full of life and fruitfulness, plans that you have prepared for me. Fill me with your hope so I can step forward boldly into a future not defined by my past, but prepared by you. Amen.

BE ALERT

'In order that Satan might not outwit us. For we are not unaware of his schemes.' (2 Corinthians 2: 11)

This verse has really helped me learn what it means to do spiritual battle properly.

In his book Intercessory Prayer, Dutch Sheets unpacks the proper meaning of this verse. In the Greek it reads like this: 'Don't be without understanding of the way your enemy thinks and operates - of his plans, plots, schemes and devices'.[6]

I think we need to be serious about this - not to give credit to Satan, but not to underestimate him either. I think God would be willing to reveal the enemy's schemes to us.

Don't get focused on the enemy, but don't be ignorant of who we are really fighting against. We need to be alert and ready to win the daily battles, enforcing the victory of the cross in our lives.

In your daily walk with God, ask the Lord, "What should I be aware of" Or "Lord, what is going on here?" Walk forward in faith and not fear, learning where to fight and holding onto the truth that the enemy cannot harm a child of God (1 John 5: 18).

Father, help me today to live as a true warrior for Jesus and usher in the Kingdom of God. Amen.

BE ON YOUR GUARD

'"Simon, Simon, Satan has asked to sift all of you as wheat. But I have prayed for you, Simon, that your faith may not fail. And when you have turned back, strengthen your brothers."' (Luke 22: 31-32)

Satan is out there desiring to knock us off our faith journey. He wants to stop us from becoming all that God has called us to be. He tried it with Peter (it worked for a bit - Peter denied Jesus three times), but Jesus' prayers were answered. Not only did Peter go on to strengthen his brothers, but he also became the rock on which Jesus built His church.

A great encouragement is that Jesus, our Saviour, is praying for us today. So stand firm, so that when the tough times come, when the storms rage (which they will do), we can be sure that Jesus is praying for us, and we know that He will help us to get through and strengthen others.

So, be on your guard. Satan will do his best to knock you off course; he will use lies and situations to get you to fall, but lift up your gaze and know that Jesus is praying for you.

Jesus, may I stand firm today and, like Peter, be a rock for others to see and to be strengthened by. Amen.

IT'S REAL

'So we fix our eyes not on what is seen, but on what is unseen. For what is seen is temporary, but what is unseen is eternal.' (2 Corinthians 4: 28)

There are three realms of life: the first realm is the earth in which we live and all that we can see with our natural eyes. The second realm is where all the angels and demons operate and engage in battles on our behalf (Ephesians 6: 12). The third realm is the spiritual place called heaven. This is where Jesus is seated with God on His throne, unhindered and unchallenged, surrounded by angels and elders continually singing, "Holy Holy is the Lord God Almighty" (Revelation 4: 8).

In this verse, Paul is encouraging the believers in the Corinthian church to learn to engage with what is real and what is eternal, which will never fade or perish. Even though it can't be seen, he challenges them to open their spiritual eyes so that they can know and experience the joy of heaven.

Today, not only fix your eyes on heaven, but also have fun imagining heaven. What does it look like? What does it sound like? What does it feel like? Take your eyes off all that is going on around you, all that is temporary, and think of the reality of eternity and the joy of heaven. Experience now in the present what is to come, and allow those thoughts and revelations to give you the strength to face the day.

Father, thank you that you are real and alive. I choose today to fix my eyes on what I can't see, and believe that the joy of heaven will encourage me today. Amen.

LET US CELEBRATE TODAY

'Many people spread their cloaks on the road, and others spread leafy branches that they had cut in the fields. Then those who went ahead and those who followed were shouting, "Hosanna! Blessed is the one who comes in the name of the Lord! Blessed is the coming kingdom of our ancestor David! Hosanna in the highest heaven!" Then he entered Jerusalem and went into the temple; and when he had looked around at everything, as it was already late, he went out to Bethany with the twelve.' (Mark 11: 8-11, NRSV)

What an amazing celebration! The crowds are all cheering for Jesus; they are singing and praising His name! It must have been a great feeling to be there to witness it. Jesus had done so much in the last three years, and now everything about His life was coming to a head.

Even though I struggle to speak, (let alone make much noise these days!), I try each morning, just to thank and praise Jesus for all He has done. Normally, the first thing I do when I wake up is say, "Morning, Jesus! Morning, Father! Morning, Holy Spirit!" I start the day with this and it gets my mind set on hope and my spirit feeling alive.

Spend some time today thanking Jesus for all He has done for you, praise His name, and give Him thanks. He is the King of Kings, Lord of Lords, He is the Saviour of the world.

Jesus, today I want to praise you and give you thanks for all you have done for me. Amen.

JUMP UP AND MOVE TO HEAR WHAT JESUS IS SAYING

'Jesus stopped and said, "Call him." So they called the blind man. "Cheer up! On your feet! He's calling you." Throwing his cloak aside, he jumped to his feet and came to Jesus. "What do you want me to do for you?" Jesus asked him.' (Mark 10: 49-51)

_____

The blind man was desperate. In those days, life would have been particularly tough for people with disabilities.

I know what it is like not to be able to participate in what is going on in your surroundings, and to feel that you are missing out. However, like the blind man, I always have a desire to push through the barriers of disability, to see Jesus and to be in His presence. The blind man was persistent and Jesus heard, stopped and called him. Jesus is never too busy for you, so never give up crying out to Him.

But I also think there are times when we need to move towards Jesus. We can so easily slip into thinking that Jesus will come to our rescue, which He does. But if you are not seeing breakthrough in a particular area of your life right now, maybe it is time to come to Jesus and hear His voice asking, "What can I do for you?".

No more pleading and shouting out for help. It is time to draw near and hear those words of Jesus. He has your answer and is waiting to give it to you.

Jesus, you understand all that I am struggling with today. I will jump up from my pit so that I can hear your voice speaking to me and leading me forward to freedom and breakthrough. Amen.

LET THESE TRUTHS GUIDE YOU AND LEAD YOU

'You who live in the shelter of the Most High, who abide in the shadow of the Almighty will say to the Lord, "My refuge and my fortress; my God, in whom I trust."' (Psalm 91: 1-2, NRSV)

'For he will command his angels concerning you to guard you in all your ways.' (Psalm 91: 11, NRSV)

'Those who love me, I will deliver; I will protect those who know my name. When they call to me, I will answer them; I will be with them in trouble, I will rescue them and honour them. With long life, I will satisfy them, and show them my salvation.' (Psalm 91: 14-16, NRSV)

This has been one of my favourite Psalms over the years. It is full of great promises of protection (vs. 11-13), which I know to be true. It speaks about the importance of making God our dwelling place (vs. 1-2) - a place where we need to be every day. This is the source of our existence. It reminds us of our value and significance in God's eyes (vs. 14-15), and how He will come and fight for us, protect us and be with us in times of trouble. We are never alone. It's such a good truth to know and believe.

Many times, as Michelle and I faced battles and struggles, we declared these verses over ourselves and the family. We have been able to go to sleep at night knowing that angels are guarding us.

In the final verses, we read of the promise of a long and healthy life now and in eternity (v. 16). Wow - I am so thankful for this verse and I believe it to be so true, even at the age of 50, I am thankful that I am still living a good life!

Father, thank you so much for these wonderful promises and truths in this Psalm. May I see them come true in my life today. May I live a good, long and satisfying life. Amen.

THE 'KNOWS' OF JESUS (PART 1)

'It was just before the Passover Feast. Jesus knew that the hour had come for him to leave this world and go to the Father.' (John 13: 1)

Over the next two days we are going to look at how Jesus was able to fulfil His purpose on earth.

Jesus was secure in His schedule: He knew that His time had come to leave the world (v. 1). And Jesus was secure in His acceptance as a Son: He knew He would go to His Father (v. 1).

Security is so key in helping us move from one place to another. It helps us do the impossible. It helped Jesus fulfil His mission on earth: to die for the sins of the world. Jesus was so secure in who He was and in the love of the Father, that He could do the impossible.

Do you really know that you are accepted by God? That if you died today, you would go to heaven. Jesus knew His timetable and knew it was time to leave the earth and go to heaven.

Are you secure in these areas of your life today? Where do you need to invite Jesus in? Where do you need to trust Him more?

Jesus, help me to be more like you, to know that I am secure in all areas of my life; to be able to do the impossible because I want to make a difference; to stand out above the crowd and be secure in who I am: a child of God, loved by Him. Amen.

THE 'KNOWS' OF JESUS (PART 2)

'Jesus knew that the Father had put all things under his power, and that he had come from God and was returning to God.' (John 13: 3)

Jesus was secure in His resources: He knew that all things were under His power (v. 3).

Jesus was secure in His identity: He knew that He had come from God (v. 3).

Jesus was secure in His destiny: He knew He was returning to God (v. 3).

Again today, think about what Jesus knew and how that helped Him move forward to fulfil His mission on earth. He knew what was available to Him; He knew who He was; and He knew where He was going. That is a pretty confident young man who 24 hours later gave up His life so that you and I could be free from sin and enter into a relationship with Abba Father.

Wow! Thank you, Jesus, that you were so secure in all areas of life!

Today, have a check-up and make sure you know how you are doing in knowing who you are and where you are going. Are you as secure in these areas as Jesus was?

Jesus, thank you that you knew who you were, where you were going and that God had all the resources that you needed to fulfil your mission on earth. Help me move forward in these areas of my life. Amen.

DRAW CLOSE TO GOD

'But as for me, it is good to be near God. I have made the Sovereign Lord my refuge, I will tell of all your deeds.' (Psalm 73: 28)

It is good to be near God. The more I think about that statement, the more sense it makes. To be near God offers us a chance to be free, to be loved and accepted, to be secure, to be fulfilled and at peace. I know that's a place that I need to enjoy and to make a priority.

The more time you spend being near God, the better life will be. You will be able to tell people how good and how generous and loving a father God is, and people will see what a difference God makes in your life.

Be near to God today. He loves it when we are close to Him.

Father, I choose today to be near you. I know it will make a huge difference in my life and will impact everyone I meet today. Amen.

HE IS ALIVE

'The angel said to the women, "Do not be afraid, I know that you are looking for Jesus, who was crucified. He is not here; he has risen, just as he said."' (Matthew 28: 5-6)

"He has risen." This is another great statement for us to engage with, to believe and to live in the full reality of its truth.

If He had not risen, then my faith and your faith, mean nothing. He has risen. Jesus is alive and in the weeks that followed, He appeared to over 500 people. Since then, over the last two millennia, millions and millions of people have encountered Him and given their lives to Him.

If you are not sure that you know Him, then maybe it is time to seek Him and find Him. All you have to do is ask Him to reveal Himself to you and He will.

For those of us who do know Him, let's use this time that we have to encounter Him in a new and refreshing way. He has paid for everything we need. He is risen, and He is alive, so let's enjoy the risen Lord Jesus today.

Jesus, you are alive, just as you said you would be. Today, may I enjoy this truth even more and fully make the most of it in my life. Amen.

GRAB HOLD OF IT

'Peace I leave with you; my peace I give you. I do not give to you as the world gives. Do not let your hearts be troubled and do not be afraid.' (John 14: 27)

This scripture is so often used at the end of a funeral, just before people leave, assuring them that even though they are experiencing grief, Jesus wants to give them peace in their hearts and minds.

When our lives are in a state of emotional crisis, or when we are finding life tough and we are afraid of what might happen, these words of Jesus, when understood, can be life-changing.

Peace is not the absence of war, nor going to the library for some quiet. Peace is much more than that: peace is about being in the presence of God. Jesus says, "My peace I give you." It is a weighty, strong and indestructible peace. It seems that peace is something we have to receive and take hold of. The best place to do that is to sit and be still in God's presence and simply take hold of the peace that Jesus is giving you. It will make a difference.

So if you need some peace in your life today, maybe take a moment, be still and grab hold of this peace that Jesus has given you, and allow it to help you move forward from where you are now.

Jesus, thank you that you give freely. Today I want to receive the peace that you talked about. May I know that you are with me today. Amen.

FEEDING ON JESUS IN THE STORM

'Just before daybreak, Paul urged all of them to take some food, saying, "Today is the fourteenth day that you have been in suspense and remaining without food, having eaten nothing. Therefore I urge you to take some food; for it will help you survive; for none of you will lose a hair from your heads." After he had said this, he took bread; and giving thanks to God in the presence of all, he broke it and began to eat. Then all of them were encouraged and took food for themselves.' (Acts 27: 33-36, NRSV)

Paul had been stranded on a ship which had been buffeted by a storm for fourteen days. However, he was holding onto a promise from God (v. 22) that although the ship would be destroyed, not one of them would be lost. As they battled fear and hopelessness, Paul urged them to eat. He knew that unless they broke bread, gave thanks to God and ate, they would not have the physical, emotional and spiritual strength needed to endure what lay ahead.

This amazing story ends with Paul and everyone onboard surviving the sinking ship. God had kept His promise. Despite this epic ordeal, Paul arrived full and not empty. In fact, on arriving, Paul not only survived a deadly snake bite (Acts 28: 4), but he healed someone from an illness (Acts 28: 8).

So often, when faced with a storm in my own life, panic and anxiety can take me away from being nourished on the 'Bread of Life'. When facing the shipwrecks of life, don't pull back and survive on scraps, but rather eat more! We all need our 'daily bread'.

May we be followers of Jesus who, like Paul, are full of digested truth and ready to overflow with supernatural power, even in the trials of life.

Father, I choose to feed on you today. Help me not to pull back in times of stress or busyness, but rather increase my appetite for you, so I can be nourished and strengthened by your truth. Amen.

LET THE LIGHT SHINE

*'I have come into the world as a light, so that no-one who
believes in me should stay in darkness.' (John 12: 45)*

What a great thought to contemplate today!

Living in the light rather than in the darkness is the best place to be.
The light dispels the darkness... it removes it. My question today is:
"What does darkness look like for you? How would you define it?"

We know it's there - we just have to read the news! We know it's real, and
we know that it wants to consume us and stop us living life in freedom
and joy. Jesus says, those who believe will not stay in darkness.

Let's take Jesus at His word today. Ask Him to surround you with His light,
to touch you, and then command the darkness that is trying to overwhelm
you, to flee.

You will walk with more joy, more freedom and more peace than before.

*Jesus, thank you that you are indeed the light that shines in this world,
help me walk today in your light. I don't want to walk in darkness
anymore. Amen.*

COULD IT BE YOU?

'The older brother became angry and refused to go in. So his father went out and pleaded with him. But he answered his father, "look! All these years I have been slaving for you and never disobeyed your orders, yet you never gave me even a young goat so I could celebrate with my friends. But when this son of yours who has squandered your property with prostitutes comes home, you kill the fattened calf for him!"' (Luke 15: 28-30)

Author Henri Nouwen describes this outburst by the older son as 'frozen anger'. Nouwen writes this: 'there are so many elder sons and daughters who are lost while still at home. And it is this lostness characterised by judgement and condemnation, anger and resentment, bitterness and jealousy - that is so pernicious and damaging to the human heart... there is so much frozen anger among the people who are so concerned about avoiding sin'.[7]

It shocked me as I thought about how I can so easily resemble the elder son, with outbursts in my own life of 'frozen anger'. I may be good at avoiding a sinful life but there is something missing, something that needs to shift in my heart so that I can know the love of the Father more deeply, instead of being angry or bitter or jealous towards others. I need to be able to celebrate and rejoice more than I do now.

Is there 'frozen anger' in you that needs to melt away so that you can receive more of the love of the Father? Then you will be able to love others more deeply and freely, to join in and celebrate with them and Father God.

Father, help me see any 'frozen anger' within me. Help me see where I can be quick to judge or quick to condemn. Help me move forward and learn to enjoy all that you have given me. Amen.

HE IS SPEAKING

'Thinking he was the gardener, she said, "Sir, if you have carried him away, tell me where you have put him and I will get him." Jesus said to her, "Mary." She turned towards him and cried out in Aramaic "Rabboni" (which means "Teacher").' (John 20: 15-16)

Mary did not recognise Jesus at first. It might have been that her tears clouded her vision or because her back was turned towards Him, but when Jesus spoke her name, she immediately knew His voice. It must have been a wonderful feeling for her as she turned round to see the risen living Jesus. I love her response to His voice: she cried out, "Rabboni". Straight away she recognised the voice of her teacher... the one who had shown her a new way to live; the one who had brought her freedom from darkness; the one who had shown her grace and wiped away her shame. She knew Jesus' voice; she was a sheep who knew her Shepherd.

We can so easily miss Jesus speaking to us. With the busyness of life, the pressures of work and family commitments, rushing from here to there. It can leave us with no time to listen to Him speaking His words of life, which are so crucial for us to hear.

Are you confident that you can hear Jesus calling your name today? He is speaking and will have something important to say to you... something that will bring hope and transformation to your heart and mind.

Take a moment to tune into heaven and listen to Him calling you.

Jesus, open my ears today. Help me to recognize your voice speaking to me. Amen.

PATIENCE IS A SKILL TO LEARN

*'I waited patiently for the Lord; he inclined to me and heard my
cry. He drew me up from the desolate pit, out of the miry bog, and
set my feet upon a rock, making my steps secure. He put a new
song in my mouth, a song of praise to our God. Many will see and
fear, and put their trust in the Lord.' (Psalm 40: 1-3, NRSV)*

Two things jump out at me when I read these verses: the word 'patiently'
and the phrase 'put a new song in my mouth'.

The Psalmist David was going through a tough time, but he believed and
trusted that Father God would hear and would come to his rescue - he
waited patiently. That is a challenge for any of us who are struggling,
either with health issues, work problems, family disunity, financial
pressures, or anything else. We would all like quick answers from God.
But what does it mean to learn to wait patiently? David waited and God
came through for him. He lifted him and set his feet back onto solid
ground.

Can I encourage you, in whatever you face today to keep waiting, with
trust and patience because He has heard your cry. David sang a new song
and rejoiced in his rescue. Today in the waiting, let us sing new songs to
Father, giving thanks for the things He has already done and believing for
the things He will do.

Trust in Him, because however hard your circumstances are, Father has
heard and He is coming to your aid.

*Father, I know you have heard my prayers, I know you are with me. Help
me trust you and be patient for you to act. Please bring a new song to
my heart and mind. Amen.*

AN INTIMATE RELATIONSHIP IS POSSIBLE

'And when Jesus had cried out again in a loud voice, he gave up his spirit. At that moment the curtain of the temple was torn in two from top to bottom. The earth shook and the rocks split.' (Matthew 27: 50-51)

On Good Friday in 1989, my Dad told me that I had cancer with a 50/50 chance of living. Over the last 30 years I have had three doctors tell me I am lucky to be alive. I have had numerous operations and have lost my ability to hear and eat, and my vocal chords and neck and shoulder muscles are significantly damaged. However, I celebrate, because Jesus' death on the cross tore the curtain in two and opened up an amazing opportunity for an intimate relationship with His Father, the Lord of Lords. This relationship that has kept me going, has been an amazing journey of discovering how much I am loved by Father God, and how much He cares for me. Even in my lowest points, I have found hope in Him.

So this remarkable relationship is made possible by Jesus' death on the cross. Not only are our sins forgiven and we can be saved - body, mind, spirit - but it has also opened up a doorway to a heavenly relationship with Father God. There is no longer a barrier; it was torn in two.

So join with me and take some time, not only to thank Jesus for what He did for us on the cross, but also to celebrate that there is an open door in heaven for an intimate and loving relationship with Father God. There is hope.

Jesus, thank you so much for making a way to have a real and intimate relationship with your Father. Today, I choose to pursue this and connect with Father God. Amen.

OPEN YOUR MINDS TO SEE

'On the first day of the week, very early in the morning, the women took the spices they had prepared and went to the tomb. They found the stone rolled away from the tomb, but when they entered, they did not find the body of the Lord Jesus. While they were wondering about this, suddenly two men in clothes that gleamed like lightning stood beside them... the men said to them, "Why do you look for the living among the dead? He is not here; he has risen!"' (Luke 24: 1-3; 5b; 6a)

This is one of the greatest encounters in the whole of scripture.

Here we have grieving women who are determined to bless the dead body of Jesus, but their lives are about to be changed forever. The stone has been rolled away, the tomb is empty and the angels are declaring that Jesus is alive. Their eyes are opened and a journey of mourning turns into a journey of amazement and joy.

I read this quote recently, which I think is a really good way to describe the amazing benefits of what Jesus achieved for you and me on the cross: 'The empty tomb means, Jesus forgives and heals our past and gives us hope for our future, but the empty tomb also means it's not just pie in the sky when we die, but cake on our plate while we wait! He set us free to live fully in the present, to find his abundant life today.'[8]

Don't miss out on this abundant life that Jesus won for us.

Jesus, you conquered death and rose again. The tomb is empty and life in all its fullness is available. I choose today to enjoy this abundant life that you have won for me. Amen.

IN THE VALLEY

'When they came to the disciples, they saw a great crowd
around them, and some scribes arguing with them. When the
whole crowd saw him, they were immediately overcome with
awe, and they ran forward to greet him. He asked them, "What
are you arguing about with them?"' (Mark 9: 14–16, NRSV)

Peter, James and John, had just had an amazing mountain-top experience
with Jesus and the Father. They were on a high and may well have wanted
to stay there, but the reason they had this experience was so that when
they came down into the valley they would be able to make an impact. As
Oswald Chambers writes, 'We are not made for mountains, for sunrises,
or for the other beautiful attractions in life, those are simply intended to
be moments of inspiration. We are made for the valley and the ordinary
things of life, that is where we have to prove our stamina and strength.'[9]

We need to live for His glory in the valley as well as on the mountain top.
These 'mountain-top' experiences are about making us into something
new so that we can shine in the valleys below.

Don't believe the lie that your spiritual life is dull or uneventful, or that
your 'mountain-top' experience wasn't worth anything, rather, know that
you are called into the valley for a reason, for God's purpose: to reveal His
glory.

*Father, help me to walk in the valley that you have called me to, so that I
can bring your presence and glory where I am. Amen.*

LIVE IN RELATIONSHIP WITH JESUS

'Not everyone who says to me, "Lord, Lord," will enter the kingdom of heaven, but only the one who does the will of my Father who is in heaven. Many will say to me on that day, "Lord, Lord, did we not prophesy in your name and in your name drive out demons and in your name perform many miracles?" Then I will tell them plainly, "I never knew you. Away from me, you evildoers!"' (Matthew 7: 21-23)

If you were to bump into Jesus today, would He really know you? Would He wink at you as if He was your friend? Would He acknowledge you with a hug or give you a high five?

How is your relationship with Jesus growing? Are you spending quality time with Jesus?

Allow Him to get to know you by sharing your heart, your thoughts, your feelings, your dreams and ideas, and let Him discover more about you. He will share stuff with you as well. Don't just go through the motions of being a 'good' Christian. Be an active follower of Jesus who is fully alive; be ushering in the Kingdom of heaven in your environment where you live and work, so that you can be confident that on that day, Jesus will say to you, "I know you."

Jesus, today I want you to know me more. Help me share my heart and dreams with you. Amen.

IGNITE A FIRE OF HOPE WITHIN YOU

*'May the God of hope fill you with all joy and peace as
you trust in him, so that you may overflow with hope
by the power of the Holy Spirit.' (Romans 15: 13)*

Need a top up today? Feeling a bit down, or feeling a bit overwhelmed?
Why not receive some extra joy and peace in your life today! Simply ask
the God of hope to fill you up so that you can overflow with joy and peace
and in turn be a blessing to others.

Viktor Frankl, a psychiatrist and survivor of the Holocaust wrote about
his experience: 'The prisoner who lost hope in the future - his future - was
doomed'.[10]

Whatever your circumstances are today, the God of hope can fill you
with joy and peace and change you and help you face the day. The Holy
Spirit will ignite a fire of hope within you that is not easily put out, and
will allow you to move forward in confidence. Let the God of hope ignite
within you the joy and peace you need.

Why not start today just by giving thanks to God for all He has done for
you.

*Father, thank you that you are full of hope, joy and peace. Today, may
I receive these wonderful gifts in order that I may be blessed and be a
blessing to others. Amen.*

IT'S TIME SOMEONE ELSE
TOOK CHARGE OF YOUR LIFE

'So he said to me, "This is the word of the Lord to Zerubbabel: 'Not by might nor by power, but by my Spirit,' says the Lord Almighty.' (Zechariah 4: 6)

I was chatting with a good friend of mine about this verse and how significant it is in our lives as followers of Jesus. I thought to myself, "How much of my life is actually led by the Spirit these days?"

So I decided to pray this verse over my life every day for a week and really live it out. Wow... I not only discovered how much I was doing in my own strength and power, but also that when I actually do allow the Spirit to lead me, how much freer I become! It has been incredible to see and feel. I realise that I am less stressed, less concerned about work, about life and what other people think of me. It is as if there is a new release of freedom upon me!

I would encourage you to give it a go and see what happens. As one American pastor once said, "don't make the Holy Spirit a prisoner, make sure you release Him every day."

Holy Spirit, forgive me for when I have tried to live the Christian life on my own and made you 'a prisoner'. I invite you to come into my life today so that I rely on you and not on my own strength or power. Amen.

BE CONFIDENT

'Surely God is my help; the Lord is the one who sustains me...
For he has delivered me from all my troubles and my eyes
have looked in triumph on my foes.' (Psalm 54: 4; 7)

David, the writer of this Psalm, had just discovered that he had been betrayed and that King Saul was on his way to capture him. But David knew in his heart that God would not betray him, that God would protect him and that he would triumph over his foes. He had his confidence rooted in God and, as verse 4 says, he believed that God would 'sustain' him through this difficult time.

Whatever you are facing today, is your confidence like David's? Is it in God, believing that you will see victory and not defeat?

Don't feel downcast, but move forward in confidence. Walk tall, trust God and He will lift up your spirit and you will see God at work.

Today, I will be full of confidence, because I know that the Lord will sustain me, He will uphold me, He will deliver me from all my troubles. Amen.

IT IS OUR MISSION NOW

'The Spirit of the Lord is on me, because he has anointed me to preach good news to the poor. He has sent me to proclaim freedom for the prisoners and recovery of sight for the blind, to release the oppressed, to proclaim the year of the Lord's favour.' (Luke 4: 18-19)

This is a well-known piece of scripture that describes the ministry that Jesus was called to. He lived it out 100% and made such an impact on all those He encountered. It is so good to read the gospels and see Jesus fulfilling His mission. I love reading the stories of Him setting people free from oppression, and healing all those with disabilities and sickness. His message of good news is still so relevant for society today and Jesus' mission is our mission now.

The Holy Spirit has anointed us, (see 2 Corinthians 1: 21), but we can ask the Holy Spirit to anoint us afresh, so that we will have the ability and faith to live the life that Jesus lived.

There are people around you today who need to encounter Jesus through you, who need to discover the freedom that God has for them.

As Jesus was called, so are you...

Holy Spirit, thank you that you have anointed me to live the life that Jesus lived and make Him known. Fill me afresh to move in power so that everyone I meet today may encounter the freedom that Jesus offers. Amen.

LEARN TO DO LIFE TOGETHER

'All the believers were together and had everything in common. Selling their possessions and goods, they gave to anyone as he had a need.' (Acts 2: 44-45)
'There were no needy persons among them. For from time to time those who owned lands or houses sold them, brought the money from the sales and put it at the apostles' feet, and it was distributed to anyone as he had need.' (Acts 4: 34-35)

I have often pondered on these powerful and challenging verses from the early church.

How do we live out these verses in our culture and society today? Was it easier for them back then? How do we, as believers, and as family, do life together and live inter-connected in this way?

I think a good way to start is simply asking Father God to show us each day where there is a need or who is in need, and how we can help them.

I know a family who recently bought a new car and, instead of selling their old car or exchanging it, gave it to a family who needed it. When we live out of the revelation of 'everything in common', we begin to release what is God's, rather than consider it to be ours, and then allow it to flow into and out of our lives freely.

Let's be looking for ways to live out this verse in the communities in which we worship.

All I have is yours, Father. Help me learn to do life with the community that I am in; to be alert to the needs of others, and to see where I can make a difference. Amen.

BE LED BY THE SPIRIT

*'During the night Paul had a vision of a man of Macedonia
standing and begging him, "Come over to Macedonia and
help us." After Paul had seen the vision, we got ready at
once to leave for Macedonia, concluding that God had
called us to preach the gospel to them.' (Acts 16: 9-10)*

Paul was at the start of his ministry, and as he was pushing for doors to be opened, it seemed that he was travelling from place to place, being led by the Holy Spirit. He was keen to go to every place that was in front of him, but not all doors were opening (vs. 6-8). It must have been very frustrating for Paul, but he was prepared to listen and obey the Spirit's guidance. So when the Holy Spirit spoke to Paul through a vision and showed him where to go, he was ready. He got up and left immediately, confident that Macedonia was where God was calling him to preach the gospel.

This is a good reminder for us to be open to the Spirit's leading in our own lives. This is so key for all of us to discern what God wants us to do. It is so easy to be working hard but actually missing out on where God really wants us to be.

When was the last time you asked for the Spirit's guidance? If we are not being led by the Spirit or even obeying the Spirit, we might end up in a wrong situation, a wrong place, or even a wrong relationship.

God always has something new to show us, so let's be open to His Spirit in this season of our lives, and find out all that God has for us.

Holy Spirit, thank you that you led Paul in the right direction many years ago, so that the gospel would expand around the world. Please direct me today so that I will be walking in step with you and doing what is right. Amen.

MAKE HIM KNOWN

'Then the woman said to Elijah, "Now I know that
you are a man of God and that the word of the Lord
from your mouth is the truth."' (1 Kings 17: 24)

Has anyone recently said to you, "I know that you are a follower of Jesus"?

Elijah had just done a remarkable thing: he had brought the woman's son back to life! She was overwhelmed and realised that Elijah really was a man of God.

Today, people need to know and see that God is real and alive. How will you make Him known with those around you, including your family, friends, and work colleagues?

One of the ways that Michelle and I do this is to use the prophetic gift which we have all been given. We have sat in restaurants or cafés, or been chatting to people, and we simply ask, "Father, is there anything you want to say to this person?" And then we share it with them.

Continue to be led by the Spirit and see what opportunities come your way today to make God known. It's so simple, but so powerful as words of truth come forth. Give it a go!

Lord, today I want people to know you. Help me find ways to do this so that your Kingdom may grow. Amen.

IT WILL HAPPEN

'Now Sarai, Abram's wife, had borne him no children. But she had an Egyptian maidservant named Hagar; so she said to Abram, "The Lord has kept me from having children. Go sleep with my maidservant; perhaps I can build a family though her."' (Genesis 16: 1-2)

Sarai does what was quite normal in those days... she offers her maidservant Hagar to her husband to see if they can have a child and start their family that way. It would seem that Sarai had lost hope in God's promise for her to have a child of her own (see Genesis 15).

Are you still waiting on God for a promise to be fulfilled? Or have you given up hope and are thinking, "What can I do to make this thing happen?" That's what Sarai was doing: taking matters into her own hands.

May I encourage you today that God is faithful. He will come through on His promise, or the prophetic words spoken to you. You will see His goodness, you will see Him act.

So do not lose heart. Keep your faith pure and holy. Don't go looking for other solutions. It didn't work out well for Sarai...

Father, I want to trust you more today. I will hold on to what you have spoken to me, and I believe I will see it happen. Father, may your promises for me come true. Amen.

HE SEES YOU

'So she gave this name to the Lord who spoke to her:
You are the God who sees me, for she said, "I have now
seen the One who sees me."' (Genesis 16: 13)

This remarkable story of Sarai and Hagar continues in Genesis 16 and the maidservant Hagar is pregnant and kicked out of the house by a jealous Sarai. She is heading back home to Egypt and encounters the Lord himself in angelic form. He speaks to her and commands her to return to her mistress Sarai, but not before He encourages her and releases hope through prophesying about the future of her unborn child.

I just love it! God saw Hagar's situation and intervened. He cares so much for Hagar, a mere maidservant, the lowest of the low. Hagar encounters the Lord; she sees Him and realises that His love has no boundaries; His care has no limit and His heart is to set her free from her misery. She declares a new name for the Lord: 'El Roi' which means, 'I have seen the Lord and the Lord has seen me'.

Take some time today and fix your eyes on the One who sees you and hear what He has to say to you. When we allow Him to fully see us, we are changed forever, so learn to see the One who sees you.

Father, thank you that you see me and you know me through and through. Today, I will walk in confidence that you are with me and will never leave me on my own. Amen.

LET'S KEEP OUR FOCUS ON GOD

'All who worship images are put to shame,
those who boast in idols.' (Psalm 97: 7)

What I am learning in life is that images and idols are not worth boasting about or spending time focusing on. Possessions, social media, screen time, image and popularity, to name a few, steal my attention and take my eyes off God, and I often end up feeling ashamed that I have spent time focusing on them. They can neither speak nor act, and in the end make no lasting difference in my life. It is my hope to walk well with my Heavenly Father and to be listening to Him, because He does speak from His word and He does act in my life.

Are there idols or images in your life that you tend to focus on which you think will give you a chance for glory, popularity or satisfaction? If so, take the good opportunity to ask Father God for help and to seek His forgiveness.

May today be fruitful as you discover that God has so much more to offer you than these worthless idols and images that steal your attention or focus. A life focused on God will be a life that is packed full of adventures. God speaks today, so be listening to His word.

Father, will you show me which images and idols are robbing me of living my life to the full. I want to focus on you today because you are real, you are alive and you do speak to us. Amen.

STAND STRONG IN HIS POWER

'Finally, be strong in the Lord and in His mighty power.
Put on the full armour of God, so that you can take your
stand against the devil's schemes.' (Ephesians 6: 10)

This is a familiar verse of scripture that many of us know, and it has three amazing truths to take hold of and live out. Today, I want to focus on one of these truths which is that we are to stand strong in God's mighty power.

Years ago, as I was beginning to understand this truth, I remember that I was helping with car parking at a conference and across the road there was a park. A mother and her two children came out of the park and the children were screaming and shouting at their mother. I saw this and quietly declared peace over the children in Jesus' name. Immediately, they became quiet and walked off hand in hand with their mother. I was chuffed! I learnt that God's power is there for me to use in Jesus' name.

How often do we actually remember to live out in our everyday situations that we are to stand strong in God's mighty power? We need to learn and know that we can exercise the mighty power of God in the name of Jesus. He has won the victory over the enemy and we must remember that we can take our stand because we are fully armed and equipped to win against the enemy's schemes and tactics... that is why Paul writes, 'be strong in the Lord and His mighty power'.

Take your stand against the enemy and be working out this truth today. You can change any atmosphere if you remember who you are in Christ. You have authority over the enemy. You can defeat him.

Father, open my eyes to see the real battle. Help me know who I am in Christ Jesus, walk in that truth and take back what the enemy is trying to steal. Amen.

STEP OUT IN FAITH AND WATCH

'And what more shall I say? I do not have time to tell you about Gideon, Barak, Samson, Jephthah, David, Samuel, and the prophets, who through faith conquered kingdoms, administered justice, and gained what was promised; who shut the mouths of lions, quenched the fury of the flames, and escaped the edge of the sword; whose weakness was turned to strength; and who became powerful in battle and routed foreign armies.' (Hebrews 11: 32-34)

I love these verses in Hebrews! I wish the writer had more time and more ink to write down their thoughts on each one of these people of faith and their ministry - it would have made a great read!

The question to ask today is not how much faith do I have, but am I prepared to give what I already have into the hands of God, and see what He will do with it?

If we do that, then God will move in our lives and many exciting adventures will come our way. There are times in my life when I sense God asking me to do something, to step out in faith and watch what He does through me.

As the writer in Hebrews points out, these great men and women of faith in the Old Testament, did just that, and look at what they achieved!

Lord, thank you for the men and women of faith who have stepped out in faith and trusted you. I would love to do the same today: to step out in faith and watch you in action. Amen.

WHAT ARE THEY SAYING?

'Then I heard the voice of the Lord saying, "Whom shall I send? And who will go for us?" And I said, "Here am I, send me!"' (Isaiah 6: 8)

This is a well-known verse, but recently I was reading a book that brought new revelation to me. The author suggests that the prophet Isaiah overheard the conversation between God and His Son who were talking between themselves. Isaiah was not involved, he just happened to be there and he heard it. I had never seen that before and I realised how little time I give to listen to what God is saying. More often, it is me telling God what is on my heart and mind.

I reckon Father God has some good things on His mind today that He would love us to hear and respond to, just as Isaiah did. So let's make sure we have time in the throne room - that is where Isaiah was - and may we hear what Father God is saying. That is certainly what I want to grow in. It just might be that what you hear will upgrade you in your walk with God and take it to a whole new level! It did for Isaiah - he responded and he became one of the greatest Old Testament prophets.

Father, thank you that you have something for me to hear today. I know it will change my life and move me forward to see even greater things. Amen.

LOOK BEYOND YOURSELF

*'Each of you should look not only to your own interests, but
also to the interests of others.' (Philippians 2: 4)*

This simple but powerful truth of learning to look beyond our own
interests would be so countercultural if lived out each day by every one of
us. Surely we would see the Kingdom of God breaking out! Isn't that what
we would all love to see?

So why not start today? Why not look beyond your own interests and go
out of your way to bless someone else, or see how you can help someone?
A good way to do this would be to ask the Lord, "Who is it that you want
me to help or bless today?"

*Jesus, thank you for putting others before yourself. Today, I want to
reach out beyond myself so that your Kingdom will grow on earth.
Please show me how I can do this today. Amen.*

I AM A CHILD OF GOD

'Yet to all who received him, to those who believed in his name,
he gave the right to become children of God.' (John 1: 12)

There is a remarkable truth in this one verse. God gave us the right to become His children. We did not earn it, it was given to us. It's a free gift to be enjoyed and lived out if we have made Jesus our Saviour.

So often I forget this truth in my daily walk and therefore try to do things to please my Heavenly Father. I try to say the right things, thinking that hopefully, somehow, He will accept me as His child. I try to do the right things so that everyone is happy and God is pleased with me. But we must learn to live from a place of acceptance rather than striving to be qualified.

Are you certain that you know that you are a child of God? 100% certain, and enjoying this identity that He has given you? Remind yourself of this truth today and begin to enjoy it.

Live it and believe it today - even declare it! Join in with the song by Jonathan and Melissa Helser, 'I am a child of God'. Know who you are and that you are accepted by the One true living God. It will transform your day and it will transform your life.

Father, thank you so much that I am your child. Thank you, Jesus, that you died for me so that I can be a child of the Father. Give me confidence today to believe it and live it out. Amen.

ONE SMALL ACT

'Our people must learn to devote themselves to doing what is good, in order that they may provide for daily necessities and not live unproductive lives.' (Titus 3: 14)

There is a simple yet powerful truth in this one verse of scripture today. It was written to Titus, who was being encouraged to stand firm in his faith and to challenge the early Christians in Crete to do good, to live productive lives and to be different to the culture in which they lived.

It is the same for us today. How will you do good today? How will you be productive in your life? How will you be different? What does goodness and productivity look like in the Kingdom of God?

Recently our church set up a foodbank, to which people can donate food which is then given to those in our community who are in need. It's amazing that doing good in this small way is making an impact in the lives of people and in our community. People are asking questions, and it's wonderful to see how a small act of kindness can open up hearts to Jesus.

Allow the Holy Spirit to inspire you today from the life of Jesus. He is our benchmark.

Jesus, will you show me how I can make a difference and how I can bring you to the people I meet today. Amen.

BE IN HIS PRESENCE

*'O Lord, remember in David's favour all the hardships he endured;
how he swore to the Lord and vowed to the Mighty One of Jacob; "I
will not enter my house or get into my bed; I will not give sleep to
my eyes or slumber to my eyelids, until I find a place for the Lord, a
dwelling place for the Mighty One of Jacob."' (Psalm 132: 1-5, NRSV)*

At the time of King David, God was looking for a location to dwell...
a place where people could come and worship Him, seek His face and hear
Him speak. David knew he had to find the best spot for the Mighty One
of Jacob, and he would not slumber or sleep until he found that place. He
found it in Jerusalem, and that is where the ark of God was moved to. And
David even leapt and danced as the ark was moved! (see 2 Samuel 6: 16).
That's real passion!

Today, we are under a new covenant and we don't have to look for a place
for God to dwell because He dwells within each one of us. But my question
today is this: do we pursue His presence with as much determination and
effort as David did? How good are we at seeking to dwell with God? I am
more convinced than ever that the more time I spend connecting with the
Mighty One, the more likely I am to live life to the full. I need to pursue
Him with a passion.

Will you?

*Jesus, thank you that you have made it possible to live in my heart
through your death on the cross. I choose today to worship you and be
in the presence of the Mighty One, my Father, so that I may be full of life
again. Amen.*

PURSUE PEACE AT ALL COSTS

'Therefore, since we have been justified through faith, we have peace with God through our Lord Jesus Christ.' (Romans 5: 1)

How are you doing? Stuck in a rut? Struggling to shake off feelings of worry or anxiety? Got an issue with someone? I have realised time and time again that I can so easily end up trying to rid myself of this concern or that problem, but the more I try, the more annoying it becomes! It just doesn't seem to go away.

I remember once when I was really struggling with a health issue, it just wouldn't improve and I was getting more and more concerned and anxious about it. But then I decided, "This is not right!" And I sat calmly in God's presence and asked for His peace to take over. Wow, what a difference that made! The problem was still there, but I was one with God, and my troubles and concerns just seemed to fade away because being with God changed my perspective. And God even opened up an opportunity for me to see a specialist!

This amazing truth of scripture can really help. Not only are we right and justified before God, we also have peace with God. That means that you and God are friends, and He is the best friend to have in any situation.

So why not today, sit down with God as your friend and allow that peace to saturate you. You don't need to do anything - it is already there for you to enjoy because Jesus obtained it. Seek that peace with God first, and everything else will begin to loosen its grip on you. God takes care of His children.

Father, today I need to know that you and I are at peace, that you are with me and for me. Thank you that it is possible to be at peace in every situation because you are my friend and nothing is too big for you. Amen.

SHARE YOUR BURDENS

'Cast your cares on the Lord and he will sustain you; he will never let the righteous fall.' (Psalm 55: 22)

———————————————

Have you had a difficult week? Then this verse is perfect for you, as it was for me.

During a difficult season of my life, I had to sit down with my journal and cast all my cares, worries and anxieties at the feet of the Lord and say, "Over to you, my dear friend; you need these and I need to be sustained by you. Will you help?"

He sure did! He is so faithful and I had such a good few days; all the tension, all the thoughts and fears were taken from me. The lesson learned is we must do this daily; we must cast our cares on Him as quickly as we can so that He can step in and not only sustain us through tough times, but draw near to us as well.

So today, cast your cares on Him and watch what happens, because His promise is that you will never fall, and you will never be overcome.

Father, thank you for this wonderful promise to sustain me and get me through difficult times. I choose to hand everything over to you today in order that I may be free to enjoy the day even more. Amen.

THE GATE OF HEAVEN IS OPEN

'He was afraid and said, "How awesome is this place! This is none other than the house of God, this is the gate of heaven."' (Genesis 28: 17)

Jacob had just had an amazing revelation through a God-given dream. He discovered that the God of heaven dwells on earth as well. He had seen angels descending and ascending into heaven and had seen and heard the Lord speak (vs. 14-16). Jacob's response to this revelation was not only to recognise that God was in 'this place', but to declare, "How awesome is this place...this is the gate of heaven".

Should we not be saying the same? Wherever you find yourself today, whether walking or driving, in a meeting or having a coffee or even shopping, take a moment to be aware that heaven is here and God's presence and His angels are with you. Then like Jacob declare, "How awesome is this place - God is here!"

Who knows what might happen as you turn your attention to the reality of God's presence with you, and release the fullness of heaven on earth! Atmospheres will shift, circumstances will change and supernatural opportunities might just pop up that you didn't expect when you acknowledge His presence. Give it a go!

Lord God Almighty, help me recognise your presence in my life and in the place where I am today. Thank you, Jesus, that you dwell in me by your Holy Spirit, that fullness of life can flow through me. Amen.

YOU ARE SAFE

'My sheep listen to my voice; I know them and they follow me. I will give them eternal life, and they shall never perish, no-one can snatch them out of my hand.' (John 10: 27)

This is a good reminder to us to keep listening to Jesus' voice as He is the Good Shepherd and we are His sheep. We can always ask Him for help and advice, but also make space to hear His voice. He has some great stuff to say to us, so let's be listening - it might just help out in a tough situation, a tricky conversation or He might show us the way forward.

Personally, this is one of my favourite verses in scripture. It was given to me in 1989, a month after I had been diagnosed with cancer, by a woman who I had never met, during a ministry time at the end of a church service. It was the night before I was going to hospital to have an operation, she came up to me and said, "This verse is for you", and she prayed over me. I had never experienced that before, and the verse spoke volumes to me, removing a lot of fear, and reminding me that Jesus was with me, and that I would be ok, whether I died from cancer or not.

The final sentence holds a wonderful promise: 'no-one can snatch them out of my hands'. This is a glorious insight into the heart of Jesus: He cares for you, He will protect you and He will fight for you. He is on your side.

Lord Jesus, will you guide me today. Help me hear your voice leading me forward to the green pastures that I need. Amen.

THERE IS NO TIME FOR EVIL

'He went on: "What comes out of a person is what defiles them.
For it is from within, out of a person's heart, that evil thoughts
come - sexual immorality, theft, murder, adultery, greed, malice,
deceit, lewdness, envy, slander, arrogance and folly. All these
evils come from inside and defile a person."' (Mark 7: 20-23)

This is a challenging verse today. At the heart of what Jesus is saying is, "How is your heart? What is stored up inside of you? What is your attitude to your boss at the moment, to your spouse, your friends and your children? Where are your thoughts going?"

We need to be asking the Holy Spirit to fill us daily, so that we can be feeding our hearts and minds on Him, so that we reflect His nature and His goodness. We have the mind of Christ, and we are called to carry purity in our hearts, so that what we say or think today will be uplifting, encouraging and full of truth.

If you know that you are harbouring 'evil thoughts' in your heart, try to engage with them so that you can be set free from their hold over you.

Jesus, thank you that you came to set me free from evil. Please show me where my thoughts are not pure. I confess them to you and I am sorry, please forgive me. Please fill me with your Holy Spirit so that my heart may carry the fruits of the Spirit. Amen.

BREAKTHROUGH

'Now to him who is able to do immeasurably more than all we ask or imagine, according to his power that is at work within us.' (Ephesians 3: 20)

This simple yet powerful verse gives us the opportunity to see God's Kingdom break into our lives, our families and our communities.

I am more convinced than ever that God is waiting for us to dream and imagine things where we would love to see breakthrough, and then to declare them out loud: 'to Him who is able to do more than I can ask or imagine, according to His power that is at work within me'.

Why not spend a few moments thinking of some areas in your life where you would love to see breakthrough. Write them down and then begin to believe and declare them, because His power is at work within you.

Father, thank you for the power within that comes from the Holy Spirit. I choose today to believe in you for breakthroughs in my life, family, work and ministry. I will see your Kingdom grow. Amen.

CHANGING YOUR HEART IS THE SECRET

'Blessed are the pure in heart, for they will see God.' (Matthew 5: 8)

This one verse holds the key to seeing more of God.

Do you have a hunger to see God? How pure is your heart? What are you feeding on? What are you pursuing? What are your desires and your dreams? What is it that you need freedom from in order to have a pure heart and to see God more clearly?

Take a few moments today and ask the Holy Spirit to search your heart. Don't hold back but choose repentance and purity. Receive a heart transformed by God's love, power and grace.

You will be blessed; you will see God more clearly.

Father, I want to see you more clearly than I have ever done before. I give permission for the Holy Spirit to search my heart and remove anything that is stopping me from seeing you today. Amen.

LET'S BELIEVE FOR MORE

"'Have faith in God," Jesus answered. "Truly I tell you, if anyone says to this mountain, "Go, throw yourself into the sea," and does not doubt in his heart but believes that what he says will happen, it will be done for him."' (Mark 11: 22-23)

I remember looking up at Table Mountain in Cape Town, South Africa and saying to myself, "Wow, I could never throw that into the sea! It would be impossible!" So what was Jesus trying to teach His disciples in these two verses about faith?

The first thing is that we must speak to the 'mountains' in our lives. Jesus said, "If anyone says to this mountain..." Jesus is putting the emphasis on us to take action by speaking to the mountains that we are facing. I think Jesus is saying something along these lines: "My child, you speak, you command or you declare, and the mountain will be moved." In other words, you have the authority and power to move this mountain; you have the supernatural power of the Holy Spirit in you, so be encouraged and believe it.

Secondly, when we speak to these 'mountains', we must speak from a place of confidence and not doubt. Jesus said, "...and does not doubt in his heart but believes." How many of us carry doubt because of seemingly unanswered prayers. I know I do, but recently I have learned that faith in God is about fully believing that what is written in His Word is true. I must believe and know this in my heart so that when I speak to the mountain it will move - there is no room for doubt; it just does not belong there.

So today, whatever mountain is in your life, face it, speak to it with confidence and believe in your heart with no doubt and it will move. Have faith in God today, nothing is impossible for Him.

Jesus, may I learn to walk in greater faith than I have ever done and as I speak to the mountains in my life, believing in faith and without any doubt in my heart, they will move. Amen.

ENJOY BEING LOOKED AT (PART 1)

'Jesus looked at him and loved him. "One thing you lack," he said. "Go sell everything you have and give it to the poor, and you will have treasure in heaven. Then come and follow me." At this the man's face fell. He went away sad, because he had great wealth.' (Mark 10: 21-22)

Over the next two days, we are going to explore this one verse.

'Jesus looked at Him and loved Him'.

Jesus was the exact representation of the Father while He walked on earth (see Hebrews 1: 3). Today, this is what Father God is doing with you right now: He is looking at you and He loves you deeply.

If we could grasp that and really believe it, we would have a foundation on which we would truly flourish and thrive; a foundation that would enable us to be who we are really created to be, without any need to impress or strive to be satisfied. It is a truth we need to grasp in our heads and our hearts in order to live life in all its fullness, and to see God's Kingdom move powerfully amongst us.

Father, thank you that you accept me for who I am today. When you look at me, you love me. Help me believe, and then walk confidently in this amazing truth. Amen.

ENJOY BEING LOOKED AT (PART 2)

'Jesus looked at him and loved him. "One thing you lack," he said. "Go sell everything you have and give it to the poor, and you will have treasure in heaven. Then come and follow me." At this the man's face fell. He went away sad, because he had great wealth.' (Mark 10: 21-22)

'He went away sad'.

Why did the rich young man go away sad? One suggestion is that he had a 'false belief' about God - perhaps something that he had inherited from his religious upbringing. The young man was wealthy (there's nothing wrong with that), but he was not able to grasp the truth of what Jesus was saying: "Sell everything and you will have treasure in heaven." He couldn't believe that God would look after him; that God would provide for him if he sold everything. He had a false belief along these lines: 'God can't fully satisfy me; I need something else.' He needed his wealth to make him secure and feel satisfied. That's why he walked away sad, because he couldn't grasp the truth of what Jesus was saying.

Is there a 'false belief' about God that you might be living under today which you may have picked up over the years? Like the young man, you may not be aware of it, but it is always good to ask Father God to show you if you are living under a false belief about Him.

Seeing Father God as He truly is brings us freedom. So give Him permission to search your heart today.

Father, please show me the areas of my life where I am not trusting you 100%. I know that you will provide for me. Help me walk in joy and not sadness. Amen.

WALK IN A VICTORY-MINDSET

'And having disarmed the powers and authorities, he made a public spectacle of them, triumphing over them by the cross.' (Colossians 2: 15)

What a great day in history - Good Friday!

Let's be thinking today of this great spiritual battle that Jesus won on the cross and how that affects our lives. He disarmed all the evil powers and authorities and He triumphed over them.

When a Roman General won a great battle, he would return to Rome with the captive King or General and there would be a powerful triumphant entry into the city. Everyone would turn out and cheer this victory. This is what Paul is comparing Jesus' victory to. It was spectacular and triumphant.

As followers of Jesus, let's be reminding ourselves today that we too can enjoy this triumphant victory. Let's not only cheer Jesus and thank Him, but let's also live in this victory. We can disarm the enemy; we can walk in victory, and we can take back all that the enemy has stolen.

We are victorious. Let's be living this out in our hearts, minds and souls today.

Jesus, today I will not only celebrate your great victory over the enemy, but I will walk and talk in victory and believe that the enemy has lost and he cannot overwhelm me. Amen.

HAVE A GOOD CLEAN OUT

'Woe to you, teachers of the law and Pharisees, you hypocrites! You clean the outside of the cup and dish, but inside they are full of greed and self-indulgence. Blind Pharisee! First clean the inside of the cup and dish, and then the outside will be clean.' (Matthew 23: 25-26)

This strong and challenging word from Jesus is so relevant for us today as well.

At the heart of what Jesus was saying, is that it is all about making sure our hearts are right. It is not about looking good and saying the right thing; it is all about making sure our hearts are pure and holy.

Don't allow the desires of 'I want more' or 'it's all about me' or 'I'm right', to direct and command your heart. Today, examine your heart and see what it is driven by and what is making it tick. Allow the Lord to show you where greed and self-indulgence have a grip, and begin to establish a clean 'inside'.

A clean heart is the secret of enjoying life even more than you are now.

Lord, help me make sure today that my heart is right. Show me if there is any greed or self indulgence going on in me. I want to be clean on the inside. Amen.

THERE IS MORE YOU CAN DO

*'A man in the crowd answered, "Teacher, I brought you my son, who
is possessed by a spirit that has robbed him of speech. Whenever
it seizes him, it throws him to the ground. He foams at the mouth,
gnashes his teeth and becomes rigid. I asked your disciples
to drive out this spirit but they could not."' (Mark 9: 17-18)*

Weeks earlier, the disciples had been driving out demons at a rate of knots, healing the sick, raising the dead and now they could not do it - it seemed as though their prayers were not working. Does that sound familiar to you? They must have felt humiliated and were probably feeling a bit less sure of themselves. What was the lesson they learned from this and what can we learn from this scene?

I think the lesson here, for them and for us, is the importance of spending time resting in the presence and grace of God. This is where Jesus had been the previous night - on top of a mountain, in His Father's Presence (Mark 9: 2-7).

We need this in our lives daily. Time in God's presence will equip us, not only to be more secure in who we are, but also will make us more effective in facing the challenges of each day. Time with God will give us the necessary tools to do the impossible. It is the secret of seeing more of the miraculous in our lives and in the communities in which we live. More time with God in secret will give each of us enough faith to see things we have not yet seen.

*Father, may I spend more time with you today and may you fill me with
your presence and power so that I can see new miraculous powers in my
ministry and in my life. Amen.*

LET THEM FLOURISH

"'Teacher," said John, "we saw a man driving out demons in your name and we told him to stop, because he was not one of us." "Do not stop him," Jesus said, "No-one who does a miracle in my name can in the next moment say anything bad about me."' (Mark 9: 38-39)

In these verses, Jesus lays down a key foundation that we must learn to live by: we must learn to allow others to flourish and to bless and rejoice when we see and hear of what Jesus is doing through them. The disciples were either acting out of jealousy or pride, effectively saying, "This is our ministry, not yours."

So many of us can become narrow-minded and so intolerant that we cannot conceive the possibility of anything else happening outside of our way of doing things. Jesus is challenging us in these verses not to be 'me-focused' but instead to be 'Kingdom-focused'. We must be rejoicing and celebrating what God is doing everywhere and not just focusing on others joining our movement or our work, but instead joining in with His Kingdom.

So ask the Lord to show you if you are harbouring an intolerant spirit towards others today. Jesus wants us all to be rejoicing in what He is doing all around the world.

Jesus, I want to see your Kingdom flourish all over the world. Help me today to bless and encourage everyone I see who is expanding your Kingdom. Amen.

LET'S HONOUR HIM

'When this became known to the Jews and Greeks living in Ephesus, they were all seized with fear, and the name of the Lord Jesus was held in high honour.' (Acts 19: 17)

Today, Jesus' name is often associated with a swear word, or it carries very little authority and power, and people have very little regard for what He has done and continues to do.

I heard a story from a good friend of mine who was praying for sick people in the name of Jesus outside a mosque in The Gambia in Africa. The sick were healed and as word of this spread, he said, "They went nuts and started rushing towards us, just like in the gospels! I asked the translator, 'What are they saying?' He replied, 'They recognise that you are followers of Jesus and people are being healed in Jesus' name.'"

Wow! I love hearing stories like that - I get so excited!

If you truly believe He is alive today, then may I encourage you to be praying for opportunities to demonstrate that Jesus' name is to be honoured.

Jesus, thank you that even today your name is respected. Help me to honour you in all that I do and say, so that people will think differently about you. Amen.

GOD HAS DONE SO MUCH

'For the Lord God is a sun and shield, the Lord bestows favour and honour; no good thing does he withhold from those whose walk is blameless.' (Psalm 84: 11)

I love this Psalm. It was the reading at our wedding.

It seems from what the Psalmist has written that God's nature is to bestow favour and honour on His children. He doesn't want to hold anything back; He has so much to give to us. But the Psalmist also suggests that our walk on earth needs to be blameless, i.e. without fault.

Why not today give thanks for all God's favour and blessing on your life in the last month or so, but also search your heart and mind to make sure that your walk on earth is blameless and without fault.

He has so much more for you. Don't allow anything to hold you back from experiencing the fullness of God's goodness in your life.

God is good. Do you really believe that today?

Father, thank you that it is your nature to bless and pour goodness on your children. You are such a good Father. May I walk upright and true for you today. Amen.

POWER FROM ON HIGH

'I am going to send to you what my Father has promised; but stay in the city until you have been clothed with power from on high.' (Luke 24: 49)

Jesus is about to leave earth and head back home to be with His Father. He has promised His disciples that they will receive 'power from on high' to continue His mission on earth: to grow the Kingdom of God.

In the last few years, I have had the privilege of seeing this 'power from on high', not only change my life, but also change the lives of many people around me. I have seen salvations from teenagers to elderly people; I have seen and witnessed many healings, both physical and mental and have seen the power of the prophetic break through so many barriers. We cannot live this Christian life without this 'power from on high'.

Ask the Father today for a fresh anointing of this power. It is what the Kingdom of God is all about.

Father, will you clothe me with power from on high today. May I receive a fresh outpouring of your Holy Spirit. Amen.

BE STRONG AND DON'T GIVE IN

'"I will not speak with you much longer, for the prince of this world is coming. He has no power over me."' (John 14: 30)

What does Jesus mean by 'he (Satan) has no power over me'?

Mark Stibbe in his devotional book on John's gospel gives the original Greek translation of this verse as this: 'On me, he has nothing.' He goes on to say 'I love that! Jesus tells His disciples, "The devil is on the way, but don't worry, he's got nothing on me."' [11] Jesus had a clean slate, a pure heart, a clear conscience, He was faultless and He was in His Father's presence. The devil could not get at Jesus. I love that too!

All of us have a past and have things going on in our lives right now. We know that the devil is a legalist and is very active, 'prowling around like a lion' (1 Peter 5: 8). Our challenge today therefore, is to be free from our past and to be free from any sin that we might be entertaining right now. We cannot give the devil a chance to have a hold on us. His desire is to steal, kill and destroy. If we really want to walk as Jesus did, it starts with us breaking free from collaborating with sin and our earthly desires. That is why Jesus put such a big emphasis on repentance and forgiveness. We must choose this path so that that the enemy cannot get a hold on us.

So do search your heart and make sure the devil doesn't have a hold on you and is not stopping you from living out the truths of the Kingdom of God today.

Jesus, thank you that you fulfilled your mission on earth. Help me today to believe who I am in you and not allow the enemy to hold me back. Please show me if I am sinning in any way. Amen.

WALK IN CONFIDENCE

'Do not let anyone look down on you (Timothy) because you are young, but set an example for the believers in speech, in life, in love, in faith and in purity.' (1 Timothy 4: 12)

Timothy was a pastor of one of the earliest churches to be established in Asia Minor around AD 64. Here we read that he was being encouraged by his mentor Paul, to lead more by example than anything else. As a well-known phrase says, 'it is better caught than taught'.

Paul's words to Timothy are a challenge to us today. He highlights five ways to live out the faith:

1) Let your speech be honest and truthful.

2) Set out to be an example to others today.

3) Let your love for others be unconditional.

4) Let your faith be active.

5) Let your heart be ruled by purity.

These five examples spur us on not only to 'say' what we believe, but also to 'show' what we believe through how we live.

I encourage you today to start putting these five examples into action in your own life, and watch what happens around you.

Lord Jesus, help me today to live a life that draws people to you. Amen.

WALK BEFORE GOD

*'And Solomon said, "You have shown great kindness to
your servant, my father David, because he was faithful to
you and righteous and upright in heart."' (1 Kings 3: 6)*

This is a challenging word today and continues the theme of how to live a
different life by walking closely with Father God.

King Solomon reminds us how his father, David, knew the great and
steadfast love of the Lord during his life on earth. David walked faithfully,
righteously and 'upright in heart' towards God. As he did this, he
experienced the love of God that enabled him to fulfil his destiny. That is
what his son Solomon remembered about his father.

What will people say about you in the years to come? What will be written
about you? What would your children or grandchildren write about you?

*Jesus, help me walk in your ways and show people that you are real and
that you make a huge difference in my life. Amen.*

YOU ARE NOT ALONE

'I am with you and will watch over you wherever you go, and I will bring you back to this land. I will not leave you until I have done what I have promised you.' (Genesis 28: 15)

God is speaking to Jacob in a dream in the middle of the desert. He has just started his journey. (Actually, he is on the run from his big brother who wants to beat him up!)

In this one verse there are some extraordinary promises that God makes: 'I am with you; I will watch over you; I will bring you back; I will not leave you'. Sure enough, that is what happened - Jacob did return to the land and became the father of a great nation.

One of the promises that stands out for me is the first one: 'I am with you'. It is also a promise that Jesus made to His disciples: 'And surely I am with you always' (Matthew 28: 20). It is God's heart to be with His children, to walk with them and not abandon them, or distance himself. He is 100% with you today. That has not changed.

Take a moment to enjoy this truth. Allow it to sink deep into your being and believe it. He is with you; you are not on your own.

Thank you, Father, that you do not leave me on my own, but you are always with me. Whatever my situation, I know that I am not alone. Amen.

HOW WILL YOU DO IT?

'As it is written: "God's name is blasphemed among the Gentiles because of you."' (Romans 2: 24)

The apostle Paul wrote this challenging word to the church in Rome.

The questions we must ask ourselves today are: How will I be a good witness for God so that His name is not blasphemed? How will I demonstrate God's love today? How might I help change what people think of God today?

I encourage you to use the gifts that God has given you to open up people's eyes to the truth of who God really is.

Be praying for opportunities to use the prophetic gift so that the love of God can break into people's lives.

Father, today help me make every effort to ensure that you are honoured, respected and valued. Amen.

HE IS THE BEST COMFORTER

'The Lord is the strength of his people, a fortress of salvation for his anointed one. Save your people and bless your inheritance; be their shepherd and carry them forever.' (Psalm 28: 8-9)

Here, in these verses, the Psalmist is giving us an image not only of a God who saves us and is our strong 'fortress', but also He is our Shepherd who will carry us.

Can you remember the last time you were carried? Maybe you are in a season now when you are carrying your own children. As a parent, do you enjoy carrying them?

Will you let God carry you today? Will you snuggle up in His huge arms of love and allow Him to lead you to 'green pastures', and to those 'quiet waters' for much needed refreshment?

Today, don't walk but instead imagine yourself being carried by the Great Shepherd. He is the best one to wrap you in His arms of love.

Father, I invite you to carry me through this day. May I learn to relax in your arms and enjoy the places and meetings you take me to. Amen.

WE ALL NEED A BIT OF WISDOM

'God said, "Ask for whatever you want me to give you." ..."So give your servant therefore a discerning heart to govern your people and to distinguish between right and wrong. For who is able to govern this great people of yours?"' (1 Kings 3: 5b; 9)

King Solomon was at the beginning of his reign when God said, "What would you like me to give you?" Solomon could have asked for so many other things but, the more I think about it, what he asked for was spot on! Simply put, he was asking for wisdom so that he could rule God's people well.

What would you ask God for today if He asked you that same question? When was the last time you asked God for wisdom? We need wisdom so that we can not only discern things more clearly, but also be distinguishable in how we conduct our lives. Embracing wisdom will reveal more of the nature of God to the people with whom we spend our time and share our lives.

Godly wisdom is precious. Ask God today for His wisdom.

Father, will you fill me with your wisdom today so that I may make a difference to the people I meet. Amen.

THERE IS GOLD WITHIN YOU

'Saul answered, "But am I not a Benjamite, from the smallest tribe of Israel, and is not my clan the least of all the clans of the tribe of Benjamin? Why do you say such a thing to me?"' (1 Samuel 9: 21)

The prophet Samuel had just spoken to Saul and had said that he was the person Israel was looking for - their new leader. Saul could not see that in himself, instead what he thought was the opposite: he did not think he could do the job; he felt totally insignificant.

Low self-esteem robs us of seeing the truth of who we are, what we carry, and what we can do.

For many years, and even today at times, my first thought about a task or a situation I am facing is to think, "I can't do that... someone else is better equipped than me". We have to learn to walk in the truth of how God sees us and know that He has placed gifts and talents within each one of us, to do more than we think we can. He supernaturally equips us.

So today, whatever you face, be confident in who you are and what you can do with what God has placed within you. In addition, help others who you encounter today - friends, colleagues, members of your own family - to learn to see the gold within themselves and then call it out in them.

When we live knowing our significance, we can be used by Father God to impact the world around us.

Father, today I will not allow self-pity or low self-esteem to win the day. I will walk tall in who I am in your eyes, and make a difference wherever I am. Amen.

TAKE YOUR DREAMS SERIOUSLY

'But after he had considered this, an angel of the Lord appeared to him in a dream... And having been warned in a dream not to go back to Herod, they returned to their country by another route.' (Matthew 1: 20; 2: 12)

Here in the beginning of the book of Matthew, God was using dreams to communicate. It is one of the many ways in which God speaks to us.

God had not spoken to His people for over 400 years and suddenly in a short space of time, the silence was broken and God began to speak. He used dreams to get His message across.

God still speaks through dreams today, He is not silent. I have begun to experience this myself more recently. When we are asleep, we have no distractions so God has our 100% attention. Our nights and our rest time is not wasted time.

I encourage you not to ignore your dreams. You never know what God might be saying to you. He is still speaking and has your best interests at heart. (If you are interested in looking more into dreams, I recommend a book that has given me greater revelation into understanding dreams. It is called Understanding your Dreams Now by Doug Addison, published by Lightning Source Inc, 2013. It's a very easy read.)

God is speaking to us through our dreams now and we can learn to discern what God is saying.

Father, thank you that you still speak to us in dreams. May you open up my mind to what you are saying and showing me through my dreams. Amen.

LET'S MAKE A DIFFERENCE TODAY

'So Daniel was brought before the king, and the king said to him, "Are you Daniel, one of the exiles my father the king brought from Judah? I have heard that the spirit of the gods is in you and that you have insight, intelligence and outstanding wisdom... Then Daniel answered the king, "You may keep your gifts for yourself and give your rewards to someone else. Nevertheless, I will read the writing for the king and tell him what it means."' (Daniel 5: 13; 17)

Daniel was a remarkable man who made a huge impact, not only on the kings of that era, but also on the nations and the known world even though he was in exile (Daniel 6: 25).

Why did he make such an impact? Firstly, Daniel did not live by his own strength or wisdom but he had the Spirit of the Lord within him. This is what made such a difference and allowed him to do what others could not.

Secondly, he did not pursue riches, power and prestige. His identity was firmly rooted in God, therefore he could walk in humility trusting God to meet all his needs.

Today, let's invite the Spirit of God to fill us so that we can walk in humility, free from selfish ambition and the desire for recognition; free from the need to establish ourselves through wealth or power; with our identity firmly rooted in how God sees us and not what the world can offer us. Then, like Daniel, we can have an impact in the environment in which God has placed us.

Holy Spirit, will you fill me afresh so that I can go out into this world with you as my strength and wisdom. I need your help today so that I can be different from the world around me. Amen.

MAKE THAT BOLD STEP

*'With this in mind, we constantly pray for you, that our God
may count you worthy of his calling, and that by his power
he may fulfil every good purpose of yours and every act
prompted by your faith.' (2 Thessalonians 1: 11)*

This is a simple but challenging verse for us today.

How active has your faith been recently? What act have you done in
faith that has either changed the atmosphere around you or influenced
someone's situation? I recently heard a story of a young man who felt
prompted by God to go into his local supermarket, with the instructions
from heaven that he would find someone who was unwell. He called out
in a loud voice, "Is anyone here sick and need healing?" All the shoppers
ignored him initially, but he persisted and finally a woman approached
him and told him that she had cancer. He was able to pray for her and
minister God's healing. He acted in faith, confident of God's power.

However big or small, Father God is waiting for us to go for it! As we step
out in faith, He will release His power so that He can fulfil His purposes
in you.

Let's be active in everything we do today and see God's power at work
through us.

*Father, today help me to step out in faith and confidence to do
something that I have not done before. I trust you to fill me with your
power so that I may do your will. Amen.*

YOU HAVE DONE SO WELL

*'When I remember you in my prayers, I always thank my God
because I hear of your love for all the saints and your faith
toward the Lord Jesus. I pray that the sharing of your faith may
become effective when you perceive all the good that we may do
for Christ. I have indeed received much joy and encouragement
from your love, because the hearts of the saints have been
refreshed through you, my brother.' (Philemon 1: 4-7, NRSV)*

What wonderful words to hear! They are so uplifting and honouring.
Philemon, the believer who Paul was writing to, must have been 'the
real deal'.

Would someone write such wonderful words about you? Or would you be
able to encourage someone today and affirm them about their faith
and life?

In these verses, we are challenged to be active in sharing our faith. So
today, why not do both: seek fresh revelation into ways to share your faith,
but also ask the Lord, if there is anyone He wants you to encourage today.

***Father, give me the opportunity today to share my faith with someone in
a way that will bless them and give them joy. Amen.***

YOU WILL GET THROUGH

'Even when I walk through the dark valley of death, I will not be afraid, for you are close beside me. Your rod and your staff protect and comfort me.' (Psalm 23: 4, NLT)

This one verse has given me hope over the many years of trials and suffering. It was one of the first verses God showed me after I had been told I had cancer with a 50/50 chance of living. It has continued to be a great foundation for me.

A few years ago, we bought a wonderful painting from a local shop. The picture is of a dark wood with a path leading into a beautiful green field. We bought it at a time when we had nowhere to live, no income and no work. It spoke to us, that despite this hard time, there is always a 'green pasture', always a better place to get to than where we are now.

Whatever you are facing today or in life, remember this small word 'through'. It gives hope that the dark valley is only a place to go through, not a place to remain. God will lead you out of it. Stay close to Him and walk through the dark valley to the green pastures. We can so easily be stuck in our troubles, trials or tough experiences and lose our way, but we must hold on to this truth - that we will get through and we need not be afraid of the valley of darkness.

God is close to you, and He will lead you out. You will get through this time.

Jesus, thank you that you walk with me in the dark times of life and you will remain close to me and get me through this valley into the green pastures that I need. Amen.

YOU HAVE IT

'Then Peter said, "Silver or gold I do not have, but what I have I give you. In the name of Jesus Christ of Nazareth, walk." Taking him by the right hand, he helped him up, and instantly the man's feet and ankles became strong. He jumped to his feet and began to walk.' (Acts 3: 6-8)

This was one of the first bible stories that captured my imagination when I was a young child. I just loved the power and awe of this story! A man born crippled, asking for money to help him survive, got a supernatural miracle instead and his life was changed forever.

Peter and John had both recently encountered the power of the Holy Spirit in their lives. They knew they had something special, and they knew that it was worth more than gold or silver. I love the fact they knew they had it and then gave it away. It was so simple - no long prayer - just simple: 'In Jesus name, walk!' Boom! The miracle happened!

We must learn to know what we have, and we must learn how to use it effectively so that the lives of people we encounter today will be changed.

You have something within you that is more precious and more valuable than gold or silver; more powerful than any form of medicine to use for Jesus' glory.

It is time for the Kingdom of God to expand through you, like it did for Peter and John.

Jesus, help me learn to give away what you have given me, so that others may encounter you in a supernatural way. Amen.

IT IS NOT NEAR, IT'S HERE

'But you will receive power when the Holy Spirit comes on you;
and you will be my witnesses in Jerusalem, and in all Judea
and Samaria, and to the ends of the earth.' (Acts 1: 8)

Jesus said that we would receive the supernatural power of the Holy Spirit and would be His witnesses to the ends of the earth.

Recently, I saw a poster that said, 'Live as if the Kingdom of God is near'. However, I believe it should have said, 'Live as if the Kingdom of God is here'! The Kingdom of God is here for us to experience and live in. It is not near... it is here!

We are called to be witnesses for the Kingdom of God today and, in the power of the Spirit, we can be effective witnesses to the fact that the Kingdom of God is here, and is real in increasing measure in our lives.

Let's believe in more of the supernatural power of the Holy Spirit in our lives and that the Kingdom of God is here.

Jesus, thank you for making it possible for the work of the Holy Spirit in my life today. May I receive the power of the Holy Spirit in my life so that I can be a witness for your Kingdom. Amen.

LET'S ACTIVATE OUR FAITH

'My eyes will be on the faithful in the land, that they may dwell with me.' (Psalm 101: 6a)

_____

Learning to dwell with God by 'being' and not 'doing', is one of the great spiritual disciplines we must learn to master. To dwell with God, with no other agenda than spending time with Him, is such a good way to start the day. It's a choice that takes great faith, but in the stopping, in the silence and in the stillness, you will be with God and He will be with you.

How do we ensure that God's eyes remain on us so that we can dwell with Him and He with us?

I find that one of the best ways to get my faith active is to start each day by just stopping everything, being still and silent in the Lord's presence.

Father, I know you want to spend time with me today. Help me move forward in my faith by learning to do nothing but dwell with you. Amen.

NO FAITH

'He got up, rebuked the wind and said to the waves, "Quiet! Be still!" Then the wind died down and it was completely calm. He said to his disciples, "Why are you so afraid? Do you still have no faith?" They were terrified and asked each other, "Who is this? Even the wind and the waves obey him!"' (Mark 4: 39-41)

This is a great story and a glimpse into the disciples' journey of discovering who Jesus was and what He was able to do. As they walked with Jesus and as their faith grew, the early disciples also began to see impossible things happen: the dead raised, prison doors opened, cripples healed and storms stilled.

Recently, I was out walking my dog on the South Downs and the wind was blowing and the rain was pouring as I came to the top of a hill. As I stood there, I thought, "Let me see if I can do anything about this." I straightened up, rebuked the wind, and told the rain to stop. Guess what? There was a small break in the clouds and it did stop raining for a minute... then the heavens opened up again and I got even wetter! However, I felt encouraged that I was exercising my faith in Jesus and in the power of the Spirit to see the impossible happen.

So today, let's be stepping out more in our faith and believing for more of the impossible to happen. God is waiting to see active faith so that He can release His supernatural power through us. So why not take those steps today.

Jesus, you calmed the storm for your early disciples and they grew in their faith and understanding of who you were. Help me to move forward in my faith and to step out and calm the storms that surround me today. Amen.

REPENTANCE IS WONDERFUL

'After John was put in prison, Jesus went into Galilee, proclaiming the good news of God. "The time has come," he said. "The kingdom of God is near. Repent and believe in the good news!"' (Mark 1: 14-15)

Why did Jesus tell the world to repent in His opening message? It's a hard word to hear and receive, but true repentance opens up the opportunity not only to be free from sin, but gives us access to a living relationship with Father God. Now that is good news!

We should never take repentance lightly, nor underestimate the power and influence of sin in our lives. Jesus knew that sin is the barrier that stops us from moving forward in our relationship with the Father. That is the one thing Jesus desires most for each of us, which is why repentance is key to life.

I have found it useful over the years to learn to recognise sin or lies which are subtly influencing me. The more I do this, the freer I am, and the more I get to experience the fullness of being in the Father's presence.

I encourage you to invite the Holy Spirit to help you recognise where sin might be in your life, repent of it and enjoy the benefits of the good news: a real and living relationship with Father God.

Holy Spirit, will you help me recognise where I am falling into sin, or listening to and believing in lies that stop me from being fully alive in the presence of Father God. Amen.

DESIRE TO BE IN HIS PRESENCE

'When his parents saw him, they were astonished. His mother said to him, "Son, why have you treated us like this? Your father and I have been anxiously searching for you." "Why were you searching for me?" he asked. "Didn't you know that I had to be in my Father's house?"'
(Luke 2: 48-49)

For the Jewish people, the temple was where God dwelt and where His presence was.

Jesus was to be found in God's presence in the temple. When His parents finally located Him, His response to His mother was quite remarkable: "Did you not know I must be in my Father's house" or as some translations say, "be about my Father's business". Jesus was ushering in a new era and a new understanding by saying this. It is the first time that Jesus uses the phrase 'my Father'. In doing so, He reveals the possibility of an intimate relationship with God which was something totally new. Jesus was aligning himself with His Father, seeking Him and being with Him. He knew that being in His Father's presence would be the most significant thing in His life.

Today, I encourage you to spend time in the Father's house, to pursue His presence, and know Him more deeply.

Jesus, you knew that the best thing in life was to be in your Father's house. My desire is to make that my priority too. Amen.

MORE FUEL ON THE FIRE

'A shoot will come up from the stump of Jesse; from his roots a
Branch will bear fruit. The Spirit of the Lord will rest on him—the
Spirit of wisdom and of understanding, the Spirit of counsel
and power, the Spirit of the knowledge and of the fear of the
Lord—and he will delight in the fear of the Lord.' (Isaiah 11: 1-3)

The prophet Isaiah is speaking about the future and is prophesying about Jesus, who would be born some 700 years later.

What strikes me about these verses is the mention of the word 'Spirit' four times in these three verses. Whenever there is an emphasis on a particular word, it's worth taking note. It would seem that without the Spirit, Jesus would not have been equipped to do what He did. He needed the Spirit, and Isaiah was showing what the Spirit brings.

The Spirit has so much to give you today so welcome and acknowledge Him at work within you. He is already within you so pour fuel on the fire within you today. Set the fire going and be listening to the Spirit's promptings as you go about your day.

Holy Spirit, I ask today that you will be alive in me, that I will walk in step with you, listening and being guided by you. Amen.

STOP WORRYING

'Therefore I tell you, do not worry about your life, what you will eat or drink; or about your body, what you will wear. Is not life more important than food, and the body more important than clothes? Look at the birds of the air; they do not sow or reap or store away in barns, and yet your heavenly Father feeds them. Are you not much more valuable than they? Who of you by worrying can add a single hour to his life?' (Matthew 6: 25-27)

Jesus knows that worry is a great temptation for us. He explains that we are more valuable than the birds of the air which God takes care of. Jesus is revealing a simple truth: not only are we extremely valuable to His Father, but we can trust God to take care of our all needs and not let worry become our focus. This can be a tough balance to get right.

Someone said to me recently: "Worrying is the way the enemy gets worshipped and gets attention." Shortly afterwards, someone sent me a worship song with the lyrics, 'God's not worried, why do I worry?'

Let's remember that we are more valuable and loved than anything else God has created and that He will take care of all our needs. What He desires more than anything else is for us to step out in faith and trust Him. So let's stop worrying, and instead focus on Him who can do the impossible, then we can step out in faith in the area of our lives where worry is trying to gain a foothold.

I am more valuable than anything else that God created - He will take care of all my worries today. I choose to trust Him more and believe that He will come through for me. Amen.

GOD IN ACTION

*'They overcame him by the blood of the Lamb and by the
word of their testimony; they did not love their lives so
much as to shrink from death.' (Revelation 12: 11)*

We need to build a habit of testifying to God's goodness in our lives every day.

Testimonies can abound in our communities because of Jesus' sacrifice. Spoken or written, small or wondrous, testimonies renew our courage and help us triumph over the enemy.

In 2014, I made the painful and challenging choice to step down from leading a church. Due to increased hearing loss and damage to my vocal cords, communication had become very difficult, resulting in increasing inability to hear others, or to be heard. My wife Michelle and I felt that we were stepping into an abyss. How would we cope financially and emotionally?

Eight years on, our life is a testimony of God's faithfulness in action. His closeness and comfort meets my family's needs in ongoing detailed and significant ways, such as the unexpected financial gift which enabled us to take a much-needed holiday; or church members who felt prompted to offer us their old washing machine. (Unbeknownst to them, ours had just broken! The gift turned out to be an upgraded and perfectly working model of our broken one.) These unexpected blessings significantly strengthened us and I remain convinced that these small miracles were the direct outworking of His goodness in action at a time I needed testimony to triumph.

Keep seeking the Father's presence; be persistent and watch for 'doors' to open so that you can experience His unexpected miracles. He loves having fun and blessing your household in unforeseen ways. He is honest and He is good. Testimonies are powerful, and they break any power the enemy might have in our lives.

*Lord, I declare that in my life I will see the power of the testimony of your
faithfulness to me. Amen.*

IT'S SHOWTIME

'They will be called oaks of righteousness, a planting of the Lord for the display of His splendour.' (Isaiah 61: 3b)

These words from the prophet Isaiah have been spoken over my life numerous times by people who did not know me, as well as by friends and family. It is such a wonderful image to hold onto and to be encouraged by.

A large oak tree in full bloom is a delight to see: strong, healthy and magnificent. It is a powerful image of who we can be if we are fulfilling the spiritual call on our lives.

God has put you where you are today - whether at work, at home, with friends or with family - and you are planted there so that you can display God's splendour and His glory. The good news is that this is achieved, not through striving, but by flowing with the Spirit who lives inside you.

Wherever you are today, whatever you do, say and think, allow your roots to draw deeply on the waters of the Spirit and you will bring glory to God.

Father, thank you that in you, I am a mighty oak tree. Today I will seek to display your glory with everyone I see and come into contact with. Amen.

REVIVAL IS ON OUR DOORSTEP

'They gave to everyone as he had need. Every day they continued to meet together in the temple courts. They broke bread in their homes and ate together with glad and sincere hearts, praising God and enjoying the favour of all the people. And the Lord added to their number daily those who were being saved.' (Acts 2: 45b-47)

I love this chapter in Acts. There is so much good stuff being released from heaven. This is the first ever recording in the scriptures of the birth of a revival.

The Spirit was released and poured out onto all people who were utterly amazed at what was happening and by the end of the first day, 3000 people repented and were saved. The Church of Jesus Christ was born and continues to grow today. At the heart of it is this: they met every day, broke bread, looked after each other where there was need, and praised God with grateful and sincere hearts.

Is it time to start pursuing revivals again in our families, and the communities in which we live? Let's return to these simple but powerful principles and live them out the best we can. Try, each day (or at least once a week) to have a focused time together, to break bread, to spend time with Father God, to praise Him with thankful hearts, and to be looking out to find new ways to help your friends and neighbours. If we do these well, I believe the Lord will indeed add to our number those who are being saved.

Let's be expectant to receive what heaven is releasing.

Lord, help me live a life that reflects these foundational truths of what it means to follow you today. Amen.

BE ALWAYS CHANGING

'Neither circumcision nor uncircumcision means anything; what counts is a new creation.' (Galatians 6: 15)

This is a strange verse which the Lord brought to my attention.

Paul, the author of the letter to the Galatians, is challenging them not to hold onto an old way of life, but to be changed into the new creation that Jesus Christ makes possible.

As I entered my third week of lockdown in 2020 during the Covid-19 pandemic, I began to experience a deeper understanding of what it means to become 'a new creation'. The old habits, views and lifestyle seemed not to mean as much as they had done three weeks earlier. I realised I had been changed into someone new.

A friend said to me during this time, "Let's hope that the by-products of this terrible situation are stronger families and each one of us becoming better people." I agreed with him. I was determined to use this time as a season for change in my life, in my thinking and in my family. I know I came out of lockdown a changed person. That season didn't stop the new creation growing in me.

Today is no different. We need to be changing. Allow the Holy Spirit to work in your life, as it is only through Him that can we become new creations.

Holy Spirit, you bring something fresh every day. I choose today to accept what you have for me and allow it to change me into a better person. Amen.

NO RETIREMENT IN THE KINGDOM

'Even youths grow tired and weary, and young men stumble and fall; but those who hope in the Lord will renew their strength. They will soar on wings like eagles; they will run and not grow weary, they will walk and not be faint.' (Isaiah 40: 30-31)

Over the years, Michelle and I have had the great privilege of discipling many young adults. Their energy and passion for God is always so infectious and we are constantly inspired by their commitment for reaching the lost. At times though, this has left us both wondering if we are 'past it' or a bit 'redundant'. Surely there is nothing we can bring to the Kingdom to match their fire?

However, these great words from Isaiah say something different. Endurance and influence in the Kingdom of God does not have a sell-by date; it is not confined to those in the prime of their lives. It is found instead through hoping in the Lord. Even the youthful zeal of the young will eventually fail. Only 'hope in the Lord' will keep them strong.

So today, I encourage you to deal with any false or counterfeit hopes in your life which we can start to build and depend upon. These could be money or property, work, image or relationships. Repent and replace them with hope in the Lord. Then, whether young or old, whether running, walking or 'soaring', we will not grow weary or faint. Instead, we will be able to stay strong in the Lord right until the end of our days.

Father, thank you that in you there is life and strength. Today, I shake off any lies that say I am redundant or past it, and I take hold of all that you have for me. Expose every false hope in me, so that I can be strengthened through hoping in you alone. Amen.

GENEROUS AND GOOD

'Then Moses said, "Now show me your glory." And the Lord said, "I will cause all my goodness to pass in front of you."' (Exodus 33: 18-19)

Moses asked to see God's glory, and God showed him His goodness. It would seem that God's glory and the goodness of God are one and the same thing. I love this: goodness and glory wrapped up in a powerful combo. God is good and that is foundational to who He is. If we believe this, then our whole concept and image of God will change.

A close friend has taught me a simple yet powerful saying: "God is good and the enemy is bad." This helps me hold onto God's goodness and recognise that even in confusing and stormy times, what God gives is always good.

So often people view God as harsh or torrid. However, He is good and He wants to show us His goodness. When we encounter His goodness, we are changed - in our lives and our situations and, like Moses, even in our very countenance (Exodus 34: 30).

Every day, as I continue to seek healing for long-term health struggles, I have to remind myself of this powerful truth: He provides healing, not sickness. There is no sickness in heaven for God to give. He is good.

Have you asked God recently to reveal more of His goodness to you? There is nothing wrong with asking your Abba Father to bless you with His goodness. It will make a huge difference in your life.

Father, thank you that you are generous with your goodness towards me. Today, I seek more revelation of the goodness of your glory. Amen.

IT'S TIME TO KNEEL

'When they came to the crowd, a man approached
Jesus and knelt before him.' (Matthew 17: 14)

'He knelt before Jesus'. This is a very humbling act to do.

During the season of lockdown in 2020, I rediscovered how good it is to be on my knees before Jesus. The very act of adopting a kneeling posture provided an opportunity to stay focused on Jesus and bring something new into my spiritual life.

As we kneel before Him, we are humbling ourselves in recognising just how awesome and powerful, yet caring and compassionate God is. One of my favourite quotes is from John Wesley: 'Every work of God can be traced back to men and women on bended knees.'

As the man knelt before Jesus and shared his heart, telling Jesus what his son was struggling with, Jesus responded and the man's son was healed (v. 18). I love it when Jesus acts like that! He still does it today.

Is it time to be on your knees? Whatever circumstances you may be facing today, I encourage you to kneel before Jesus and share your heart with Him. I believe Jesus will respond to your prayers in the same way as the man who knelt before Jesus. He will act for His Kingdom purposes to be seen on earth.

Jesus, I kneel before you today. I recognise who you are and what you can do. Hear my prayers and may your Kingdom come on earth as it is in heaven today. Amen.

ONE DAY... IT WILL HAPPEN

'One day Peter and John were going up to the temple at the time of prayer - at three in the afternoon. Now a man who was lame from birth was being carried to the temple gate called Beautiful ... He jumped to his feet and began to walk ... For the man who was miraculously healed was over forty years old.' (Acts 3: 1; 8; Acts 4: 22)

'One day'.

I was recently reading a book that brought home to me the significance of 'one day'. These two words remind us to believe that God can do anything - we just have to keep trusting and persevering.

The man who was healed by Peter and John that day was born lame and he was healed some 40 years later.

'One day' gives us hope; 'one day' your situation will change; 'one day' the money will come in; 'one day' your prodigal will return; 'one day' the sickness will be under control.

'One day' is such a powerful phrase to hang onto wherever you find yourself today. It is coming; God has heard your prayers. Keep praying, keep trusting and keep persevering because today could be that 'one day' for you.

Father, thank you that you have heard my prayer, so I will not lose hope, I will still trust you to move in my life, to change my situation and to bring healing to me. This will be my 'one day'. Amen.

PASS ON THE BATON OF FAITH

'O God, from my youth you have taught me, and I still proclaim your wondrous deeds. So even to old age and grey hairs, O God, do not forsake me, until I proclaim your might to all the generations to come.' (Psalm 71: 17–18, NRSV)

Here are some wonderful verses of scripture for us to take hold of today and live out until we do indeed grow old and have grey hairs! Let's be full of hope! Let's be praising Him! Let's be sharing our stories of how we live out our faith each day, so that we see marvellous deeds amongst us.

Once a week as a family, we join with my parents and my brother's family for supper and we share highlights or stories of what we have seen God doing in our lives during the week. We are telling our children what God has been up to in fun ways and they share their stories with us too.

How do you share your stories? How do you pass on your baton of faith?

Let's be passing on a baton that is full of life and hope for others to take hold of and be inspired by. It is a great joy to be in a relationship with 'Him who is able to do immeasurably more than all we ask or imagine' (Ephesians 3: 20).

Jesus, you have blessed me so much over the years. May I tell of all that you have done for me. Today, I believe that you will do even more than I can imagine. Help me pass on the baton of faith to the next generation of believers. Amen.

DEFEND OUR MESSAGE

'Watch out for those dogs, those people who do evil, those mutilators who say you must be circumcised to be saved. For we who worship by the Spirit of God are the ones who are truly circumcised. We rely on what Christ Jesus has done for us. We put no confidence in human effort.' (Philippians 3: 2-3, NLT)

Paul, the author of this verse, was on cracking form when sharing something that is close to his heart! He uses quite strong words: 'Watch out for those dogs, those people who do evil, those mutilators'. I am sure he would be in a bit of trouble if he used those words today! It is clear that he not only dislikes religious zealots, but also any form of religious rules, such as circumcision.

So what is he so passionate about? In these two verses, he is defending the gospel of Jesus Christ. He does not want the gospel to be diluted from its true message in any way. Jesus has done everything by His death on the cross and His resurrection. There is nothing else that needs to be done to be accepted by Father God. No human effort will make salvation possible.

I love saying to my daughter: "So, why do I love you?"

She replies, "Because I am your daughter!" She doesn't have to achieve anything or do anything to make me love her. I just love her. She's my daughter. It's the same with our salvation. We are saved because Jesus has done everything.

So today, let's be really clear on the message we share with people: it is finished; it has all been done by Jesus. All you have to do is accept Jesus as your Saviour and make Him Lord of your life. That's it.

Jesus, may I have the opportunity to share the message of the cross today; to tell people that is it all done; everything is paid for and ready to be received. Amen.

GROW IN HIS PRESENCE

'Meanwhile, the boy Samuel grew up in the presence of the Lord... And the boy continued to grow in stature and in favour with the Lord and with men.' (1 Samuel 2: 21b and 26)

Samuel shaped the course of history for Israel during his lifetime. He worked with God to establish the kingship for Israel and he anointed the first two kings of Israel: Saul and David. He was one of Israel's first prophets and set a standard that would be followed by generations to come. What was his secret? His secret was that he had learnt to be in the presence of God from a very early age.

When we live in God's presence, we can hear and recognise His voice; we can move forward in peace and confidence; and we can see His Kingdom displayed through us even more.

How good are you at being in God's presence? I am more convinced than ever that this discipline and lifestyle is something all of us must pursue to a greater level. One thing I try to do is to be still and wait on Him. I turn my affections towards Him to receive His love for me in my heart.

I encourage you today, to learn to pursue and practice being in the presence of God in your life. God wants to be with you. Will you let Him?

Father I need your help, I need to grow in this spiritual discipline of being in your presence each day. I know it will change my life. Amen.

HE IS SEEKING YOU

'Yet a time is coming and has now come when the true worshippers will worship the Father in spirit and truth, for they are the kind of worshippers the Father seeks.' (John 4: 23)

In this well-known conversation with the Samaritan woman, Jesus reveals more about His Father. I am struck by the word 'seeks'. This one word gives a marvellous insight into the Father's heart.

Seeking is an active expression that Jesus uses to describe what His Father is like. I love it! It shows that our Father is interested in us. He desires to be with us.

Jesus is saying that His Father no longer needs a building to be worshipped in (the temple in Jerusalem). He no longer sits distanced from us, but actually He is out there seeking, looking and searching the earth - in your home and in your community - for true worshippers.

How will you be a true worshipper in your life, in your home, in your conversations and in your thoughts today? God is seeking you out. Will He find in you a true worshipper in spirit and truth?

Father, thank you that I can worship you anywhere today. May I be filled with the Holy Spirit today, so that I can worship you in spirit and in truth. Amen.

A TEACHABLE HEART

'If you ignore criticism, you will end in poverty and disgrace; if you accept criticism, you will be honoured.' (Proverbs 13: 18, NLT)
'If you listen to constructive criticism, you will be at home among the wise, if you reject criticism you only harm yourself; but if you listen to correction, you grow in understanding.' (Proverbs 15: 31-32, NLT)

In these three verses from the book of Proverbs, we are advised not to ignore criticism or correction. Both of these are very hard to receive at times, but if we are prepared to listen and learn from others then we will benefit, grow and be better off. We need to live our lives in a way that enables us to be open to challenge and change. If not, then we will only bring more problems our way.

So today be preparing yourself so that when criticism is given, you can receive it and deal with it. One way to prepare yourself is to make sure you carry a soft and teachable heart. The best way to have a soft and teachable heart is to invite Jesus into it every day, for Him to be at the centre of all your thoughts. He is the only person qualified to change your heart, so let Him in.

Lord, help me to receive any form of correction or even criticism well, and to be prepared to change into a person who is teachable. Jesus, please will you prepare my heart. Amen.

LET'S BELIEVE IN THE PROMISES

'They came to Bethsaida, and some people brought a blind man and begged Jesus to touch him. He took the blind man by the hand and led him outside the village. When he had spat on the man's eyes and put his hands on him, Jesus asked, "Do you see anything?" He looked up and said, "I see people; they look like trees walking around." Once more Jesus put his hands on the man's eyes. Then his eyes were opened, his sight was restored, and he saw everything clearly.' (Mark 8: 22-25)

Two thoughts for today: firstly, God has made lots of promises throughout scripture. Here, the promises referred to in Isaiah 35: 5-6, are clearly manifested, where it states that 'the eyes of the blind will be open'. Jesus knew this and therefore believed it would happen. He had faith in God who has made promises for each of us to take hold of and believe in, so that whatever situation we find ourselves in, we can find a promise and believe that it will happen.

Secondly, Jesus took the blind man by the hand, led him outside the village, and then spat on him. I love it! By taking his hand, Jesus was establishing a personal relationship with the blind man which would have given him confidence and some expectation of his healing. When we have the opportunity to bring healing to someone, let's be personal, not operating out of formula or religion, but being led by the Spirit into how He wants to minister healing uniquely to that person. Then let Jesus take over and do the healing through you.

So today, believe that the promises of the scriptures will come true in your life, and be praying and seeking for opportunities to bring healing to someone. Do not give up and do not be shy.

Jesus, I am going to walk confidently in the promises that you have shown me in the Holy Scriptures. Help me believe in them and see them come to life through all I do today. Amen.

MORE POWER, LORD!

'You know what has happened... how God anointed Jesus of Nazareth with the Holy Spirit and power and how he went around doing good and healing all who were under the power of the devil, because God was with him.' (Acts 10: 37-38)

What a powerful verse for us to take on board today! Jesus brought heaven to earth by revealing the goodness of God and healing people.

Is that what you would like to be doing more of? How did he do it? Simple: God anointed Him with the Holy Spirit and with power.

Recently, I was reading a book where the author used this definition for power: 'Power is the capacity to do things'.

So today, however you are feeling, whether weary from life or desiring a new lease of life, or whether you want to see peoples' lives impacted by bringing heaven to earth, you need to allow God to anoint you afresh with the same Holy Spirit and power that He anointed Jesus with.

I encourage you to ask Father God to anoint you today so that you have the capacity to do what Jesus did.

Father, in your grace and mercy, will you anoint me with the Holy Spirit so that I can do what Jesus did on earth today. Amen.

MOVE FORWARD

'But how different it is for the righteous! The Lord embraces
their paths as they move forward, while the way of the
wicked leads only to doom.' (Psalm 1: 6, TPT)

I remember being at school, and every Wednesday afternoon we would have to do army cadet training. One of the commands that was often shouted out by the Sergeant Major was, "Move forward!" And the whole battalion would start to move forward, approximately a hundred people.

This verse encourages us to keep moving forward in our spiritual walk with God. The more we are moving forward in our learning, in our thinking, in our circumstances, even during tough times, the more opportunity it gives Father God to 'embrace our path'. If we don't move forward, however small those steps might be, and instead get stuck and bogged down in confusion, unconfessed sin, or fear, God may not be able to embrace us. He is waiting for us to move so that He can act on our behalf. He is waiting to embrace us.

So wherever you are or whatever situation you are in, find a way to move forward. It may be through praise or thankfulness; it may be through initiating a conversation; or it may be through making a change in your life. Fear can make us passive, so don't stagnate in your circumstances.

Make a move, knowing that His embrace is full of grace - we don't need to be perfect, just trusting. One small step will allow God to act on your behalf.

I take authority over fear and command it to get out of the way of me
moving forward today. I choose to take that small step and in faith, I
know that the Lord Almighty will carry me forward. Amen.

WAKE THOSE GIFTS UP!

'For this reason, I remind you to fan into flame the gift of God, which is in you through the laying on of my hands.' (2 Timothy 1: 6)

In this verse, writing to his close friend and spiritual son Timothy, Paul is saying that you already have within you the spiritual gifts, and he is reminding him 'to fan into flame' these gifts from God. Timothy does not have to work or strive to receive them - he already has them! Timothy was leading a church and Paul is encouraging him to grab hold of this truth and start operating in all that God has given him. We must learn to use what we have already received.

In his book, You May All Prophesy, Steve Thompson gives another more helpful translation of the word 'gifts' or 'charismata' as the word 'enablers' or 'spiritual empowerments'.[12] We need these to enable and empower us to live 'the Jesus life', and to extend His Kingdom.

Are you operating in your spiritual gifts or are they lying dormant within you? I encourage you today to start operating in the supernatural and to experience just how life-changing they can be for you and others you meet. Wake up those spiritual gifts and be enabled to go on a supernatural adventure with Father God!

Holy Spirit, will you ignite the flame inside and release the gifts that you have given me, so that I can make an impact for you today. Amen.

IT'S TIME TO STAND OUT

'Remind the people to be subject to rulers and authorities, to be obedient, to be ready to do whatever is good, to slander no one, to be peaceable and considerate, and to show true humility towards everyone.' (Titus 3: 1-2)

When writing to Titus, Paul wanted the church where he was based in Crete to stand out, to make a difference and to show people the proper way to live. We can do that as well, today.

During the Covid-19 pandemic, I was challenged by these verses. Many of us were left feeling that we were being stripped of our rights and freedoms, as those in authority made decisions that greatly affected our daily lives. However, these verses encourage us, that even in complicated and confusing political times, we can be known as people who bring goodness, peace and gentleness instead of slander and pain.

Today, let's pray for revelation for how best to live out these truths in whatever political climate we are in, and pray for wisdom for those in authority. Let's show people that having Jesus in our hearts makes a big difference.

Jesus, I know that we are called to be different to how the world lives and reacts. Please help me today to play my part in making the community in which I live see Jesus. Amen.

TOUGH NOT SOFT

'And the peace of God, which transcends all understanding, will guard your hearts and your minds in Christ Jesus.' (Philippians 4: 7)

So often we can think of peace as a soft or 'floaty' thing - maybe the type of peace that comes from sitting in stillness or lying down in a meditative state. However, this is not the type of peace that Paul is describing here. In the Amplified Classic Edition of this verse, it describes God's peace as having the strength to 'garrison and mount guard over your hearts and minds'. God's peace is a tough peace, a weighty peace, a type of peace that can literally surround and place a guard over your heart.

Over the years, Michelle and I have felt the power of God's peace mounting guard over us many times. One instance that stands out was during the birth of our daughter. In the final stages, Michelle was rushed into theatre to have an assisted delivery. As the panic levels began to rise in the room, I responded by praying in tongues and taking hold of God's peace. We instantly felt a shift in the atmosphere as Father's fortress of peace fully surrounded us.

Later, many of the nurses commented on how peaceful our daughter was, saying that it was unusual after such a difficult birth. They were surprised, but we weren't! We had cried out to the God of peace and He had come through for us.

Whatever you are facing, God's peace - which is tough and strong - is available for you today. It can withstand whatever opposition you are going through.

Today, I choose to take hold of the peace of God to come and garrison and mount guard over my heart and mind. Amen.

I HAVE GOOD NEWS TODAY

'Day after day, in the temple courts and from house to house, they never stopped teaching and proclaiming the good news that Jesus is the Christ.' (Acts 5: 42)

We have been encouraged in our church recently to 'rise up, get out and save lives'! Why? Because we have good news to share: Jesus is the Messiah, the Saviour of the world! That's why the early church kept proclaiming this good news.

Good news is important for people to hear, especially in the midst of all the trials of life. Our families, our communities, our country and the world all need to hear good news today. Jesus' presence can change every situation and the world needs to hear this good news. We need to tell people about Jesus and the joy that He brings and pray that people will hear it and receive it.

Let's not be afraid but instead, let our voices be heard; let this message be on our lips and in our actions. It really is good news that a Saviour has been born for all people!

So let us rise up, get out and share the good news. Have fun doing it!

Jesus, thank you that you gave up your heavenly place and came to earth to bring good news of great joy. Help me to share this good news with everyone I meet today. Amen.

PRIDE IS OUR DOWNFALL

'His fame spread far and wide, for he was greatly helped until he became powerful. But after Uzziah became powerful, his pride led to his downfall. He was unfaithful to the Lord his God and entered the temple of the Lord to burn incense.' (2 Chronicles 26: 15b-16)

This remarkable story of King Uzziah of Judah in 2 Chronicles 26 can teach us all such a good lesson in our lives today. He became King at the age of sixteen and was very successful in every area of his life: from military conquests and building cities, to large herds and abundant provisions. However, his power became too much for him and pride took over and got him into big trouble!

In all our lives, pride is lurking at the door. No-one is exempt from it. It's ready to pounce, to lift you up above everyone around you. It tells you, "You are in charge, you're the boss, don't listen to them; you know what's best; your ideas and thoughts are superior."

Sadly, Uzziah fell for it and did not listen to the advice of the priests at the crucial time in his reign. Instead, he got angry with them, dug in his heels (v. 19), probably thinking, "How dare you challenge me or speak to me like that. I can do what I like, don't you know who I am?"

So today, be careful, do not allow pride into your life, into your thinking and decisions. God may have raised you up to a powerful position, but be careful how this impacts you. Take some time today to ask Father God to highlight anything which pulls you away from Him or is allowing pride to step in and have its way. As scripture says, 'God opposes the proud but gives favour to the humble.' (see James 4: 6)

Father, today I don't want to make the same mistake as King Uzziah. May I walk humbly and I ask you to show me where I have let pride into my life. Amen.

ARE YOU STILL HEARING FROM GOD TODAY?

'The Word of the Lord came to me: "What do you see Jeremiah?"
"I see the branch of an almond tree," I replied. The Lord
said to me, "You have seen correctly, for I am watching
to see that my word is fulfilled."' (Jeremiah 1: 11-12)

Jeremiah was at the beginning of his ministry as a prophet to the nations, which would last over four decades. However, right from the outset, God taught him a key foundation for his ministry: to learn to see what God was showing him. "You have seen correctly," God said to him. By learning this basic skill of hearing God's voice and knowing what to do and say, Jeremiah was able to have the confidence to deliver a tough message to the people of God at that time.

Are you continuing to be reliant on God to show you what He is up to, and what He is saying to you in your present situation and His call on your life? These verses are a reminder to keep our focus on God, keep our ears open to what He is saying, and our eyes fixed on the unseen. We have to be dependent on Him and see what He is showing us. It might well make a huge difference in our lives, in the lives of our families, in the community in which we live and, just maybe, in the nation in which we live.

God is asking the same question to you today: what do you see?

Lord, thank you that you still speak to me. I ask that you open my ears and eyes to see what you have to share with me today. Amen.

CALL ON GOD FIRST

'The Lord is a shelter for the oppressed, a refuge in times of trouble.
Those who know your name trust in you, for you, O Lord, have never
abandoned anyone who searches for you.' (Psalm 9: 9-10, NLT)

What a powerful couple of verses of scripture! Not only is there a promise here but also a truth that we all need to grasp and live out. Father God offers a strong and secure shelter for us and He has limitless resources to give to each person who needs help.

We will all face troubles in our life and when they come, the first place to turn to is Father God. It is so easy to try other things first.

Michelle and I have learnt over the years that God must be the first point of call when we hit a tough time. It is in His presence that we can pour out our hearts and share our deepest feelings. As verse 10 says, 'those who search for Him, He will never abandon'. There is the promise.

So whatever you face today, whatever you are going through, reach out to Father God first and allow Him to shelter you and provide for you.

Father, you never abandon us. I choose today to fall into your loving
arms. I know you will help me through this tough time. May the
resources of heaven be released over me. Amen.

HOW IS YOUR RELATIONSHIP WITH FATHER GOD GOING?

'Now this is eternal life: that they may know you, the only true God, and Jesus Christ, whom you sent.' (John 17: 3)

Before He went to the cross, in one of His final prayers to His Father, Jesus gave us a clear picture of eternal life: to know the Father, the one true God. Through His death and resurrection, Jesus gave us access to this most wonderful and transforming relationship.

So how is your relationship with Father God going? Have you spent quality time with Him recently? Have you sat in His presence, listening to Him, and inviting Him into every area of your life? Or is it just a one-way relationship: you telling Him what you want, how He can bless you, what He can do for you?

When we choose Jesus as our Lord and Saviour, this eternal life starts straight away. So today, let's enjoy getting to know Father God better. Grab hold of this incredible truth and get to know Father God more deeply.

Father, help me know you better and enjoy our relationship. I want to know you as Father and receive your love and kindness today. Amen.

HE KNOWS OUR HEARTS

'The Lord looks over us from where he rules in heaven. Gazing into every heart from his lofty dwelling place, he observes all the peoples of the earth. The Creator of our hearts considers and examines everything we do.' (Psalm 33: 13-15, TPT)

The world is so different to the Kingdom of God. Many of us today will have people looking at us, seeing how we appear; observing how we come across and wondering what our body language is saying. It can have a big impact.

However, the Lord's gaze is not on the outside. The Lord's gaze looks at our hearts. When the prophet Samuel chose David to anoint as King, God said, "People look at the outward appearance, but the Lord looks at the heart" (1 Samuel 16: 7). That is so different from how the world views us.

We cannot hide anything from God. He knows our hearts and can see all that is going on: our struggles, our fears, our frustrations, our joys and our happiness.

So today, why not allow His loving gaze, healing hands and kind words to touch your heart. He is the only one qualified to release your heart into true freedom and true joy - to release you into your full potential.

Father, thank you that you don't judge me by how I look or by what I say and do, but instead you know my heart. I open my heart to you and ask that you will help me change. Amen.

HE HAS A SOLUTION

'God heard the boy crying, and the angel of God called to Hagar from heaven and said to her, "What is the matter, Hagar? Do not be afraid; God has heard the boy crying as he lies there. Lift the boy up and take him by the hand, for I will make him into a great nation." Then God opened her eyes and she saw a well of water. So she went and filled the skin with water and gave the boy a drink.' (Genesis 21: 17-19)

The Egyptian slave Hagar and her young son were cast out of Abraham's home into the desert. They were left to survive on their own in the wilderness and they had run out of water. It was such a desperate situation that Hagar expected the child to die. She faced this frightening and emotional time with no likely solution.

If you are facing the unknown and it feels overwhelming, know this: the Lord listens; He understands; He is with you; He steps in with solutions and He gives hope. He opened Hagar's eyes to see a well of water and rescued her and the boy.

So many times in life, we can miss out on what God can do. Therefore, our challenge today is to be attentive today to hear His words, so that we can see the strategies and solutions that He has for each specific situation we face. Panic can blind us but we are His children and He wants us to thrive.

Lord, thank you that you understand and that you are with me. I need your help today. Please restore my situation and open my eyes to see your solutions to my troubles. Amen.

WHO AM I?

'One day the evil spirit answered them, "Jesus I know, and I know about Paul, but who are you?"' (Acts 19: 15)

What a challenge - 'Who are you?'

The enemy always tries to undermine our identity. He tries to get our attention and to lie to us about who we really are. The enemy wants to make us believe that we are nothing or that we are not able to do this or do that. Don't believe his lies. Replace the lies with truth of who you are.

Why not remind yourself who you are in Christ? Here are a few ideas to get you going: you are loved by God - 100%; He is very proud of you; He is well pleased with you; He delights in you; you are His son or daughter; you are seated with Jesus in the heavenly realms far above anything else; you are chosen by God; you are unique; God has a purpose for you.

Today, you can walk in confidence because of who you are in God's eyes. Don't listen to the lies of enemies.

I choose to walk in who I am in your eyes, Father. I am your child: fully equipped to stand tall and be about your work today. I lack nothing, I am able to do more than I can imagine. Amen.

HE HAS THE BEST PLANS FOR YOU

"'Woe to the obstinate children," declares the Lord, "to those who carry out plans that are not mine, forming an alliance, but not by my Spirit."' (Isaiah 30: 1)

In today's verse we see that Isaiah did not hold back. The message he had to relay was tough but he was faithful and said what God had told him to say. It still continues to be a weighty truth for us to hear and receive. It is always tempting to follow our own plans but the key truth to hold on to today is that God wants to be part of our everyday lives. He wants us to trust Him completely.

Michelle and I have a fridge magnet that says: 'We plan, God laughs'. I find it a helpful reminder to involve God in all we do and allow Him to lead us.

Today, the challenge is to allow Him to guide and direct our lives: our plans, our friendships, our work, our ministry or calling and even our holidays! Learn to submit to Him as He who knows all things and He has the best plans for our lives. We need to live in line with what the Spirit of God is saying.

So whatever you are planning, get God involved!

Father, I recognise today that I have made plans in which you have not been included. I am sorry. I will submit all my plans to you. I ask that by your Spirit you will show me what is the best way forward to fulfill all that you have for me. Amen.

KEEP CHANGING

'Therefore we do not lose heart. Though outwardly we are wasting away, yet inwardly we are being renewed day by day.' (2 Corinthians 4: 16)

This verse still speaks directly to us and helps us to see that the most important thing in life is a thriving heart that is open to change by the Spirit of God.

For me personally, even though my outer body has been wasting away, and at times, when I have been rushed to hospital or lying in bed weakened by illness, it has been my inner journey of being renewed that has kept me fighting and focused on Him who is above all things.

In this verse, Paul seems to imply that we should be being renewed day by day. Are you changing inwardly?

Are you allowing Jesus to change you into His likeness? Are you inviting the Spirit to change you? Is God's word speaking to you?

Don't get stuck in old patterns, old experiences, and old ways of thinking, or even stuck in situations you are facing right now. Continue to be renewed day by day.

Jesus I will press in for more of you. I want to be open to new things, new thinking, new insight, so that when the tough times come, I will be strong and will stand firm. Amen.

YOU ARE HIS

'For you did not receive a spirit that makes you a slave again to fear, but you received a Spirit of sonship (adoption). And by him we cry, "Abba, Father." The Spirit himself testifies with our spirit that we are God's children.' (Romans 8: 15-16)

What a wonderful truth to hear! We are God's children, adopted by a loving Father who wants us and who chose us.

As someone who has received the Spirit of adoption, are you enjoying all that the Father has for you and all that He is saying to you? Maybe stop and listen to His voice speaking to you today. Let His words confirm in you who you are: His child, His daughter, His son, His beloved. He is proud of you today.

The worship song 'No Longer Slaves' by Jonathan and Melissa Helser is based on these verses. I encourage you to sing these powerful words with all your heart! "I'm no longer a slave to fear. I am a child of God." May they bring fresh revelation to you today of your adoption.

Don't hold back - run to your Father.

Jesus, may I walk in these powerful truths today, and may I have the opportunity to introduce people to Abba Father. Amen.

BE CAREFUL WHAT YOU SAY

'John replied in the words of Isaiah the prophet,
"I am the voice of one calling in the wilderness,
Make straight the way for the Lord."'(John 1: 23)

The Pharisees and scribes from Jersulsem had travelled far to find John the Baptist. They were on a mission to find out who he was and were to report back to HQ in Jerusalem. In their previous questions to him, John had answered, "No, I am not the Messiah," but in this reply he declares who he is: a voice preparing the people to meet Jesus. John knew his mission and was able to stick to it. He was the last great prophet who pointed people to the Messiah.

What will your voice be saying today? Will it be pointing people to Jesus? Or the very opposite! The voice and the words we speak can be very powerful, they can carry blessings or curses.

So speak well today with grace and truth, and allow people to see the difference Jesus makes in your life.

Father, may my words today be words that not only point people to Jesus, but also show people the way to Jesus. Amen.

BEST PLACE TO BE LIVING

'How priceless is your unfailing love! Both high and low men find refuge in the shadow of your wings. They feast in the abundance of your house; you give them drink from your river of delights.' (Psalm 36: 7-8)

Here in this Psalm we get a glimpse of the Father's house. There's so much to enjoy and feast upon and so much to delight in from the 'river of delights'. It is a place of safety and a place where true, unconditional love is found. It's a place that accepts you, whether rich or poor, of high or low status. It's a place of peace, a place where you are loved for who you are. This is the place that Father God has prepared for you.

When was the last time you imagined what it's like to be in the Father's house? Today, ask the Father to show you more of His delights, more of His love for you and then feast upon what you see. Be creative and imagine the Father's house. You will come alive in the Father's house; you will be refreshed in the Father's house, and you will be free in the Father's house.

I encourage you to go there and to take some time to be in the Father's house.

Father, thank you that you accept me into your house today and that I can enjoy everything you have for me. Amen.

FRIENDSHIP FIRST

"I no longer call you servants, because a servant does not know his master's business. Instead, I have called you friends, for everything that I learned from my Father I have made known to you." (John 15: 15)

The truth of this verse is overwhelming. Jesus does not call us to be 'worker bees' for Him, or servants that He commands at His beck and call. No, He invites us to be His friends - intimate friends who know His business and who get to work in partnership with Him.

So often in the busyness of life and ministry, we can forget this truth. I know that I can often slip into striving and exhausting myself, focused on my own agenda. But this verse cuts through all that and brings us back to friendship and partnership. Jesus' plan is that we would all experience a friendship with Him which is so deep and rich, that it would be the singular most transformational thing in our lives.

How is your friendship with Jesus today? Are you enjoying Jesus and spending time with Him just because He's your friend? Or is your relationship with Him based on activity and productivity? Why not take some time to just 'kick back' with Jesus today, being with Him, doing nothing and allowing Him to share His heart with you.

Jesus, thank you that you want me to be your friend. May I learn to be a good friend to you. Amen.

REMEMBER WHO HE IS

'Jehoshaphat stood in the assembly of Judah and Jerusalem, in the house of the Lord, before the new court, and said, "O Lord, God of our ancestors, are you not God in heaven? Do you not rule over all the kingdoms of the nations? In your hand are power and might, so that no one is able to withstand you. Did you not, O our God, drive out the inhabitants of this land before your people Israel, and give it forever to the descendants of your friend Abraham?"' (2 Chronicles 20: 5 -7, NRSV)

King Jehoshaphat and the whole of Judah were in trouble. Facing a vast army, Jehoshaphat starts his prayer with testimony of who God is and what He has done. He doesn't panic, or seek solutions, he seeks the Lord. (Do read the rest of the chapter - it is an amazing story of God's power and might and how God rescues them from an impossible situation).

Jehoshaphat praised God and He responded back in a mighty way.

When you pray today, whether you have a vast problem in front of you or not, why not pause and take a moment, remember what God has done for you in recent weeks, months or years and give testimony of who God is.

God loves to hear our praise of Him. Worship Him first and He will bring about the breakthrough you may need today.

Father, you have done so much for me in my life. I am so grateful to you for everything. Amen.

NOTHING IS HIDDEN FROM JESUS

'He did not need any testimony about mankind, for he knew what was in each person.' (John 2: 25)

This is quite a challenging thought. Jesus 'knew what was in each person'. He not only had the ability to know what was going on inside every person he met, but also he was the only person qualified to change them.

He knows what is going on with you in every area of life: your thoughts, your actions and your emotions. You can either run from Him or turn to Him.

Jesus came to set us free. You can trust His love and grace. Don't sit and withdraw, but instead share, let go and enjoy the life He has for you today - life in all its fullness.

Jesus, today I want to let you into my heart, into my thinking, into my soul, so that I can be free and know that your love will carry me through this day. Amen.

BE REFRESHED

*'But as for me, I am filled with power, with the Spirit of
the Lord, and with justice and might to declare to Jacob
his transgression, to Israel his sin.' (Micah 3: 8)*

The Prophet Micah needed the power and might from the Spirit to do what God was asking him to do. He was given the task to show the nation of Israel their sin and wayward life. He had to challenge their leaders and speak the truth that they didn't want to hear.

This is a mission from heaven that I would not like to do unless I had the power and might of the Holy Spirit!

We need to ask the Holy Spirit to fill us so that He will equip us to do what God is calling us to do, whether that is being a good parent, a good friend to someone or moving in the supernatural gifts of the Spirit, so that God's Kingdom can be seen and heard through our message.

We need to be filled afresh with the Holy Spirit every day.

Holy Spirit, will you fill me again today so that I can move forward and bring your Kingdom on earth to all those that I see and spend time with. Amen.

BE SECURE

'Jesus answered, "Even if I testify on my own behalf, my testimony is valid, for I know where I came from and where I am going."' (John 8:14)

In this one verse, Jesus reveals two wonderful truths for us to grab hold of. Firstly, Jesus knew that He was the Son of God; He knew that He had come from heaven - that was His identity. Remember you are also a child of Abba Father.

Secondly, Jesus knew where He was going: back to heaven, to be in God's presence, in the inner throne room of His Father and to sit at His right hand. It's the best place to be! He would not let the world and all the trials and tribulation take these truths from Him. He kept focused on what He knew was true. Both of these truths are for us to enjoy today, to walk out and live out.

We live in a world that is constantly trying to label us or make us feel left out or squeezed into being something else. So today, however you are feeling or whatever you are struggling with, remind yourself of these truths and allow them to dispel the power of this world. Let these words of Jesus reassure you today of who you are and what you have.

Today, I will not allow these truths to slip from my mind. I will walk in confidence that I am a child of God and that there is a place for me in heaven. Amen.

PUT THE LORD FIRST

*'In the thirty-ninth year of his reign, Asa was afflicted
with a disease in his feet. Though his disease was severe,
even in his illness he did not seek help from the Lord
but only from the physicians.' (2 Chronicles 16: 12)*

Asa was one of Judah's great kings, who actually sought the Lord for help
for most of his reign, but here at the last hour, he did not. Why was that?

Asa was angry and resentful. Earlier on in the chapter, we read that
He had been told that what he had done was wrong. He had relied on
another king for help and not the Lord and his mistakes were exposed by
a prophet (vs. 1-11). So he was angry and lost his focus on the Lord, which
eventually cost him his life.

This is a good lesson for us to all learn. Whether we are doing really well
or we are struggling with sickness or other issues, we must seek the Lord
first and foremost.

Are you seeking help from the Lord? Are you allowing Him to be involved
in your life, or is He a last resort? Whatever is happening in your life or
your children's lives, make sure you are asking God to be involved. Seek
Him out and ask Him questions and He will respond.

*Father, forgive me if I have not sought you in recent weeks and instead
relied on my own abilities and resources. Will you show me what I need
to see and hear, so that I can walk in unity with you. Amen.*

HE WILL NOT LET YOU DOWN

'Why are you downcast, O my soul? Why so disturbed within me? Put your hope in God, for I will yet praise him, my Saviour and my God.' (Psalm 42: 5)

King David was having a tough time in life. Enemies were surrounding him and he was desperate to be in the presence of God. It was all getting too much for him. David was brilliant at engaging with his emotions, sharing them out loud and finding the answer to his struggles. He had hope in God because he knew that God had never let him down.

We are the same. Life can often throw a lot of tough stuff at us and our souls can often get downcast and disturbed. However, we must not remain in a place of self-pity or worry - we must rise up and put our hope in God. We can bring life to our souls through giving thanks to God and remembering who He is and what He has done for us.

I have had so many times when all I want to do is cry out in despair: why me? Why so long? Why this cup of suffering? However, I have found out over the years that this downcast attitude must be shared, released to Father God, and my thought patterns changed, otherwise I find I am on a downward path leading to destruction.

Today, I encourage you to rise up and find the peace, stillness and joy of heaven for your soul. Don't give up. Hope is the answer and we must rely on that, so that our focus is always a positive one.

Put your hope in God today. He will never let you down.

Father God, you are so faithful. Today, I choose to put my hope in you. I will not allow self-pity or worry to be my focus. I will focus on you. I will see your hand on my life. You are my God. Amen.

WORSHIP IS THE ANSWER TO EVERYTHING

'They rose early in the morning and went out into the wilderness of Tekoa; and as they went out, Jehoshaphat stood and said, "Listen to me, O Judah and inhabitants of Jerusalem! Believe in the Lord your God and you will be established; believe his prophets." When he had taken counsel with the people, he appointed those who were to sing to the Lord and praise him in holy splendour, as they went before the army, saying,"Give thanks to the Lord, for his steadfast love endures forever."' (2 Chronicles 20: 20-21, NRSV)

King Jehoshaphat and the nation of Judah were going out to face the huge army which had come up to wage war against them. He orchestrated something which was unheard of in all the history of Israel's wars. He sent the worshipping men out first at the front of the army. What a move! And guess what? The enemy was defeated and there was so much plunder it took them three days to collect it all! Wow, what a victory! Let's have some of that, please Lord!

Whatever is coming against you at the moment, or whatever circumstance you may have to face today, however big or small, if you choose to put your faith in God, He will uphold you and will enable you to praise Him in whatever situation you find yourself. He is a faithful and loving God. He will bring you victory.

Lord, I will sing your praises today. I will lift my voice to you so that the sound of it may be heard by you. May it be a sweet sweet sound to your ears. Thank you for fighting for me. Amen.

YOU AND THE HOLY SPIRIT TOGETHER

'May the grace of the Lord Jesus Christ, and the love of God, and the fellowship of the Holy Spirit be with you all.' (2 Corinthians 13: 14)

How is your relationship with the Holy Spirit?

The Apostle Paul seems to put an emphasis on an active relationship with the Holy Spirit. He uses the word 'fellowship'. This word implies spending time together, hanging out, communication and intimacy. Paul knew that he could do nothing on his own, he needed the Holy Spirit. He knew the importance of the Holy Spirit in his life.

I love inviting the Holy Spirit into restaurants with us and then asking for a prophetic word or picture for our waiter or waitress. It is fun sharing these moments. Also, often at times before church on Sundays, I ask the Holy Spirit for a specific word of knowledge for someone who will be there that morning so that I can give them an encouragement from the Lord. It's fun, and it's fellowship with the Holy Spirit at its best.

So let's take up Paul's challenge and not ignore the Holy Spirit in our daily walk. He is the third person of the Trinity who wants to have fellowship with us, so let's enjoy Him today.

Simply welcome Him and invite Him to be with you wherever you go. He's got so much wisdom that He would love to share with you.

Holy Spirit, you are so full of life and good gifts. Today, I choose to walk with you in close fellowship so that together we may see God's Kingdom here on earth. Amen.

MORE, LORD!

'And with that he breathed on them and said,
"Receive the Holy Spirit."' (John 20: 22)

One of the first things that the resurrected Jesus did was to give His disciples the Holy Spirit. Why? They needed Him so that they could be more like Jesus and not be reliant on their own strengths, gifts and talents.

I heard a quote recently that said, "Christians have the Holy Spirit within them, but not many allow the Holy Spirit to fully have them". The Holy Spirit is powerful and wants to be released in us so that we can do the impossible. Jesus knew this, so that is why it was important for His disciples to receive Him. They went on and did great things and moved more 'mountains' than they could imagine! The Spirit made them fully alive and active which is where we need to be! We can do nothing without Him.

When was the last time you asked Jesus to breathe on you and give you the Holy Spirit? Does the Holy Spirit have priority in your life? Simply pray from a humble heart and receive in faith. You will have a better day, a better week, and a better life if every day you ask to receive the Holy Spirit afresh.

Jesus, may I receive the gift of the Holy Spirit today. I want Him to be fully alive in me. I want to walk as Jesus did and see even greater things than I have already seen. Amen.

NO MORE RUBBISH

*'There are six things the Lord hates, seven that are detestable
to him: haughty eyes, a lying tongue, hands that shed innocent
blood, a heart that devises wicked schemes, feet that are quick
to rush into evil, a false witness who pours out lies and a person
who stirs up conflict in the community.' (Proverbs 6: 16-19)*

I don't know about you, but I certainly don't want any of these things to
be playing out in my life if they are things that God hates! It would seem
to me that many of the traits highlighted in these verses are so often
evident in the world in which we live. It's no wonder God hates them as
they are so destructive and bring so much confusion and sadness into our
world. If they were removed for just one day, how much better would this
world be!

Are any of these seven things rearing their ugly heads in you at the
moment? Have you found yourself slipping into any of these things or
allowing them to be part of your life? It is always good to ask for insight
from the Holy Spirit to search your heart and mind. If any of these are
active in your life now, may I encourage you to stop, think again, sort it
out and seek God's forgiveness. He wants to bless you and give you favour
and grace today. He wants to use you to help others to have a good day. He
wants you to carry His Kingdom forward today.

God knows the ways of goodness and love. Let's listen and obey Him.

*Father, today I will walk in the light of the truth of these verses.
Everything I say and do will bring glory to you. I will walk in the
opposite of these traits so that I may bless and encourage people
instead of putting them down. Amen.*

HELP YOUR FRIEND

'My brothers, if one of you should wander from the truth and someone should bring him back, remember this: Whoever turns a sinner from the error of his way will save him from death and cover over a multitude of sins.' (James 5: 19-20)

It is so important that we keep each other from wandering and stumbling in this world.

If you need to challenge a friend, a partner or a child, make sure that your heart is in the right place before you speak. When you take that step, always speak from a place of love and grace, and preferably face to face. In the long run, if you embrace love and grace, that person will have the chance to become a better, freer and happier person.

So don't hold back if you know someone is doing wrong, but remember, always speak with love and grace.

Father, give me courage to step forward to speak to my brother or sister. Will you fill me first with your grace so that I may speak in love and help them move forward. Amen.

PRESS IN

'As you know, we consider blessed those who have persevered. You have heard of Job's perseverance and have seen what the Lord finally brought about. The Lord is full of compassion and mercy.' (James 5: 11)

We know that Job persevered and pushed through when he lost everything but in the end all was restored. God's compassion and mercy reached beyond all that he expected. It was a full restoration for Job: more children, more livestock and more wealth than he could imagine.

How is your faith doing? Are you struggling with an ongoing problem and feeling hopeless? Is work just too much? Are relationships adding more pressure on you? Are you feeling the strain of life? Hang in there, press in - God will bless you. He will bring the peace you need. He will honour you in ways that you can't even see or imagine right now.

May God's compassion and mercy touch you today and may your perseverance be richly rewarded.

Lord, I need a breakthrough. Will you give me the strength today to persevere, to push in for more than I can imagine right now. May your compassion and mercy be upon me. Thank you. Amen.

BE ALERT

'He sends his commands to the earth; his word runs swiftly.' (Psalm 147: 15)

God is active and real, and wants to use us to step into other people's lives, to minister healing, to meet a financial need, or to be with them at a point of crisis. Are you open to hearing God's voice speaking to you today?

Recently, my 20 year old niece was out in the garden, playing with her younger sister and my daughter and, whilst doing a handstand, she collapsed onto her neck and was out cold. My wife Michelle was first on the scene trying to revive her and called for an ambulance. At that moment, she had a sense that my niece's friend Tom, who lives nearby, was meant to come over and join her in praying. So Michelle cried out to God, "Father, send Tom'"

Now Tom, who lives just a few roads away, was having breakfast and felt the Lord say to him, "Leave the house now!" He did just that - he did not even put on a pair of shoes! As he left the house and started walking, he received further instructions from God, who showed him an image in his mind's eye of walking past our house and me coming outside to meet him. Guess what? That is exactly what happened! Tom ended up being with her for the next 6 hours, praying with her whilst she was in hospital, and Father God faithfully turned disaster into an opportunity to grow in faith.

God does indeed still, 'send His commands to earth'. Let's be alert and good at hearing His voice each day and be willing to step out and respond.

Father, I know you will be sending commands to earth today. May I hear what you have to say and be prepared to act upon them. Amen.

ARE YOU IN NEED?

*'Let us then approach the throne of grace with
confidence, so that we may receive mercy and find grace
to help us in our time of need.' (Hebrews 4: 16)*

When was the last time you approached the throne of grace?

Jesus made it possible for us to approach the King of Kings with confidence. This is one of the greatest things achieved for us.

God's mercy is new every day, so whatever situation we are in or whatever we feel we have done, God is rich in mercy and will forgive us, He will accept us as we are.

You can approach Father God with confidence and share your heart with Him, and He who is able to do all things, will meet your need. He will shower you with His grace and bring you into His arms of love.

Let's not miss this amazing privilege today.

Lord Jesus Christ, thank you that I can enter the throne room of grace this day because of what you did for me on the cross. Today, I choose to approach your throne and experience all that your Father has for me. I know I will be blessed and I know my needs will be met. Amen.

MAKE THE RIGHT CHOICE TODAY

'If we claim to have fellowship with him yet walk in the darkness, we lie and do not live by truth. But if we walk in the light, as he is in the light, we have fellowship with one another.' (1 John 1: 6-7a)

John is urging us to ensure that we let go of the old lifestyle we once lived, so that the new life in Christ can flourish. As we do this, our relationship with Jesus and also with others can be massively impacted. In some ways, it can be easier to 'walk in darkness' than to walk in the light. Subconsciously, some of us may have actually grown accustomed to aspects of our lives which are lived in darkness. However, life cannot grow in darkness.

I encourage you today to sit, be still, and ask Father God to reveal any areas of your life where you are still walking in darkness and not in the light.

Are there facets of your life, perhaps in the way that you live, where you know you need to make a stand, say, "No" and walk in the opposite direction? Or perhaps in your hidden thought-life, or in issues from your past which have not been dealt with and brought into the light. It may go against the flow of our culture, but to walk in the light is what we are created for. As it says in Psalm 36, 'In His light, we see light'. Then we are fully alive and free.

May God give you the strength and courage today to choose to walk in the light and enjoy the company of other believers.

Jesus, I will walk in the light today, I will not allow the pressure and powers of darkness to overcome me. I will enjoy you more today. Amen.

HEADING IN THE RIGHT DIRECTION

'This is what the Lord says - your Redeemer, the Holy One of Israel: "I am the Lord your God, who teaches you what is best for you, who directs you in the way you should go."' (Isaiah 48 :17)

Within this verse are some tough questions to think about today.

Israel needed to hear these words so that even in exile in a foreign land they would not lose sight or direction. God was their Redeemer, and He would restore all that was lost. But they needed to be steadfast and hold on to what they had heard and wait until the Lord's will was done.

What is God teaching you at the moment? Who is really guiding you in your life today? Are you living your life in line with what God is saying to you? Are you being obedient to what He is revealing to you?

Today, allow His teaching to affect your life.

Father, even today you have things to teach me, you have plans to direct my life in the way I should go. May I be open to hear your words and be obedient to them. Amen.

DISCOVER GRACE

'Do not be carried away by all kinds of strange teachings. It is good for our hearts to be strengthened by grace, not by ceremonial foods, which are of no value to those who eat them.' (Hebrews 13: 9)

God's grace strengthens our hearts. What an amazing truth!

A story is told that the author C.S Lewis stumbled into a discussion at a conference on comparative religions, as experts from around the world debated what, if any, belief was unique to the Christian faith. Lewis responded, "Oh, that's easy. It's grace."[13]

Take a moment today to ponder and think about the word 'grace' - God's grace. You could read, listen or even meditate on the words of the hymn 'Amazing Grace'. Allow the words to strengthen your heart, mind and soul today and to stir in your heart just how much God has done for you and how grace can give you strength to face the day.

God is for you and you don't have to do anything to earn His favour. It is all paid for by Jesus.

Open my heart, Lord, to understand the power of your grace, so that I can be strong to move forward into all that you have for me. Amen.

FRUIT TO HAVE UP YOUR SLEEVE

'Let your gentleness be evident to all. The Lord is near.' (Philippians 4: 5)

The world we live in today is hard and can sometimes be a tough and violent place in which to exist.

But people are wanting to see something different, and they need something different.

As a dad, I went through a season of praying that I would be more gentle towards my daughter. This came from realising that I sometimes lacked gentleness in my response to her in the way I spoke with her. I needed to change. I am certainly not perfect, but I noticed my communication and my actions towards her began to change and our relationship blossomed.

Gentleness is a powerful fruit to carry into every situation. So today, ask the Father to give you a spirit of gentleness and you will be a light in your surroundings.

Lord, may my gentleness be evident to all this day. I ask for this to increase in my life so that others may be drawn to you. Amen.

KEEP YOUR EYES ON THE RIGHT THING

'You sympathised with those in prison and joyfully accepted
the confiscation of your property because you knew that you
yourselves had better and lasting possessions.' (Hebrews 10: 34)

Today's message challenges us not to be controlled by material possessions.

The writer here is praising the early Christians for demonstrating that the gospel message was far more important than what the world had to offer. They were experiencing the full power of the gospel in their lives; their focus was not on earthly things, but on what was eternal; their joy in life came from knowing Jesus as their Lord and Saviour.

I am not sure how I would respond to the confiscation of my home - it would be so hard to let it go. I don't think I would do it joyfully, would you?

However, what we must do with everything we own, is to keep our focus on what will last forever; to keep our eyes and our heart on eternity and the joys of that. If we do, then what we own will have less of a hold on us. If we have a healthy perspective on what is really important, then letting go may be easier.

Jesus, help me today to keep my focus on you and the joy of heaven so that whatever comes my way I will be ready to trust you. Amen.

WHO WILL YOU TRUST?

'It is better to take refuge in the Lord than to trust in man.' (Psalm 118: 8)

Let me share a remarkable set of facts about this verse. (It's sort of a bible quiz which you can use to show off to your friends!)

What is the shortest chapter in the bible?... Psalm 117.

What is the longest chapter in the bible?... Psalm 119.

How many chapters are there before Psalm 117?... There are 594 chapters.

How many chapters after Psalm 119? There are 594 chapters.

If you add those two numbers together you get a total of 1188 chapters in the bible.

So taking that number - 1188 - you could then say this: the central chapter in the bible is Psalm 118, and the verse related to this number is verse 8. So the central verse at the heart of the Bible says this: 'it is better to trust God than man'.

So today be asking yourself this question: is God the most important person in my life and am I trusting Him and making Him my place of refuge?

Man is changeable but God is 100% reliable, so entrust your life to Him.

Father, I choose today to put my whole trust in you. You are my safe place, may you be my best friend. Amen.

IT'S TIME FOR CHANGE

'The lamp of the Lord searches the spirit of a man; it searches out his inmost being.' (Proverbs 20: 27)

Our Father in heaven is a Father full of love, care, mercy and compassion. It is His desire to set us free, so that we may enjoy life to the full.

Allow His light to shine in your inmost being, and bring any secrets, fears, worries and concerns to Him, for He is gentle and His light will guide you to the freedom that you need.

Is it time to allow God into your situation?

Don't live entrapped in darkness, but come into the light.

I give you permission, Father, to shine your light into my heart so that I can see what I am carrying and give it to you. I don't want to keep any more secrets from you. Amen.

BE CREATIVE

"'The Lord bless you, my daughter," he replied. "This kindness is greater than that which you showed earlier."' (Ruth 3: 10)

In today's verse, Boaz prays a blessing over Ruth.

Blessing people is such a wonderful thing to do and gives people a chance to feel loved, valued and cared for. People need to be blessed. In the well-known Aaronic blessing, it says that when Aaron and his sons pray a blessing on the people of Israel, 'so shall they put my [God's] name upon the people of Israel, and I will bless them' (Numbers 6: 27).

Most mornings, before my daughter leaves the house and heads off to school, I say to her: "Bless someone today, Emily".

How can you bless someone today? Why not pray and think of ways in which you can bless people. It will make a huge difference to them and to you.

Lord, will you show me how I can bless people today? Help me be creative so that someone's life can change for the better. Amen.

HELP IS ON ITS WAY

'May the Lord answer you when you are in distress; may the name of the God of Jacob protect you. May He send you help from the sanctuary and grant you support from Zion.' (Psalm 20: 1-2)

Today's message from Psalm 20 is simple but powerful.

We need to continue to put our faith in God. He will answer our cries for help; He will protect us from the traps of this world; He will send help in amazing ways and offer us support in areas we can never imagine.

Do not give up if you are facing a difficult time. Press on for more so that you will see heaven on earth. You will see the breakthrough. He will lead you into the green pastures that you need.

Thank you, Father, that you will step in and help me today. You will support me and you will protect me from my enemies. Open my eyes to see your provision today. Amen.

DEALING WITH SIN

'Then David said to Nathan, "I have sinned against the Lord."' (2 Samuel 12: 13)

David had clearly done something wrong: adultery and murder. But until Nathan the prophet spoke to him, David thought he had got away with it, he didn't feel it was wrong. He was the King.

Sin can so easily slip past us. We can think we are right when actually we are wrong. We can have hard hearts and can be critical of others, thinking we are right and they are wrong. Or, we simply don't recognize our own sin or don't actually believe we could sin. It takes courage to admit and see our sin. Ultimately sin is against God, it hurts Him, it hurts us and it hurts others.

So spend some time today quietly before the Lord, and ask Him to show you, in His kind way, where you have sinned or where there is sin in your life, and then simply repent of it. Don't wait for a prophet to come and point out sin in your life - that may be a tough encounter!

Father, thank you that you will forgive me. Help me to see where I am holding onto sin or unconsciously living in sin and where I need to seek your forgiveness. Amen.

TWO POWERFUL WORDS TO EMBRACE

'Then Jesus said to his disciples, "If anyone would come after me, he must deny himself and take up his cross and follow me."' (Matthew 16: 24)

These words of Jesus are just as important for us to try to comprehend, as well as to live out the best we can.

Dietrich Bonhoeffer is one of my heroes of the faith from the 20th Century. He stood up against Nazism which eventually cost him his life. He understood the importance of denying himself and taking up his cross. His last recorded words before he died in 1945 were these: "This is the end – for me the beginning of life."[14]

Take a few moments to reflect on what comes to mind when you think of the cross. What does it mean for you to deny yourself today? How will you apply that to your life, so that you can follow Jesus more closely?

Jesus, help me today to move forward in understanding the importance of denying myself so that I can embrace all that you have for me in my life. Amen.

HAVE A REALLY FUN DAY

'Be imitators of God, therefore, as dearly loved children and live a life of love.' (Ephesians 5: 1)

'Be imitators of God'. Wow, what a challenge!

Think and pray about how you can show someone today a glimpse of who God really is. They need to see Him through you! That is the plan of God: we are to be His witnesses on earth today; we are to love as He loves; we are to bless as He blesses; we are to speak truth in love and grace just as He does.

Go for it and be good imitators of God! He is with you.

Have fun!

Father, help me today to show people who you are. Help me to love as you love and to bless as you bless. Amen.

JESUS' BIG HEART

'But Jesus came to them and touched them, "Get up,"
he said and "Don't be afraid."' (Matthew 17: 7)

The encounter on the Mount of Transfiguration was one of those that Peter, James and John would remember for the rest of their lives. They heard the audible voice of the Lord and fell to the ground terrified.

Here, we have a wonderful image of Jesus. He came to them and touched them and reassured them that everything was ok. He removed their fear and showed them His care.

I have never heard the audible voice of God. I just wonder if I would have the same reaction as the disciples... But in their encounter with God, we see Jesus' heart for them.

Jesus wants to touch you today. He wants to come to you and draw close and whisper the words that you need to hear. Will you let him? Whatever situation you are in right now, just stop and allow Jesus to touch you. It is His desire to do so.

Jesus, I need to encounter you today, I need a word and a touch from you that will enable me to keep going. Amen.

NO MORE IDOLS

'They set up kings without my consent; they chose princes without my approval. With their silver and gold they make idols for themselves to their own destruction. Throw out your calf idol, O Samaria. My anger burns against them. How long will they be incapable of purity.' (Hosea 8: 4-5)

The people of Samaria were way out of line with what God desired for them and sadly it brought their own destruction upon them.

Is there an idol in your life today? Is there something that you have done without seeking the Lord's approval? What preoccupies your mind? What do you spend time thinking about? Could that be an idol? Is what you are doing in life, what the Lord wants you to do?

Why not sit and be still and give permission for the Holy Spirit to search your heart and mind and see if there is an idol there. If so, throw it out, seek the Lord's forgiveness, and then step into the freedom He brings you and enjoy Him more.

Holy Spirit, will you show me where I need to come back in line with all that God has for me. I don't want to worship anything else. Amen.

THE SECRET IS OUT

'I know what it is to be in need, and I know what it is to have plenty. I have learned the secret of being content in every situation, whether well fed, or hungry, whether living in plenty or in want. I can do everything through Him who gives me strength.' (Philippians 4: 12-13)

The Apostle Paul had an extraordinary life: he witnessed the awesome power of God, he experienced severe beatings and shipwrecks, and was in prison when writing this letter. And yet he had discovered the 'secret of being content in every situation' that he faced. Who would not want that!

When was the last time you were really content and fully at peace? I believe that the secret of being content is knowing the intimate love of the Father, walking with Jesus and being led by the Spirit on a daily basis. If those three are all active in your life, then you have a very good chance of discovering the gift of contentment in every situation that you face.

Don't miss out on this wonderful secret. It is yours to enjoy and will give you the strength to face whatever comes your way.

Today, may I discover this wonderful secret of being content. May I know contentment even within the storm that I am facing, as well as contentment in times of peace. Amen.

YOU ARE THERE

'Where can I go from your spirit? Or where can I flee from your presence? If I ascend to heaven, you are there; if I make my bed in Sheol, you are there. If I take the wings of the morning and settle at the farthest limits of the sea, even there your hand shall lead me, and your right hand shall hold me fast.' (Psalm 139: 7-10, NRSV)

Psalm 139 is packed full of great truths. Here is another one: you cannot escape from His presence. Wherever you go, wherever you feel hidden and unseen, wherever you hide, wherever you run or escape to - God is there.

We need to understand more deeply this simple, yet mind-blowing truth: there is no place, no situation and nothing too horrible that we face, that God will not be there. It is a solid foundation as we walk through life. There is no need to run anymore, there is no need to hide. Instead we can step into the truth that God is with us by His Spirit.

The Father is waiting with arms outstretched to welcome you, to hold you and to be with you. Don't face another day relying on your own strength and willpower - turn to face Him and let God in. He is waiting for you to fall into His strong arms.

So no more fleeing. Today is a new day for you.

Father, I can't run any more. I turn to you and fall into your arms of love that will hold me fast and guide me to new pastures. Amen.

HEAVEN IS A WONDERFUL PLACE

*'Instead they were longing for a better country - a heavenly
one. Therefore God is not ashamed to be their God, for
He has prepared a city for them.' (Hebrews 11: 16)*

This is a wonderful image to try to comprehend today: a spiritual home is available for us that God has prepared through the death and resurrection of His Son Jesus. It is a place for us to hope for and believe in and even experience now.

Jesus' death means that the Kingdom is breaking out on earth now. He taught us to pray, 'Your kingdom come, on earth as it is in heaven', so heaven is available to be enjoyed today. You can enjoy the benefits of heaven today!

Are you enjoying that heavenly spiritual home? For me, the truth of this verse helps pull me through the tough days. To know that heaven is here, changes my perspective and releases hope. I can see beyond the struggles to take hold of the goodness of God.

Take some time out and imagine and enjoy this incredible place that has been prepared for you!

*Father, thank you that you have prepared an awesome place for me.
May I believe it is here and enjoy the fruits of it today. Amen.*

TWO LIVES TO LIVE

'This is what the Lord says: "Cursed is the one who trusts in man, who depends on flesh for his strength and whose heart turns from the Lord... But blessed is the man who trusts in the Lord, whose confidence is in Him."' (Jeremiah 17: 5; 7)

In these two verses, we have a choice to make: one path leads to destruction and misfortunes (see v. 6), whilst the other leads to a better and fruitful life (see v. 8).

A practical way to learn to put our confidence in the Lord is to be still, and ask Him to fill us with His Spirit so that we don't rely on our own flesh and our own strength. The more we become dependent on God, the more we will be blessed and our lives will be fruitful. It is so easy for us to trust and rely on our own strength and skills, that we can so easily become independent and lose sight of what is important.

So today, choose to rely on God and His Spirit to help you in your situation. Put your confidence in God.

Father, I need your help, I realise that I am becoming too dependent on my own flesh and skills. Please forgive me. I ask for more of your presence in my life. Today, I will trust you. Amen.

DON'T BE INACTIVE

'After that whole generation had been gathered to their fathers, another generation grew up, who knew neither the Lord nor what He had done for Israel.' (Judges 2: 10)

We must learn to give away our faith to the next generation - the quicker, the better! We must be able to let others flourish and for the next generation to carry forward what we have seen and witnessed in our lives. They need to take it to the next level so that our ceilings become their floors.

So the question today is this: is your faith making an impact on the people around you: your family, your friends and your work colleagues? Is your testimony of God's goodness still active?

Let's not be the generation that fails to live out our faith in Jesus and pass it on. Let's always be investing in others, releasing them and watching them move forward further in their faith.

Lord, will you bring me people today who I can pass my faith and testimony on to, so that your Kingdom will continue to flourish and you will be known from generation to generation. Amen.

SPEAK POSITIVELY

*'If anyone considers himself religious and yet does not
keep a tight rein on his tongue, he deceives himself
and his religion is worthless.' (James 1: 26)*

Imagine what a better world we would have if we could keep a tight rein on our tongue: no lying, no grumbling, no complaining, no anger, no gossiping and so much more.

Today, keep a check on the use of your tongue. Speak the truth, and use words that bless others and bring glory to Jesus Christ.

Jesus, help me speak only words that can be heard in heaven, words that will make a difference, words that will impact someone's life. Amen.

LET'S SHARE THE MESSAGE

'"We hear them declaring the wonders of God in our own tongues!" Amazed and perplexed, they asked one another, "What does this mean?"' (Acts 2: 11b-12)

One of the greatest days in the history of humankind, was the day the Holy Spirit was poured out on all people, and the prophecy of Joel was fulfilled - young and old, both men and women received Him, and lives were changed forever.

But what I love most about this verse is that even though these things were happening to a specific group of people, others were also being blessed. They heard the wonders of God in their own language. The message of Jesus is for all people to hear.

People need to hear about what God is doing in your life so that they can know Him.

Are you giving time for God to work in your life, or is He perhaps sidelined?

He wants to work in your in life and do wonders which you can tell others about. Don't miss out on what God has for you today.

Lord, thank you for the gift of the Holy Spirit, who gives me the opportunity for new life. May I have a chance to share about you today, and all that you have done for me. Amen.

IT'S TIME TO RISE UP

'Who is it that overcomes the world? Only he who believes that Jesus is the Son of God.' (1 John 5: 5)

The world we live in can be filled with all kinds of pressures and stresses: broken relationships, financial worries, ill-health and other concerns causing anxiety, fear, and sleepless nights, but we can overcome these! We have such a rich inheritance in Jesus to enjoy now to help us overcome our problems.

If you want to see your belief in Jesus grow to new levels, get to know Him for who He really is - the Son of God, who conquered death and rose again and overcame the world.

Spend some time today with Jesus. Believe who He is and that He has overcome the world and then live in that great victory.

Jesus, you have overcome the world and all its difficulties. I will walk in confidence in who you are and what you have done. I believe in you. Amen.

HE'S COMING

'In my distress I called upon the Lord; to my God I cried for help. From his temple he heard my voice, and my cry to him reached his ears. ...He reached down from on high, he took me; he drew me out of mighty waters. He delivered me from my strong enemy, and from those who hated me; for they were too mighty for me. They confronted me in the day of my calamity; but the Lord was my support. He brought me out into a broad place; he delivered me, because he delighted in me.' (Psalm 18: 6; 16-19, NRSV)

Wow - what an amazing image revealing a powerful truth of God's heart and passion for us! Look how He responds to our cries for help! It's no half measure for Him! He comes ready to act on our behalf. He wants to carry us in His arms and draw us close to Him, and rescue us from all our troubles.

God really does care about you and He will come and rescue you. He is so attentive to the situation that you are in, and is already fighting to bring breakthrough.

Call out to Him. Don't give up. He is responding. Victory is on its way.

Lord, you are indeed on your way to step in and help me. Thank you that you have heard my cry for help and nothing will get in the way of your rescue plan. You are coming to carry me in your arms to a safe place. Amen.

DON'T BE DIVIDED IN YOUR HEART

*'I will give them an undivided heart and put a new spirit
in them. I will remove from them their heart of stone
and give them a heart of flesh.' (Ezekiel 11: 19)*

In this one verse from the prophet Ezekiel, we begin to see God's plan and His desire to dwell in the hearts of every human being.

Most religions are about laws and rules, but with God, through Jesus, it is about relationship and intimacy. God's desire is to give us a heart of flesh, not stone; a heart that is alive with His love and full of His Spirit. God's purpose is to turn our hearts to Him and make us alive in the Spirit. He doesn't want any coldness or hurt or pain in our heart, but a soft heart of flesh, not a hard heart of stone.

So the question we must ask ourselves today is this: is my heart fully alive today or are there some areas still closed off to God?

Allow God's Spirit to remove that heart of stone today. He wants all your heart - not a divided heart.

He loves you more than you know.

Father, thank you for your desire to give me an undivided heart - a heart that is fully alive and connected to you in an intimate way. Amen.

KEEP ACTIVE

*'Now I want you to know, brothers, that what has happened to
me has really served to advance the gospel.' (Philippians 1: 12)*

Even in prison, Paul was demonstrating the message of Jesus to the prison
guards who were the elite soldiers of that time. Nothing held him back:
'no fear of man, no scheme of hell' would stop Paul advancing the gospel.

How is the gospel going to advance through you today?

The truth is that whatever circumstance you find yourself in presently,
whether rejoicing or weeping, succeeding or failing, busy or resting, the
Kingdom can still be advanced through you. In fact, God loves nothing
better than taking the knocks and disappointments of life and redeeming
them through the gospel flowing out of you in every situation.

There have been so many times when I lay in a hospital bed feeling held
back by the enemy's arrows of sickness, only to have nurses and other
hospital staff drawn to the gospel because of Jesus, 'the river of life'
flowing through me.

In every situation, God can win. Nothing can hold back the gospel
message and the Kingdom being revealed on earth.

Let's be finding ways to do the same in our own lives today.

*Jesus, thank you that your disciple Paul, advanced the gospel whilst in
prison. Help me today to advance your gospel in ways that others will
see and know that you are the Saviour of the world. Amen.*

'SHUT UP AND DIE!'

'We always carry around in our body the death of Jesus, so that the life of Jesus may also be revealed in our body.' (2 Corinthians 4: 10)

This is a challenging word from Paul today.

Carrying the death of Jesus signifies that we must learn to die to our desires, our wishes and our wants, because that is what Jesus did when He went to the cross. Jesus had given up his right to any entitlements, so must we. The more we surrender our lives to Him, the more His life is revealed in us.

My wife Michelle has a great expression she uses when faced with the wrestle of the flesh: 'shut up and die!'

Is there something that you are holding onto that you know you have to let go of?

Peace is found in surrender. So take some time today to be with Jesus, and ask Him for help, so that you can surrender and 'die'. Then you will reflect Him more powerfully in your life.

Jesus, will you help me become more alive in you than I have ever experienced before. Please show me where I need to die to something, so that the life of Jesus can be revealed. Amen.

LET'S GIVE GOD A CHANCE TO ACT

'With this in mind, we constantly pray for you, that our God may count you worthy of His calling, and that by His power He may fulfil every good purpose of yours and every act prompted by your faith.' (2 Thessalonians 1: 11)

We can allow God's power to be at work in us today so that God can extend His Kingdom as we step out in faith. As we take time to realign ourselves with Him, our thoughts, words and deeds bring glory to Him.

Some good family friends of ours shared a wonderful story of stepping out in faith and seeing God act promptly. Their daughter who had lived in Australia serving with YWAM for 3 years, was coming home and they did not have enough money between them to pay for her excess baggage. So they prayed. The daughter felt she should step out, trust God and head to the airport with her bags. As she was leaving the house, someone arrived saying, "I owe you some money." She had forgotten all about the money and it was the amount she needed for her bags, with a little bit extra left over!

Whatever our circumstances or limitations, we can still step out and respond in faith to the promptings of the Holy Spirit.

Let's give God the chance today to act as we step out in faith.

Father, I need courage so that I can use my faith in order for you to act in power. Please give me the opportunity to do this today. Amen.

IT'S THE BEST GATE TO OPEN

'I am the gate; whoever enters through me will be saved. He will come in and go out, and find pasture.' (John 10: 9)

This less familiar 'I am' of Jesus gives a wonderful picture of what happens once we enter the gate of salvation. There are pastures to be found and to be enjoyed. The image of pastures implies that there are ample supplies for all our needs, a space for us to be nurtured and fed, a space for us to rest and be safe.

Jesus is saying that in this new life you have entered, you have everything you need to live to the full. (The next verse gives the contrast: 'The thief comes only to steal and kill and destroy; I have come that they may have life, and have it to the full (v. 10).

So today, make the most of being in heaven's pastures. There are plenty of supplies for every situation you find yourself in. You don't need to worry, you don't need to be afraid, you are not alone, you are loved and you can live a more fulfilled life in the pastures of the Kingdom of God than anywhere else.

If you have never opened this 'gate of salvation' in your heart, maybe today is a good day to do that. Simply invite Jesus into your heart and enjoy all He has for you.

Jesus, today I open this wonderful gate of salvation and enter into a new life with you. I will enjoy all the wonderful and good things of heaven that are mine to enjoy. Amen.

IT WILL GET BETTER

'For you, O God, tested us; you refined us like silver. You brought us into prison and laid burdens on our backs. You let men ride over our heads; we went through fire and water, but you brought us to a place of abundance.' (Psalm 66: 10-12)

Back in 2014, we went through a very tough time in our lives. I was very ill and had to retire from a job that I loved which also left us without a home, without an income and no future ministry in church life... our dreams disappeared.

It felt like going 'through fire and water' and carrying 'burdens on our backs'. However, God spoke to me through this verse of scripture and now, as I look back, I can see that God is true to His promises - He 'brought us to a place of abundance'. I am still in awe of what He has done for us! (He brought us into a new church family, provided a home for us to live in and to share with others, and He gave us opportunities to use our gifts to bless other people.)

So today, if you are in an abundant place, spend some time thanking Him for being faithful to His promise. However, if you are going 'through fire and water', carrying burdens, know this truth: He is with you. He will bring you into a place of abundance, a place better than it is now - that is His promise to you. So hang in there!

Abba Father, thank you that you are faithful to your word, that your word is the truth and your word is real. I thank you for bringing me to a place of abundance. Amen.

HE CAN DO IT

'When Israel went out from Egypt, the house of Jacob from a people of strange language, Judah became God's sanctuary, Israel his dominion. The sea looked and fled; Jordan turned back. The mountains skipped like rams, the hills like lambs. Why is it, O sea, that you flee? O Jordan, that you turn back? O mountains, that you skip like rams? O hills, like lambs? Tremble, O earth, at the presence of the Lord, at the presence of the God of Jacob, who turns the rock into a pool of water, the flint into a spring of water.' (Psalm 114, NRSV)

This is a wonderful reminder of how awesome and powerful Father God is: the mountains tremble, the rivers depart, the sea flees! Nothing is impossible for our God! He has no limits; there are no restrictions to what He can do in any situation. He can bring water from barren rocks.

At the heart of this Psalm is the fact that God chose to dwell with Judah, to make Israel His dwelling place.

God would love to dwell with you, for you to be in His presence and enjoy fellowship with Him. It is being in His presence that allows extraordinary things to take place and for miraculous transformation in your life. There is no limit to what He can do.

Father, you can move mountains, you can stir the seas and make the earth tremble. I ask that you change the situation that I am facing now. Amen.

FOR SUCH A TIME AS THIS

"'If you keep quiet at a time like this, deliverance for the Jews will arise from some other place, but you and your father's family will perish. Who knows but that you have come to royal position for such a time as this.'" (Esther 4: 14)

God put Esther in the King's palace for a certain reason and God has put each one of us in a certain place - home, job, work, ministry - for a specific reason and in a specific season.

We need to be aware of the significance of where He has placed us, even if it feels insignificant in our eyes or in the eyes of others.

As we are sensitive to the needs around us, we can be available to God at a moment's notice. He will be speaking to us and showing us how to act, so let's be alert to His voice. Let's not miss out on the God-given opportunities that come our way today and, like Esther, let's not be afraid or hold back, but step forward and see how God changes things.

Father, thank you that you have placed me where I am today for a specific reason and I will not be afraid or hold back. Amen.

MAKE GOD YOUR FIRST PORT OF CALL

'They all plotted together to come and fight against Jerusalem and stir up trouble against it. But we prayed to our God and posted a guard day and night to meet this threat.' (Nehemiah 4: 8-9)

Nehemiah was sent by God to rebuild the walls of Jerusalem and, more often than not, there is opposition to God's work. Nehemiah teaches us that the correct route to take when things get tricky, is to seek the Lord. He gathered friends and they prayed and heard God's solution.

So often, when things don't work out as we plan, we do not seek the Lord first. Praying to God and bringing Him into our situations is something that needs to happen straight away.

Don't wait until you are at the end of yourself. Make prayer an important part of your life and watch how God works. He is listening and wants to help you.

Forgive me, Father, for when I have not sought you first but instead relied on my own wisdom or skills. Today, I turn to you and seek your way forward for my life, family and work. Amen.

ENJOY THE BENEFITS TODAY

'When they hurled their insults at him, he did not retaliate; when He suffered, he made no threats. Instead he entrusted himself to him who judges justly. "He himself bore our sins in His body on the tree", so that we might die to sins and live for righteousness; "by his wounds you have been healed." For "you were like sheep going astray," but now you have returned to the Shepherd and Overseer of your soul.' (1 Peter 2: 23-25)

These verses sum up all that Jesus did for you and for me. He took it all as a human being, without complaining, without any resentment, and died so that you and I could taste and see God's love for us. He opened up the door for amazing things to happen: a relationship with Father God is made possible; sin is destroyed; bodies can be healed and we will never be alone again. Nothing is out of our reach, because Jesus stepped up and became the perfect sacrifice. He was and still is awesome!

Today, let's not sit around and forget to take in the enormity of what Jesus has achieved for us. He wants all of us to enjoy the life that He has made possible for us.

He is the Good Shepherd and He will lead you into a life of freedom and peace.

Jesus, thank you so much for going through what you did for me. Thank you for the new life you have made possible for me. I will forever be in debt to you. Amen.

BELIEVE WHAT GOD SEES

'When the angel of the Lord appeared to Gideon, he said, "The Lord is with you, mighty warrior."' (Judges 6:12)

Gideon did not see himself as a 'mighty warrior'. He even said of himself, "I am the least in my family," (v. 15). But that is not how the Lord saw him.

God sees you differently to how you see yourself sometimes. We can so easily focus on the negative thoughts about ourselves. God has so many good things to say about you and so many gifts and talents for you to discover.

If an angel of God visited you today, what do you think he would say to you? Why not spend some time thinking about how God really sees you. Allow His thoughts and His words about you to become dominant in your mind.

Enjoy them and believe that you are someone unique and special.

Father, thank you that you see the gold in me and you see me as your child. Today, I choose to walk and live believing that I am special and unique in your eyes, and not listen to the lies of the enemy. Amen.

IS IT TIME TO WAKE UP?

'These are the words of him who holds the seven spirits of God and the seven stars. I know your deeds; you have a reputation of being alive but you are dead. Wake up!' (Revelation 3: 1b-2a)

'Wake up!' This cry is not just to the churches mentioned in the book of Revelation but to us all.

We need to connect with the Father to give life to our spirit, rather than continuing on as we are, just seeming to be alive. If we don't, there is a danger we can end up spiritually dead.

If each day is the same and nothing is really happening, perhaps that connection with the Father is lost.

Today, choose to wake up, reconnect with the Father, be refreshed in the Holy Spirit and walk in fullness of life.

Lord, I will wake up today and begin to walk in fullness of the life that you have given me through Jesus Christ my Lord and Saviour. I will wake up so that I will see your Kingdom come on earth. Amen.

RISE UP

*'Then the Lord said, "Rise and anoint him, this
is the one."' (1 Samuel 16: 12b)*

The Lord gave the prophet Samuel this command: "rise and anoint him".

Samuel did God's work. He anointed David who would rise up and become Israel's greatest king who not only established peace in the land, but found a site for the temple where the Lord God could dwell and be worshipped.

Will you rise up and bless someone today with an encouraging word? Will you be God's messenger of hope for someone today?

Let's look beyond ourselves: rise up, do God's work and extend His arm of love to people.

You never know what impact it will have. Rise up!

Jesus, will you give me an opportunity today to bless someone, to bring a message of hope for a person who needs it. Amen.

KEEP FLOURISHING

'Blessed are those whose strength is in you, whose hearts
are set on pilgrimage. As they pass through the Valley
of Baka, they make it a place of springs; the autumn
rains also cover it with pools.' (Psalm 84: 5-6)

The whole of this wonderful Psalm, and especially these verses, have become for us over the years not only a great comfort for my family, but also a promise realised, as we have experienced fresh 'springs' and 'pools' in the midst of darkness and confusion.

Here we discover that as we pass through 'the Valley of Baka' - times of weeping and hardship in our own lives - we are blessed not only to get through, but to flourish and grow, even in the valley of tears.

Whatever you are facing today, be encouraged that something exciting is waiting for you, something new, something to discover. Don't miss out - do not forget the One who is mightier and bigger than any situation you face.

So let's not lose heart, let's not give up. Let us use every opportunity to go from strength to strength, to turn tough times into springs of life and joy, and to make our lives a story of pilgrimage.

Lord, I will not sit back and stay where I am. I choose to make my surroundings into a place of blessings and I know that you will carry me to new pastures. Amen.

NEW INSIGHT NEEDED?

'When I heard these things, I sat down and wept.
For some days I mourned and fasted and prayed
before the God of Heaven.' (Nehemiah 1: 4)

Jerusalem's walls and gates were ruined; the Lord's name had been disgraced. This news was devastating to Nehemiah. He was determined that God's name would be honoured again. He sought the Lord in prayer and fasting.

Do you have the same passion and willingness to restore God's name? If so, start seeking Him now and discover new ways to bring His Kingdom on earth through you, your work and your ministry.

Jesus, help me establish your Kingdom on earth today so that your name is honoured and talked about in good ways. Amen.

HANG IN THERE

'Though I walk in the midst of trouble, you preserve my life. You stretch out your hand against the anger of my foes; with your right hand you save me. The Lord will fulfil his purpose for me; your love, O Lord, endures forever - do not abandon the works of your hands.' (Psalm 138: 7-8)

There are some wonderful promises in these two verses today, which shed light on the amazing God whom we worship.

He has wonderful plans for you. He has not abandoned you, He walks alongside you today, so take His hand and enjoy fellowship with Him. You can have confidence that He is in charge of your destiny, and nothing can hold back the fulfilment of His purposes in your life.

Don't give up, but instead trust in Father God to get you to where He wants you to be.

Father, thank you that you will be with me today, you will not abandon me. I need your presence and strength to enable me to carry on, so that I can see all that you have for me. Amen.

HE WILL ACT - LEARN TO WAIT

'Since ancient times no one has heard, no ear has perceived, no eye has seen any God besides you, who acts on behalf of those who wait for Him.' (Isaiah 64: 4)

Waiting is a hard discipline to undertake, but what an amazing promise Isaiah reveals here: God will act on behalf of those who wait.

At the time that Isaiah was writing, the world was full of gods who demanded constant placating and ritual in return for their help. That was their belief system, but Isaiah was showing the exiles that their God was different. All they needed to do was to wait on Him.

What is the best way to wait? Jesus says in Matthew 6, "Go into your room, close the door and pray to your Father," (v. 6). He is saying that we have to be intentional.

I have made an effort to have a place in my house where I can go. Once there, I sit and simply believe that God is there with me and He sees me. I sit there waiting and I pray, inviting God to speak to me. It can be hard, but you have to start somewhere, and over the years I have got better at waiting on the Lord. As that verse continues, Jesus says, "Then your Father, who sees what is done in secret, will reward you." (Matthew 6: 6).

So if you are going through a tough time, seeking direction or you would love God to move in a particular area of your life, then waiting on God will be a blessing. Waiting is a discipline that needs to be part of our lives. Give it a go.

Father, thank you that you promise to act on my behalf. You will step in and usher in your Kingdom into my life and situation. I will learn to wait on you and begin to grow this discipline in my life. Amen.

WE HAVE TO SHARE IT

'Jesus did not let him, but said, "Go home to your family and tell them how much the Lord has done for you, and how he has had mercy on you." So the man went away and began to tell in the Decapolis how much Jesus had done for him. And all the people were amazed.' (Mark 5: 19-20)

Good news is hard to find in today's society.

This man who had just been healed by Jesus, had so much good news to tell people. His whole life had been completely changed, and yet it is so important to hear what Jesus says to the man: "Go home - go to your own people and tell them how much the Lord has done for you." The man did what Jesus told him and later on in Mark's gospel, Jesus goes back into the Decapolis area and the sick and the lame are brought to Him and He heals them (Mark 7 and 8). The Kingdom of God advanced on earth because the man shared the good news of what Jesus had done for him.

If God has touched you or blessed you this week, or just been there for you, or has shown incredible mercy to you, why not tell someone. Jesus would love us to do that. The more we share and sow seeds, the greater the opportunity people have to encounter Jesus.

Don't let fear stop you from sharing the good news. Let it be foremost on our lips.

Jesus, you have done so much for me already. Help me to share this good news with people that are close to me and with those whom I meet today. I will step out and tell people about you. Amen.

WILL IT TAKE ROOT?

'And he said to them, "Do you not understand this parable? Then how will you understand all the parables? The sower sows the word. These are the ones on the path where the word is sown: when they hear, Satan immediately comes and takes away the word that is sown in them. ...And these are the ones sown on the good soil: they hear the word and accept it and bear fruit, thirty and sixty and a hundredfold."' (Mark 4: 13-15; 20, NRSV)

We may know this famous parable, but do we really understand it and allow the gospel message to grow in us? Today, we know that God, (represented here as the farmer), is still sowing seed - He has never stopped. Is His Word taking root in good soil in your heart and growing and producing a crop? Or is Satan snatching it away?

In his book The Screwtape Letters, author C. S Lewis sums up this 'snatching away' really well. The book on spiritual warfare is written in the form of a series of letters from a senior demon to his subordinate:

'I note with grave displeasure that your patient has become a Christian... there is no need to despair; hundreds of these adult converts have been reclaimed after a brief sojourn in the Enemy's camp and are now with us. All the habits of the patient, both mentally and bodily are still in our favour.'[15]

Is your life bearing good fruit? Are you teachable with a soft heart, ready to learn, or are you still stuck in old sinful habits? God is still throwing seed out today, seed with powerful revelation to change you. May it take root in your life in 'good soil' in your heart, bear much fruit and never be snatched away.

Jesus, may my heart be soft and ready to receive your message today so that it will take root in good soil and produce a bumper crop. Amen.

BE JOYFUL

*"'I have told you this so that you will be filled with my
joy. Yes, your joy will overflow!'" (John 15: 11, NLT)*

Jesus has just shared with His disciples some amazing teachings in these
last chapters of John's gospel. As He enters the final hours of His life, Jesus
shares with them this truth: if they remain in His love, they will be filled
with His joy. He wants all of us to grab hold of that truth as well.

Jesus' joy was knowing the Father on an intimate level, and He wants to
share that joyous relationship with us. His incredible invitation is for us to
be drawn intimately into the wonderful relationship between Himself, the
Father and the Spirit.

How close are you to Jesus today? His desire is for all of us to be filled with
His joy. Whether you are going through a good patch or bad, draw close to
Jesus. Then you will overflow and have the joy you need at this time.

*Jesus, thank you for giving me the opportunity to be filled with your joy.
I receive it and may this joy of heaven overflow into others and bring
happiness and joy to people I meet today. Amen.*

NO LIMIT TO WHAT GOD CAN DO

*'"Ah, Sovereign Lord, you have made the heavens and
the earth by your great power and outstretched arm.
Nothing is too hard for you."' (Jeremiah 32: 17)*

There is no limit to God's amazing power and there is no limit to what
He can do. The astonishing thing is that the Creator of the universe, who
created us and who loves us, wants us to work with Him and partner with
Him.

As we surrender, and lay down our lives and follow Him, He promises
to get to work doing the impossible in our lives. It sounds like a
brilliant exchange!

Is there something you need His help with today?

Why not ask Him?

*Father, nothing is impossible for you today. I ask that you will step in
with your great strength and power to help me. Amen.*

WHAT YOU SAY WILL MAKE A DIFFERENCE

'Do not let any unwholesome talk come out of your mouths, but only what is helpful for building others up according to their needs, that it may benefit those who listen.' (Ephesians 4: 29)

We live in a culture that tends to speak negatively and put people down. In fact many of us find it easier to offer a word of criticism rather than a word of encouragement.

Why not ask the Holy Spirit today, to make you more aware of how you talk to people in your home, in your place of work, with your spouse and with your children. Which way does the balance tip? Ask Him to begin to change the way you talk, helping you speak words that will encourage, strengthen and build people up.

I find that the difference can even be seen physically as people go from a posture of looking deflated and curved in on themselves, to becoming buoyed-up, upright and open before your very eyes!

Choose to speak words that bring life today.

Jesus, you have called me to be different, to live a life that reflects you and your presence. May I speak today with words of love and kindness, and help me to see where I am not saying the right things. Amen.

IT'S TIME TO BE HONEST

'You know my folly, O God; my guilt is not hidden from you. May those who hope in you not be disgraced because of me, O Lord, the Lord Almighty; may those who seek you not be put to shame because of me, O God of Israel.' (Psalm 69: 5-6)

David, the author of this Psalm knew he had done something wrong. He couldn't hide it from God and he knew this would cause a problem for others as well.

We all make mistakes and sometimes our mistakes hurt not only ourselves, but they hurt and confuse others, and can even affect their relationship with God. Therefore, the most important thing to do is not to hide, but bring before God anything we know we have done wrong. We can always approach Him.

In our relationship with our daughter, we have tried to create an atmosphere where nothing is hidden, nothing is covered up, nothing is so bad or so wrong that it can't be brought out into the open and talked about. This makes for some very open and gritty conversations at times, but our desire is for her to know that in the same way she does with us, she can bring anything before God.

Are there things you are hiding or covering up? Whether it is in the past or is more recent, seek the Lord's forgiveness and love, and bring it out into the light. The more we are free from our folly, the bigger the impact we will have on those who observe us. When they see the Father's grace lavished on us, they will want it for themselves.

Do not hide, but instead be free from guilt and shame, and give testimony of God's goodness that will change the lives of others.

Father, you know me through and through, so I come to you today seeking your love and forgiveness. I want to change so that I can be a good witness for you and be the child you want me to be. Amen.

NEVER BE ON YOUR OWN

*'For those who are led by the Spirit of God are
the children of God.' (Romans 8: 14)*

In the original Greek, the tense for the verb 'led' is the continuous present tense. In other words, it reads 'as many as are regularly led by the Spirit of God, these are the children of God'. Also, the Greek word for 'children' implies a degree of maturity as opposed to a little child.

In light of this, are you being led by the Spirit on a daily basis and is your faith maturing? If you feel you are not living these words out today, I encourage you to seek the Lord's grace and mercy, so that every area of your life reflects His glory.

Don't do it alone. Walk in step with the Spirit.

Holy Spirit, will you come alive in me today, so that I can be led by you and do remarkable things for the sake of the Kingdom of God. Amen.

GET YOUR MIND FOCUSED

'Do not conform any longer to the pattern of this world, but be transformed by the renewing of your mind. Then you will be able to test and approve what God's will is - his good, pleasing and perfect will.' (Romans 12: 2)

Renewing our minds enables us to make choices founded upon heaven's values whether in regard to relationships, lifestyle, family, work, or even money. If we are free from the world's patterns of thinking and acting, then we will be able to make choices that are good and pleasing. Knowing His ways of thinking and living is so much better than conforming to the patterns of this world.

Is it time to take a rain check? How much does the world influence your mind at the moment? Have you allowed some of the world's values to slip through the net and shape who you are - independence, pride, selfishness and worry - to name a few?

Sit down today and take a few minutes to realign your mind and get your focus back on Jesus. It may be that you will need to repent of something specific. When our minds are renewed and we are no longer thinking like the world, then transformation can take place.

Jesus, I no longer want to live conforming to the patterns of this world but instead live in God's perfect will for my life. I can't do this on my own, please come and help me to renew my mind and be different. Amen.

IT'S TIME TO THROW IT AWAY

*'Let us throw off everything that hinders and the sin
that so easily entangles.' (Hebrews 12: 1b)*

Sin repeated over time can become ingrained in our lives.

Is there a habit, or a thought pattern that you find yourself constantly battling with? Or a lie from the enemy that you speak over yourself or listen to? It's time to throw these things off. But how can we do that?

Take some time and ask the Holy Spirit to take you to the cross where Jesus' blood paid for those things you are struggling with (you can even visualise this as you do it). Then, repent and exchange your old ways of thinking for new ones. Receive forgiveness, and take time to drink in the Father's love and grace for you.

The final and most important step is to walk in the opposite spirit and the opposite way of thinking. I have found that this is really powerful and is actually true repentance. I find a particular scripture that speaks heavenly truth which is the opposite to that habit or thought pattern. Then I refer to it each day, so when the thought or sin tries to creep back, I not only see it, but replace it quickly with the truth from scripture. I find that declaring it out loud is also very powerful and when we do this, there is evidence that it literally changes our neural pathways. By doing this, I am filling my mind with His Word which strengthens my foundation, so I am not easily entangled again.

*Jesus, I recognise that I have allowed sin to entangle me. I want to
be free and walk enjoying a fuller life than I am now. Thank you that
you died so that I can be free. I will break free today and be rid of sin
through the power of the cross. Amen.*

I NEED HELP

'I thank Christ Jesus our Lord, who has given me strength, that he considered me faithful, appointing me to his service.' (1 Timothy 1: 12)

There is so much we can thank Jesus for - He has done so much for us.

Paul, the author of this letter written to his friend Timothy, had so much to be thankful for. He was once a persecutor and a blasphemer (v. 13), but Jesus showed grace and mercy and called him to serve and bring the gospel to the known Gentile world. He needed every ounce of strength to fulfil this task and Jesus did not let him down. He will not let us down either.

Looking back at the seven years during which I led a church, I can bear witness to the fact that God does give us strength to carry out the tasks that He appoints for us to undertake. This whole season was marked with tremendous health struggles. However, Michelle and I saw God bless us daily with strength: strength to endure confusion; strength to overcome sickness; strength to lead others despite weakness; strength to hold onto hope; strength to deal with disappointment and strength not to withdraw, but instead to share our journey with others.

Today, He wants to give you His strength to face all that comes your way. Ask for it and He will give it to you, so that you can carry out all that He has planned for you.

Jesus, thank you that you have called me into your service, to help advance your Kingdom on earth. I ask that you will give me extra strength today to fulfil all you have for me. Amen.

NO RETREAT, NO SURRENDER

"'If we are thrown into the blazing furnace, the God we serve is able to save us from it, and he will rescue us from your hand, O king. But even if he does not, we want you to know, O king that we will not serve your gods or worship the image of gold you have set up.'" (Daniel 3: 17-18)

Shadrach, Meshach and Abednego were about to face a terrible thing: death by burning. However, their hope was placed in something and someone higher than even their survival. They were placing their hope and faith in God, whatever the outcome, no matter what happened. Even if God didn't save them, they would still hold the course; they would still only worship Him and not bow to other gods. They were trusting that whatever happened, God would make it all good in the end.

We may face fears and terrors in our lives. Sometimes it is only through facing them that we can stop feeling intimidated.

Michelle and I have had to face many fears over the years. However, for us, breakthrough has come when we have looked these fears straight in the eye and said to ourselves: "Even if they happen, we will still hope and trust in God. We trust He will come through for us and make it all good in the end."

So today, take a moment to check that your hope in God is not dependent on certain outcomes. Will you only trust and follow Him if things work out? Bring any issues you are facing to God and the fears that they stir up, then lay them down. He will come through and work everything for good in the end.

Father, I bring to you my fears and the conditions I can place on you. I surrender again, choosing to place my hope and faith in you... no matter what happens. Amen.

LET'S BE ACTIVE

"'Ask and it will be given to you; seek and you will find;
knock and the door will be opened to you. For everyone
who asks receives; he who seeks finds; and to him who
knocks, the door will be opened.'" (Matthew 7: 7-8)

Jesus speaks these words to us today to encourage us to be active in our walk with Him, to allow Him to be involved in our lives.

Are we letting God into the situations that we are dealing with?

One day, during a busy time at work, I remember feeling quite stressed, so I stopped and simply asked the Holy Spirit to help me. I can testify that I felt at peace immediately and found a way forward with my busy workload.

It makes such a difference to be active in our daily walk, applying these simple truths to everyday life. Jesus gave these instructions so that we, as His disciples, can be productive.

So let's be asking, seeking and knocking and see how He moves in our lives and in the situations that we face. The door will be opened. He will answer.

Jesus, thank you that it's your desire to open doors for me in every
situation that I face. Help me be active in my walk with you today, to be
seeking you and getting you involved. Amen.

THAT IS AMAZING

'How precious to me are your thoughts, O God! How vast is the sum of them! Were I to count them, they would outnumber the grains of the sand. When I awake, I am still with you.' (Psalm 139: 17-18)

Read those verses again. How can that be? God thinks about you!

He has so many thoughts about you, and all of them are positive and good - not just half a dozen or so but millions and millions of good and loving thoughts! He loves you so much. That is an amazing concept!

Sit for a moment today and ponder these amazing verses. Ask Father to share some of His thoughts about you.

Remember, God is there for you, just wanting to love you and for you to know how much He is interested in you, and how much good He sees in you.

Father, thank you that you hold me in the palm of your hand and that you think such good thoughts about me. Today, may I discover more of how you see me, love me and care for me. Amen.

MAKE THE MOST OF IT

*'But you have an anointing from the Holy One, and
all of you know the truth.' (1 John 2: 20)*

We live in a world which often feels at war with the truths that Jesus
teaches us. I know that I can often feel confused and powerless. However,
this verse shows us that each one of us has an anointing from the Lord
today. Each one of us can have the power needed to move, speak and live
in truth.

This is so encouraging and transformative for how we live our lives.
Power and truth are available for work, for parenting, for maintaining
strong relationships, for dealing with crises and for living in relationship
with Jesus.

Let's take hold of this and believe it today. Let's be out in the world
bringing truth from heaven.

You will make an impact, because the Holy One has anointed you. Know
you are anointed, believe it and live it.

*Jesus, thank you that you have anointed me with your presence and your
power. Help me today to walk in confidence of this and to speak truth in
love and grace where truth needs to be spoken. Amen.*

OPEN MY EYES, LORD

'Then their eyes were opened and they recognized him.' (Luke 24: 31a)

The encounter on the road to Emmaus is a wonderful story to read. Here we find two people who are mourning and in shock, having just witnessed the death of Jesus. They had been with Jesus for part of His ministry on earth, but now walking with Him, they did not recognise Him or understand the words He spoke.

Could it be that their grief was preventing them from recognising Jesus; that their current experience was overshadowing the truth that Jesus was actually walking with them? I love the fact that their moment of recognising Jesus comes when they finally sit, rest and eat with Him.

It is in the difficult times we go through, that we learn to recognise that Jesus is with us, walking with us. Whatever we are facing, however hard our situation is, we must learn to stop, to sit, to welcome Him and then our eyes will be opened to recognise that Jesus is with us.

Just as Jesus walked with these two people during their crisis, He is walking with you. Jesus wants your attention; He wants to step in; He wants you to recognise Him; and He wants to bring you hope.

Allow Him to open your eyes so that you can recognise Him today. He is there.

Jesus, thank you that you are with me. May you open my eyes to see you and to know your peace and love that I need right now. Amen.

YOU HAVE A BLESSING COMING YOUR WAY

'"I tell you the truth, anyone who will not receive the kingdom of God like a little child will never enter it." And he took the children in His arms, put his hands on them and blessed them.' (Mark 10: 15-16)

In this verse, Jesus makes it very clear that the Kingdom can only be accessed by those who are willing to be like a little child and, at the end of the verse, we have a wonderful image of Jesus taking children and blessing them! We are His children. He would love to do the same with us.

Today, why not take a moment to do an audit on your 'childlikeness'? How childlike are you feeling today? How much are you filled with wonder and awe, with hope and trust, joy and expectancy? Is your faith in Jesus based on relationship or information? Are you expecting good things in your future? Believe that He wants to bless you and then spend a few minutes receiving from Him. Don't let busyness and doubt stop you from receiving His blessing.

Ask the Holy Spirit to show you any areas in your heart and in your life that need to be refreshed and made childlike again. Like a child, be trusting and expectant of good things.

Step forward into His presence with confidence.

Jesus, thank you that I am your child and that your desire is to bless me. Help me to understand this today and to receive your blessing with open hands and an open heart. Amen.

LET JESUS TOUCH YOU

'A man with leprosy came to him and begged him on his knees, "If you are willing, you can make me clean." Filled with compassion, Jesus reached out His hand and touched the man. "I am willing," He said. "Be clean!" Immediately the leprosy left him and he was cured.' (Mark 1: 40–42)

The man recognised who Jesus was and knelt before Him and begged. This was a sign of respect and submission, as well as desperation.

Here, Jesus demonstrates the Father-heart of God: filled with compassion, Jesus reached out and touched him. He was willing to step in where no-one else would. Leprosy was a total 'no-go' area in their culture. Lepers were 'untouchable', but that did not stop Jesus from stepping in. He was willing and He was full of compassion. He had a desire to bring change to that person's life.

Is there something that desperately needs changing in your life or in a friend's life? Where do you need God's compassion to step in and change a situation? Do you need to feel God's compassion for you?

Get on your knees and allow Jesus to touch you today, allow Him to act in your life. He is willing, so bring it to Him. He changed that person's life forever, and He wants to do the same for you.

Jesus, thank you that you are willing to help me today. I come before you and kneel and ask you to step in and touch me in my situation. Amen.

HE IS NEAR AND WILL ACT

'Seek the Lord while he may be found; call on
him while he is near.' (Isaiah 55: 6)

Two active words here are 'seek and call'.

Let these words be in your life today as you face all that comes your way. Seek the Lord, call on Him and He will answer. Don't try and survive on your own as His ways are better than our ways, His thoughts are better than our thoughts.

A few years ago, the daughter of a close friend of mine was in a horrific speedboat accident. He was first on the scene and on seeing the situation, the damage to his daughter and hearing her cry, "Daddy am I going to die?", his first response was simply to call out, "Jesus, help!".

Jesus did help through an extraordinary sequence of events which happened so quickly and saved his daughter's life.

May our first response be to seek the Lord and call on Him. He is near.

Heavenly Father, you are with me today. When I call to you, please come and hold my hand; when I seek you, please reveal yourself. Amen.

LIVE IN WORD AND SPIRIT

'He (Nicodemus) came to Jesus at night and said, "Rabbi, we know you are a teacher who has come from God. For no-one could perform the miraculous signs you are doing if God were not with him."' (John 3: 2)

What can we learn from this one verse today?

The senior theologians in Jesus' time were noticing two things about Jesus as he started his ministry: the first was that He was a teacher of God's word, and the second was that He was moving in the supernatural power of the Holy Spirit.

Jesus knew the scriptures and He demonstrated the power of the Holy Spirit. These are two powerful qualities which we must take on board in our own spiritual walk today. Only by spending time in God's Word, will we increase in knowing Him. Only by spending time with Jesus, will we be able to demonstrate the supernatural work of the Spirit in our lives.

For the Kingdom of God to be growing today, we need to be growing in both the Word and the Spirit and only then will people see a real difference in us.

They certainly saw it in Jesus.

Jesus, thank you that you have shown me how to live and extend your Kingdom on earth. May I learn from your life and be a person of the Word and the Spirit. Please teach me how to become a better follower of you today. Amen.

NEED A GOOD DRINK?

*'As the deer pants for streams of water, so my soul pants
for you, O God. My soul thirsts for God, for the living God.
When can I go and meet with God?' (Psalm 42: 1-2)*

Have you had a tough week? If so, these two verses will really help you.

Twice the writer uses the word 'soul' which, in our understanding, is
made up of our minds, character, thoughts, and feelings. It can be where
all our anxious thoughts, worries and fears sit, robbing us of peace.

The Psalmist is in need of God; his soul is dry and in need of refreshment
from the living God. However, unlike the Psalmist, we do not have to go
anywhere to find God. We live in the light of the New Covenant, so all
we need to do is sit and pour out our soul to the Living God, and let Him
refresh us with His streams of Living Water, and we will never be thirsty
again (see John 3: 10-14).

I often find that the more honest and real I am with God, the more
refreshing His streams of water seem to be.

If you are having a tough time, I encourage you to take time to pray, write
down your thoughts, and read the rest of the Psalm, as it will give you
some good truths to focus on, and then drink deeply from Jesus and His
life-giving Holy Spirit.

*Father, only you can truly satisfy me. I need to be refreshed by your
presence and by the Holy Spirit today, I know that you are here for me.
Amen.*

IT'S TIME TO SEE MORE

'He got up, took his mat and walked out in full view of them all. This amazed everyone and they praised God, saying, "We have never seen anything like this!"' (Mark 2: 12)

How many miracles have you seen lately? Have you heard of a healing testimony recently? Jesus healed everyone who asked for healing and people were blown away by it.

Miracles are still happening today. It is important that we don't box God in; so keep increasing your expectations, get rid of doubts and believe, and be amazed at what God can do. Our God is the God of the impossible. Let God become bigger in your heart and you will see amazing acts of the supernatural as you step forward in faith.

I remember praying for a friend of my daughter's who had hurt her wrist quite badly. She didn't believe in Jesus and I wanted to see healing as I had not prayed for someone for a while. So in front of her parents and my daughter, we prayed for the wrist to be healed.

You should have seen the look on their faces as the pain left immediately! I will never forget that small miracle. It was just amazing!

Jesus, thank you that you healed everyone. Help me to step up and believe for more healing in my life. I want to do what you did and see people healed. Amen.

LIGHT SHINE IN ME

'When Jesus spoke again to the people, he said, "I am the light of the world. Whoever follows me will never walk in darkness, but will have the light of life."' (John 8: 12)

Following Jesus means total surrender of oneself. It means choosing to be reborn and to allow the life and light of Jesus to grow and flourish in us. It means His thoughts, His plans, His power, His ways... in us.

Are there areas of your life that you have not yet surrendered to Jesus? Are there habits, thoughts, attitudes or even places of darkness that need the Light of the World to shine on them? So often in life, we can find it hard to recognise the areas that are holding us back, the patterns that keep us in darkness. However, the kindness of God means He can shine His light, bringing clarity and revelation that leads to our freedom.

Come to Jesus today, and let the light of life shine on you. Let the light shine deep into your heart and dispel the darkness. Surrender to Jesus and let Him give you life in all its brightness.

Jesus, I want to change. I don't want any darkness in my life. You are the Light of the World. I invite you to shine in me to dispel all the darkness, so that I can live a full and healthy life. Amen.

ARE YOU READY FOR YOUR CALL

'In Damascus there was a disciple named Ananias. The Lord called to him in a vision, "Ananias!" "Yes, Lord," he answered.' (Acts 9: 10)

Ananias was simply a disciple who knew the voice of God and was ready to respond. God's message to him was urgent and needed to be heard and delivered. It changed a man's life forever, and in turn, that man - Paul - impacted the whole world.

God may well be calling to you to do something today.

Are you giving time to hear God's voice and respond with a 'yes'? Or is the busyness of life, or the worries of this world stopping you from hearing God speaking to you? He has something to say and it might just be the turning point needed either for you or for someone else.

So today, God might just have something for you to do which will have a huge impact in the world.

Be sure to be ready to hear God's voice today.

Lord, I am ready to hear your voice today telling me the right direction to go or the right words to say. I do hear your voice and I will respond. Amen.

WHAT A WONDERFUL TRUTH!

'"They will be mine," says the LORD Almighty.' (Malachi 3: 17a)

What a wonderful statement of truth!

Take a moment today to sit and be still and enjoy those words the Lord says to you in light of what Jesus has done for us: "You are mine".

That is such a powerful image to grasp and enjoy - whatever your past, whatever your present, whatever your concerns for the future.

Allow those words to sink into your heart today. They will give you such strength as they become real to you and you realise that you are a child of God.

Lord, you love to say to me today, "You are mine". I am so thankful that I am yours and I will allow this amazing truth to sink in and change my life. Amen.

OTHERS

"'As the Father has sent me, I am sending you.'" (John 20: 21b)

We have been commanded to go to others: "I am sending you".

God sent Jesus to us; Jesus sent us to others. The world needs to be loved and people need to be loved. Jesus is the best way to show love.

Be praying today about who it is you can share the love of God with; who needs to be blessed; who it is who needs to know God's love. Be asking for creative ways to share the love of Jesus to others today.

Have fun!

Jesus, thank you that you have called me to help others. I am ready to go out today and show people who you are, and what you have done for them. Amen.

IT IS TIME TO LISTEN

*'"This is my Son, whom I love; with him I am well
pleased. Listen to him!"' (Matthew 17: 5b)*

This was one of the greatest experiences for the three disciples, Peter, James and John. They heard the audible voice of God and were in His presence.

The account on the Mount of Transfiguration is a classic story to read and engage with. This one verse from the story shows us just how important it is for us to learn to listen to Jesus. If God says we must listen to Jesus, then we must listen because He has many things to say to us.

When my wife Michelle was younger, her church youth group leader encouraged her to, "Just read the red." These were the words spoken by Jesus highlighted in red italics in her bible. The youth leader knew that reading these would change the lives of the young people.

Jesus' words will bring you the everlasting peace you are looking for and show you what you need to know. Make sure that you take time to listen to Him or spend more time in the gospel accounts, and get to know what Jesus has said already.

Have a great time listening to Jesus today, either by reading the Word or listening to the Spirit.

Jesus, you have something to say to me today. Your words will change my life. Help me hear what they are. Amen.

HOPE IS SO GOOD

'My mouth is filled with your praise, declaring your splendour all day long ...But as for me, I shall always have hope; I will praise you more and more. My mouth will tell of your righteousness, of your salvation all day long.' (Psalm 71: 8; 14-15a)

What a wonderful set of verses to take on board today! We are encouraged to have praise flowing out of us.

It really delights Him when He hears His children praising God and giving Him thanks for all He has done. Thanksgiving will increase your hope by enabling you to recall all that God has done throughout the earth and in your life. It will also deepen and strengthen your hope. Hope brings so much change to our lives.

Steve Backlund, a pastor at Bethel Church in Redding California has a ministry called 'Igniting Hope'. In his book on Igniting Hope, he says this: "Remember there are no hopeless circumstances, there are only people who do not have hope. Once people get true hope, the circumstances can't stay the same."[16]

Take some time today to praise God, to give Him thanks for who He is, what He has created and what He has done for you and your household.

Press in with praise and see hope grow.

Father, you have done so much for me, you have given me hope when my life needed it. Today, I will sing and share about all you have done for me. Amen.

STAND FIRM AND DON'T GIVE UP

'Therefore, my dear brothers, stand firm. Let nothing move you. Always give yourselves fully to the work of the Lord, because you know that your labour in the Lord is not in vain.' (1 Corinthians 15: 58)

How are you doing? Is your relationship with God on solid foundations or is something not right? Do you wobble when you are told bad news? Do you fear what might happen if...?

Paul encourages us to stand firm and not to be moved or shaken.

Trials may come and go, but we are to stand firm and not be moved and not give up. You will reap a reward and breakthrough will come, maybe not now, but it will come, so stand firm in who you are: a child of the Living God. The work you do will not be in vain, however big or small. Every seed sown, every step taken will not be in vain.

Keep going, keep pressing in for more, and keep focused on what God has called you to do.

Father, will you sustain me today. Will you open up the door so that things will change for me. I will stand firm, I will not be shaken and I will press in for more. Amen.

NEVER TOO OLD TO BEAR FRUIT

'They will still bear fruit in old age. They will stay fresh and green, proclaiming, "the Lord is upright; He is my rock and there is no wickedness in Him."' (Psalm 92: 14-15)

Some of us may already be living these words out, but many of us still have a long way to go!

How can we be preparing ourselves for old age, to continue to be fresh, to be bearing fruit, to speak about the goodness of God, and to stand on the Rock when the storms come.

Here are four suggestions:

1. Know the Father more intimately

2. Walk with Jesus more closely

3. Be filled with the Spirit daily

4. Live out the truths of the Word of God continuously

Which one do you need to focus on in this season of your life so that you will continue to bear fruit and be fresh?

Father, thank you that you have so much in store for me today. May I bear fruit and keep fresh so that your Kingdom may grow in and through me today. Amen.

BE CREATIVE AND HELP PEOPLE BELIEVE

"'My prayer is not for them alone. I pray also for those who will believe in me through their message.'" (John 17: 20)

Someone passed on the message of Jesus to you, it changed your life and now you in turn get to pass it onto others in your own unique way. Each one of us has a responsibility to share our powerful story of what Jesus has done for us.

In what creative ways are you thinking of spreading that message? Be thinking of ways to communicate the message of Jesus to others. Jesus has prayed for everyone to respond and believe in Him. We must be sharing the message and bringing people into contact with Him.

So let's go for it and spread the good news today so that Jesus' prayer may be answered as it was for you.

Thank you, Jesus, that your prayer for me has been answered and I know you and walk with you. Today, I choose to take bold steps to help the people that I meet to believe in you. Thank you that I have the privilege of being part of the answer to your prayer for them. Amen.

MAKE HIM KNOWN TODAY

"'Righteous Father, though the world does not know you, I know you, and they know that you have sent me. I have made you known to them."' (John 17: 25-26a)

One of the key features in Jesus' message to His disciples was the wonderful news that they could know His Father. It would have been mind-blowing for them to understand this!

Jesus wanted His first disciples to know His Father intimately and He wants us to know His Father in the same way, for us to experience just what an awesome Dad He is! So we must desire to know Father God more - this is so key to our lives.

For me, in my early Christian walk, the image I had of God was of one of a judge, at a distance, ruling through laws. I certainly did not know Him as Abba Father, and I think that this was probably the initial image the disciples had as well. It was probably only after many years of being a Christian that I began to know and experience God as a loving Father.

However, we also have a responsibility to make the Father known. Jesus said, "The world does not know the Father." We who know the Father, have a responsibility to let others know Him.

So how will you be active today in making the Father known to the world? Will people see Jesus in you today? Will you attract people to the Father by your actions, by your words and by being yourself?

Just imagine if we were all this active. How many more people would come to know the Father!

Jesus, help me today, like you did with the first disciples, to show and tell people what the Father is really like. Help me make Him known today. Amen.

GET THAT TONGUE UNDER CONTROL!

'Likewise the tongue is a small part of the body, but it makes great boasts. Consider what a great forest is set on fire by a small spark. The tongue also is a fire, a world of evil among the parts of the body. It corrupts the whole person, sets the whole course of his life on fire, and is itself set on fire by hell.' (James 3: 5-6)

The apostle James talks frankly and boldly and gets to the point very quickly. His message is for all of us to take on board today. We must be careful what we say. Often our response to this scripture is to focus on our words to others, but today I want to take a moment to focus on the words we speak to ourselves.

Take some time today and listen to what you are speaking over yourself, whether out loud or silently in your mind. So often we can be very harsh with the words we use on ourselves, speaking a dialogue that we would never ever say out loud to someone else about them! "You are always getting things wrong."... "Buck up!"... "You're so fat!"... "They probably don't like you very much."... "I'm so stupid!" Recognise any of those? The tongue can corrupt you and make you think you are worse than everyone else. We need to be aware of the tongue's power and rein it in.

Today, let's have victory over our tongue, both in our private inner dialogue, and in what we speak out over others.

Jesus, help me today to speak the right words to people, so that they will be blessed and honoured, but also show me where I need to change what I say and think about myself. Amen.

290   HAVE A GOOD DAY

LET THE LIGHT OUT

"'You are the light of the world. A city built on a hill cannot be hid. No one after lighting a lamp puts it under the bushel basket, but on the lampstand, and it gives light to all in the house. In the same way, let your light shine before others, so that they may see your good works and give glory to your Father in heaven."' (Matthew 5: 14-16, NRSV)

This is a challenging and thought-provoking word from Jesus.

Is it time to lift the lampshade and allow the light to shine out of you? Why remain hidden? Each one of us has a wonderful message to share with others, we must not hide it. Each of us has a gift which will enable us to share the light in different ways. Let's not hide, but let the light shine out.

Be thinking of something you can do today to bless someone. Or is there someone who needs to see the Father's love in you? We are the light in a dark world, may we shine today and enable others to see and praise God.

Holy Spirit, will you give me the strength and insight to shine the light of Jesus into the world today. I need your help and wisdom in finding ways to do that, so that people may know and praise the Father today. Amen.

TROPHIES FROM THE BATTLE

'O Afflicted city, lashed by storms and not comforted, I will rebuild you with stones of turquoise, your foundations with sapphires. I will make your battlements of rubies, your gates of sparkling jewels, and all your walls of precious stones.' (Isaiah 54: 11-12)

———————————

What wonderful verses describing the restorative power of God!

Gemstones, like the ones mentioned here, are all created in atmospheres of great pressure. Isaiah is speaking here of a work of God so full and powerful in our lives that it can bring beauty out of pressure, turning things of pain into things of beauty. God will take things that are desolate and destroyed and make them strong and fortified. What a promise for our lives today!

For the last 25 years, Michelle and I have stood on the promises in these verses. We both experienced great pain, loss and damage in our lives from the ages of 18 to 23. However, God promised to rebuild. We can honestly say that God has done what He promised and both our lives - through His grace - display the gemstones of His restoration plan, and we look forward to the many more that He will continue to add.

Whatever damage you may have experienced through destructive storms in your past, the Father promises to rebuild you. Furthermore, He promises not only to rebuild you, but also to make you strong, dazzling and beautiful! Displaying - for all to see - the gems you have won under great pressure.

Father, let me not lose heart but open up my eyes to see your work of restoration in my life. Help me recognise all you have done, and give me hope for all that you will do. In you, I will be restored and built up again. Amen.

CONTINUE TO TRUST GOD

"'But blessed is the man who trusts in the Lord, whose confidence is in him. He will be like a tree planted by the water that sends out its roots by the stream. It does not fear when heat comes; its leaves are always green. It has no worries in a year of drought and never fails to bear fruit.'" (Jeremiah 17: 7-8)

What an encouraging picture of a tree that is always bearing fruit, never worrying, has no fears and is always green! Wouldn't that be good if we were all like that? It is simply about trusting God and having 100% confidence in Him. It is easy to say that, but at times difficult to live out.

As a family we recently went through a testing time with our finances. We had to learn more about trusting God and not allowing fear to come in. At times, I was confused and struggled to know the peace of His presence. I had to push through and trust in Father's character and stand on the testimonies of His provision over my life up to that time. He did not let us down. He came through for us and my trust in Him grew.

Is there an area of your life where you need to trust God today? If so, spend some time with Him and learn more of His unlimited ability to help you. Don't give in to fear, but instead live in trust.

Father, what a wonderful picture of a strong tree flourishing in the world for me to hold on to today. I will put my trust in you. Amen.

HOW LONG?

'How long, O Lord? Will you forget me forever? How long will you hide your face from me? How long must I bear pain in my soul, and have sorrow in my heart all day long? How long shall my enemy be exalted over me? Consider and answer me, O Lord my God! Give light to my eyes, or I will sleep the sleep of death, and my enemy will say, "I have prevailed"; my foes will rejoice because I am shaken. But I trusted in your steadfast love; my heart shall rejoice in your salvation. I will sing to the Lord, because he has dealt bountifully with me.' (Psalm 13, NRSV)

How long, Lord, will I have to wait for my healing? How long, Lord, until I see a breakthrough in a relationship, in my finances, or in this challenging situation? Many of us will have or maybe are asking these two powerful words: How long?

Like David, it is right for us to share our heart and feelings with God and to keep asking for His divine intervention. However, as David reminds us in the last verse, it is so that we can remain full of hope and always praising and thanking God for who He is and what He has done already. He is good and He is faithful.

Healing and breakthrough will come... keep praising Him, keep believing, keep hoping.

Abba Father, you know how long I have been waiting for an answer. Help me to continue to trust you and to be positive in both my mind and in my words. You will step in, I know. Amen.

IT'S TIME TO LET GO

'Cast all your anxiety on Him because He cares for you.' (1 Peter 5: 7)

So many people carry anxiety and worry. I know that I can. Anxiety and worry can cripple and destroy us so easily.

This wonderful truth of scripture is for us to believe in today. God is so pleased when we cast our anxiety on to Him. He doesn't want us to be weighed down by it. He cares for us so much and is waiting for us with a big smile and big hands to receive all our fears, worries and concerns.

When our daughter feels worried or anxious, we sometimes act out grabbing hold of all these thoughts, put them in her open hands and ask Father God to take them, and we throw them up to Him. It's a simple act, but very powerful.

So why not, right now, sit down and pass them on to Him. He cares for you so much, He wants you to be free to enjoy life, so why not chat with Him, get Him involved and cast everything on to Him. Nothing is too big for our God to take from you, or so small that He thinks it is insignificant.

Father, thank you for carrying my burdens and my anxiety today. I want to let them go and give them to you so that I can be free. Thank you for taking them away. Amen.

REMOVE THAT PLANK FROM ME

'"Why do you look at the speck of sawdust in your brother's eye
and pay no attention to the plank in your own eye? How can you
say to your brother, 'Brother let me take the speck out of your eye'
when you yourself fail to see the plank in your eye? You hypocrite!
First take the plank out of your eye, then you will see clearly to
remove the speck from your brother's eye."' (Luke 6: 41-42)

This is another hard-hitting word from Jesus, but it is such a good truth to live by.

The challenge for us is to make sure that our own hearts and minds are right with God first before we find fault with others. We can be so quick to judge others without first checking whether we are right.

Don't judge other people if you yourself have not yet removed all the rubbish from your own life. You can see and think so much more clearly when you are in the right place with God.

So take some time out today to be with God and know Him and see things from His viewpoint, not how you see them. Press deeper into God so that there are no planks in your own eyes.

Lord, will you help me see the planks in my own eyes today, so that I can then see more clearly and know the right way to approach others. Amen.

BE CARRIED TODAY

*'He tends His flock like a shepherd; He gathers the lambs
in His arms and carries them close to His heart; and
gently leads those that have young.' (Isaiah 40: 11)*

What a wonderful image of God!

Why not today just enjoy being in His arms and allow Him to carry you
through the day.

Be close and hear and feel His heart beating and the words He wants
to say to you. You don't have to face today on your own or in your own
strength.

Let Him carry you.

*Abba Father, thank you that you will be carrying me today. Help me feel
your arms around me all day. I need you to do this for me. Amen.*

WHAT IS GOD SAYING

'Then the Lord said to Jacob, "Go back to the land of your fathers and to your relatives, and I will be with you."' (Genesis 31: 3)

It must have been hard for Jacob to comprehend: "go back to your home, land and relatives". Jacob had been on the run for 25 years from his brother Esau, who had threatened to kill him and, in his present situation, he had fallen out of favour with his father-in-law and brothers-in-law. He left to go back with no idea how God would take care of him, no idea what route to take, and no idea what would happen when he met his brother, but he left knowing that God would be with him.

One of the most important and well-known promises of the bible, spoken by Father God and then by Jesus to His disciples in the New Testament is this: "I will be with you".

Maybe God has asked you to do something that seems impossible. Maybe there is a risk you need to take, or maybe a relationship that needs restoring. As you move forward, know that God will be with you. If you can keep this promise at the forefront of your thinking, you will have great courage as you step out into all that Father is calling you to do.

You are not alone, He is with you.

Father, you were faithful to Jacob and showed him the way forward. Today, I ask that you will be with me as I take those few steps of faith. Amen.

MOVED BY THE SPIRIT

*'It had been revealed to him by the Holy Spirit that he would
not die before he had seen the Lord's Christ. Moved by the
Spirit, he went into the temple courts.' (Luke 2: 26-27a)*

'Moved by the Spirit, he went...'

The issue today is not, is God speaking, but rather are we listening?

Are you open and ready for the Spirit's prompting in your life today? He
has things to say to you and things for you to do.

A friend of mine tells a great story, that whilst in the gym one day, he
had a strong sense of God's love on him and the Holy Spirit saying, "Go
and speak to that guy over there about my love for him." He eventually
plucked up the courage and got an opportunity to tell this guy - who he
had never met - that the Lord loved him. When he shared this word, it
rang true for him and opened up a fascinating conversation about Jesus.

Be moved by the Spirit today, be listening to His voice and promptings
and let Him be active in your life. It is always a fun thing to do to be led by
Him and a day led by Him will always be full of surprises.

Let's be open to the Spirit today.

*Holy Spirit, you have something really good to tell me today. I look
forward to receiving, obeying and sharing it if necessary. Amen.*

GOD REALLY DOES LOVE YOU

'But God demonstrates his own love for us in this: While we were sinners, Christ died for us.' (Romans 5: 8)

This verse in scripture is an amazing statement! If you were the only person in the world, Christ would have still have died for you, because God's love for you is so great.

I remember when I was at university, walking down a street late at night with a friend and I shared this truth with them and that night they gave their life to Jesus.

Take some time today to let that sink in and realise how much God loves you, and then respond and tell God how much you love Him, because He has done so much for you.

We didn't deserve any of it as we were steeped in sin, but that sums up the love of God for us. It's huge!

Finally, if you have a chance to share this truth with someone today, then go for it!

Abba Father, thank you for sending Jesus into this world to die for me, a sinner. Your love is so big for me, I will enjoy that today and I will let you know how much I love you. Amen.

HE WILL SAVE YOU

'Though the Lord is on high, he looks upon the lowly, but the proud he knows from afar. Though I walk in the midst of trouble, you preserve my life; you stretch out your hand against the anger of my foes, with your right hand you save me. The Lord will fulfil his purpose for me; your love O Lord endures forever - do not abandon the works of your hands.' (Psalm 138: 6-9)

In 2011, Michelle and I had been invited to stay at a game farm in South Africa which was an amazing experience. During the evening, I experienced an episode of Acute Adrenal Crisis which meant I became very ill. Isolated, we couldn't access medical help until the following day and that night, this Psalm became a reality as we found ourselves 'walking in the midst of trouble'. Our only choice was to throw ourselves fully onto God. We prayed scripture, we sang scripture, we declared scripture. As the night wore on, we experienced Father God flexing His strength and stretching out His 'hand against the anger of His foes'. By morning His 'right hand' had saved us and peace reigned. Only years on, and with a greater understanding of my medical needs, do we fully appreciate what a miracle happened that night. Without the Lord's intervention, I could have died.

The Lord will preserve your life and walk with you through tough times and fulfil His purposes for your life. Whatever you are facing in life right now, whether disappointments, a broken heart, a broken relationship, work-related problems, or troubling matters, the Lord is with you. He is closer than you think and He certainly has an abundance of love to give you.

Today, don't miss out on the Lord, let Him save you and fill you with His love and carry you forward into His peace.

Father, I need your saving right hand and presence in my life today, will you bless me and be with me. Amen.

RELY MORE ON GOD

'We do not want you to be uninformed, brothers, about the troubles we experienced in the province of Asia. We were under great pressure, far beyond our ability to endure, so that we despaired even of life. Indeed, in our hearts we felt the sentence of death. But this happened that we might not rely on ourselves but on God, who raises the dead.' (2 Corinthians 1: 8-9)

Paul, the author of this letter to the church in Corinth, is sharing his hardship, and what he went through and the lessons he learned. At the heart of it, he learned to rely on God.

Learning to trust and depend on God is the secret of negotiating the way through every situation you find yourself in. He who is able to raise the dead, can raise you up and move you on.

Trust Him today and do not rely on your own strength and skills. Invite Him into your situation and see Him work.

Father, nothing is impossible for you. I ask for your help today. I let go of all that I am and I rely on you today. Amen.

KEEP YOUR EYES ON JESUS

'Christ in you, the hope of glory.' (Colossians 1: 27b)

———————————————

What an amazing truth this is: Christ lives in you!

The living Lord Jesus delights to dwell within you. It is too much to comprehend for small minds, certainly for my mind! It's as though we have a jewel inside us, which we can't see, but we need to believe is there. We need to hold this amazing truth at the forefront of our minds.

Our gaze needs to be upon the One who lives in us, and our focus needs to remain on Him. Jesus needs to have a throne established in us where His glory can shine.

Does something need to shift so that Christ can be your focus? Or is it time to sit down and take in this wonderful mystery that is within you and believe it and live it out.

Jesus, I choose to make this truth a reality within me today, so that I can live for you and help others see you more clearly in my life. Amen.

SEEK AND LIVE

"'Seek me and live, do not seek Bethel, do not go to Gilgal, do not journey to Beersheba, for Gilgal will surely go into exile and Bethel will be reduced to nothing. Seek the Lord and live.'" (Amos 5: 5-6a)

"Seek me and live," says the Lord.

Life can throw all sorts of unexpected things at us. When it does, how do you respond? What places do you go to? If we turn to God, there will be hope for us. Rather than seek other things first, seek relationship with the Father who loves you and He will come and embrace you.

When I tested positive with Covid-19, I made it my priority to go and sit with Father and seek Him out, not to allow all the fears and lies to run riot in my mind. I sought Him out and He led me to a wonderful Psalm that gave me peace and the assurance that I was not alone.

Seek Him first, wait for Him and He will carry you through. Seek Him today, and He will be found. Don't look elsewhere.

Abba Father, forgive me where I have sought other places for help, where I have not focused on you and sought your help that leads to a better life. I choose to seek you first today. Amen.

LET THE SPIRIT BE ACTIVE IN YOU

'"But when He, the Spirit of Truth, comes He will guide you into all truth. He will not speak on His own; He will speak only what He hears, and He will tell you what is yet to come. He will bring glory to me by taking from what is mine and making it known to you. All that belongs to the Father is mine. That is why I said the Spirit will take from what is mine and make it known to you."' (John 16: 13-15)

This amazing piece of scripture that John wrote cannot be ignored.

All the wealth, insight and wisdom of the Father and Son is known and administered by the Holy Spirit. The Spirit is the steward of the 'storehouse of heaven'. It will be for our benefit to grow and deepen our friendship with the Holy Spirit, and to allow Him to be fully alive within us.

Be open to Him, so that you can not only benefit from the storehouse of heaven, but also know what the Father and Son want to tell you and give you.

Holy Spirit, please fill me afresh today with your presence so that I can enjoy the benefits of the Father and the Son. Amen.

ENTER INTO HIS THRONE OF GRACE

'Since, then, we have a great high priest who has passed through the heavens, Jesus, the Son of God, let us hold fast to our confession. For we do not have a high priest who is unable to sympathise with our weaknesses, but we have one who in every respect has been tested as we are, yet without sin. Let us therefore approach the throne of grace with boldness, so that we may receive mercy and find grace to help in time of need.' (Hebrews 4: 14-16, NRSV)

By His death, Jesus has created a wonderful opportunity for us all: we can approach the throne of grace and mercy. All we have to do is simply pursue Him. The wonderful thing is, that God is waiting for us to approach His throne so that He can pour out His grace on us in order to bless us and so that we can receive His mercy.

There are so many blessings God wants to give you today, and so much He wants to help you with, so don't miss out. He knows your needs. Enter the presence of His throne room today with confidence and experience the wonderful grace and mercy of God.

Jesus, thank you that you have made it possible for me to enter into the throne room of grace and mercy. Today, I choose to step in and enjoy it and see Father God meet all my needs. Amen.

YOU ARE PROTECTED

'No weapon formed against you shall prosper; and every tongue which rises against you in judgement thou shalt condemn. This is the heritage of the servants of the Lord and their righteousness is from me, saith the Lord.' (Isaiah 54: 17, KJV)

We are in a battle each day which can be nasty, emotional and confusing. However, we can know that God has covered us with a robe of righteousness and this is what protects us.

Don't try to survive in your own strength or wisdom - God is covering you. He will step in and the enemy will be defeated - he will not prosper, he will not get his way. The Lord has spoken and He is faithful to His word.

We have a wonderful heritage as servants of the Lord; make sure today that you use it and enjoy God's protection.

Father, thank you that the enemy cannot win, he is defeated. I choose today to walk in righteousness and trust you in every situation that I am facing. Amen.

KEEP YOUR MIND FULL OF HOPE

'O Israel put your hope in the Lord both now and forevermore.'
(Psalm 131: 3)

Has hopelessness got a hold of you in any area of your life?

Today is the day to turn that around. Don't listen any longer to the voice of hopelessness, but instead begin to move in the direction of hope. Seek the loving and caring arms of your heavenly Father. As you read this verse, put your name in the place of 'O Israel' and begin to see the Lord set you free.

Having a mind full of hope each day enables me to live in peace and overcome any obstacles, and not allow debilitating illness or infirmity to become my focus. The more hope I have, the less power these things have over me.

Keep hope alive in you today. Look to the Father and let hope arise within you.

Father, today I choose hope instead of hopelessness. Amen.

GET GOD-FOCUSED

"'Those who turn back from following the Lord and neither seek the Lord nor enquire of him.'" (Zephaniah 1: 6)

The people of Judah were in trouble: enemies were approaching its borders, and fear and worry were causing havoc. Zephaniah's words were a challenge to them to get their focus back on the Lord their God as their focus had obviously been elsewhere.

This one verse is crucial for all of us to get hold of and understand its importance.

We need to seek the Lord, and enquire of Him for the way forward in our lives.

Have you forgotten to enquire of the Lord? This is such an important discipline to have: to seek Him, to be silent in His presence. He is waiting for you to enquire of Him so He can guide you and tell you what is on His heart. He knows what you need and He knows how to help you.

Lord, thank you that you know my situation. I seek you today to find the road that you want me to walk on. Amen.

KEEP BELIEVING

'Against all hope, Abraham in hope believed and so became the father of many nations, just as it had been said to him, ... Without weakening in his faith, he faced the fact that his body was as good as dead - since he was about a hundred years old - and that Sarah's womb was also dead.' (Romans 4: 18-19)

Abraham placed his hope in the one true God and God did not let him down. His wife did give birth to a child, and the promises of God were fulfilled. Abraham believed and became the father of many.

Is there something in your life that needs changing, or something where hope is needed? If so, God is the person to turn to. Put your hope in Him today and see Him work. Don't keep trying in your own strength and effort. Learn to keep believing that God will not let you down. His promises will come through.

Father, thank you that you don't let your people down, you are faithful, you are everlasting and your promises are true. Today, I choose to walk in faith, like Abraham, so that you can do even more through me than I can see now. Amen.

HE FIRST LOVED US

'We love because he first loved us.' (1 John 4: 19)

Speaking at a conference in America, well-known author and Christian speaker Brennan Manning said this: 'I am now utterly convinced that on Judgement Day, the Lord Jesus is going to ask each of us one question and only one question: "Did you believe that I loved you?"'[17]

Three times in this one chapter the apostle John uses the phrase 'loved us' (v. 10; 11; 19), all referring to Father God. It is as if the Lord wants us to grab hold of this statement with such an intensity that we will truly believe it and live it out.

How do we grasp this amazing truth and let it affect the way we live? Do we really believe this truth and allow our lives to flourish knowing that we are loved? If we really believe this, then all our troubles, fears, woes and concerns, would have no hold on us. We would be free and able to enjoy our day. We have a heart that is created to love, but we must allow our heart to receive this free and unconditional love each day. It is what we were created for.

Let's ensure that today we live out this transformative truth that we are loved by Father God and by Jesus, not only believing it in our hearts and minds, but also living it out through our actions. Let's move forward in learning to receive this love more deeply into our lives.

Father, may I learn to believe this truth in a new and deep way, to feel your love in my heart so that I can have the capability to love others as you do. Amen.

VENGEANCE IS THE LORD'S

'Strengthen the feeble hands, steady the knees that give way; say to those with fearful hearts, "Be strong, do not fear; your God will come, He will come with vengeance. He will come with vengeance, with divine retribution. He will come to save you."' (Isaiah 35: 3-4)

God has come, He has not let you down. For everything stolen from us in life, His promise is that there will be 'vengeance and divine retribution'. He will step in, He will come and save us. This is a work that only He can do, we don't have to conjure up a miracle, but rather remain strong and expectant.

The day we found out that Michelle was pregnant with our daughter was a day of exploding joy and tears of relief! For us, it was a day of 'vengeance and divine retribution' as Father stepped in and gave back what the 'thief' had stolen from us (see John 10: 10). Twenty-two years earlier, when I had been diagnosed with cancer, I had received a promise from God that He would heal me and restore everything that the enemy would try to steal from me. Fertility was one of those 'stolen' things. However, after five years of fertility treatment, and Michelle and I learning to stand strong and expect good things from God, breakthrough and restoration finally came!

The enemy had tried to take my life, but I had defied expectations and lived and was now passing life on to the next generation! He had come!

Trust Him today. He will come and He will step in and make a difference. However long it takes, He will bring justice.

Father you will come; you will sort out my situation; you will bring justice to the situations I have lived through, and to those who have hurt me. I choose today, to remain strong, to stand tall and not give in to the pressures that surround me. I will let go and choose to trust in you knowing that you will come. Amen.

IT'S GOING TO BE AN AMAZING DAY

'Joshua told the people, "Consecrate yourselves, for today the Lord will do amazing things among you."' (Joshua 3: 5)

The walls of Jericho fell that day without a weapon being fired. That is amazing!

However, Joshua did say to the people that they needed to 'consecrate' themselves. In our context, today, I believe this means making sure we are right before God and before our friends and family.

Do you believe that God is still doing amazing things today? I do. He loves doing amazing things, so don't miss out, don't be distracted, focus on Him and see His glory!

Be in His presence on your knees and ask the Holy Spirit to show you if there is anything holding you back from seeing God working in your life. Don't let sin or hidden thoughts get in the way of God doing amazing things for you today.

Father, thank you that you still do amazing things in our lives today. I declare that I will see your goodness and power in my life today. Amen.

HE IS LOYAL

'God said, "Never will I leave you; never will I forsake you."' (Hebrews 13: 5b)

This one verse has been a cornerstone for me. It was one of the first verses the Lord showed me after I was diagnosed with cancer back in 1989.

I turned 50 recently and took the opportunity to look back at my life and I was overwhelmed by the truth of this scripture. Yes, at times things have been very hard, but the Lord has never forsaken me, He has always stepped in at the right time with the right solution. He has always been there. I know I am valuable to Him and He has never left my side.

Wherever you are in your spiritual walk with God, whether you are old or young, continue to seek Him and He will not forsake you, He will not leave you nor abandon you. He is the most loyal person I know and the One in whom we can trust.

Today, take a moment with the Holy Spirit to look back over your life - the places you have been and the circumstances you have found yourself in - and see how God has indeed been faithful to His promise of never leaving you. You have never been alone. Then respond to these fresh revelations of His faithfulness in worship and praise.

Father, you have been so faithful to me over the years, you have fulfilled this promise in my life. I am so grateful that in the worst times of my life you have never left me nor forsaken me. Thank you that I am valuable to you. Amen.

BE JOYFUL

'O Lord, the king rejoices in your strength. How great
is his joy in the victories you give!' (Psalm 21: 1)

King David was full of joy and thanks for all the Lord had done for him.
He had seen God at work, and had not only seen many victories in his life
that the Lord had ordained, but he knew Him in a very personal way as
well and had seen Him do amazing things.

Like David, we worship an all-powerful God who wants to help us. Are
you rejoicing because He is working in your life? Is He the one you are
inviting in to help you win the battles you need to win?

Be with Him today and draw on Him for all you need and find the joy of
His presence.

Father, like King David, I want to be full of joy and remember everything
you have done for me. I know you have so much more to show me and I
look forward to rejoicing with you. Amen.

WHAT DO YOU NEED TODAY?

'For God did not give us a spirit of timidity, but a spirit of power, of love and of self-discipline, so do not be ashamed to testify about our Lord.' (2 Timothy 1: 7-8a)

God has given us a spirit of power, of love, and self-discipline and we need to remember to rely on these constantly. The more we engage and rely on the Spirit's gifts, the more effective we will be in testifying about the Lord Jesus. His gifts will be a sign for others to see Jesus in us.

We cannot do this Christian life walking in our own strength - we need help from the Holy Spirit.

So which one of these three gifts of the Spirit do you think you need more of today? Or which one do you need to develop more in your life? Is it power, love or self-discipline?

Why not ask God to release it to you today?

Father, thank you that the Holy Spirit is full of abundant gifts which you give to your children. I ask that today I may be a living testimony of those gifts working in me. Amen.

BE OPEN FOR WHAT GOD WILL SHOW YOU

'The hand of the Lord came upon me, and he brought me out by the spirit of the Lord and set me down in the middle of a valley; it was full of bones. He led me all around them; there were very many lying in the valley, and they were very dry. He said to me, "Mortal, can these bones live?" I answered, "O Lord God, you know."' (Ezekiel 37: 1-3, NRSV)

There are two things to point out today. Firstly, it was God who was taking the initiative: 'He brought me... He asked me... He said to me... His hand was upon me...'

Who is taking the initiative in your life?

Secondly, I love the response of the prophet when he was asked if the bones could live. He was honest and real with God about the situation that he faced. He didn't rely on his own initiative, wisdom or power, but instead he spoke the truth: "O Sovereign Lord, you alone know". Then the Lord spoke to Ezekiel and gave him one of the great prophecies of the Old Testament.

Let's be real and honest with God on how we are doing and let Him interact with us today. He might have a message to share with you that will impact you, your family and even the nation!

Father, as you spoke to Ezekiel, may I be ready and willing to hear what you have to say to me. Amen.

GOD IS WORTHY OF OUR PRAISE

'Great is the Lord, and most worthy of praise, in the city of our God, his holy mountain.' (Psalm 48: 1)

The word 'great' can also be translated as 'awesome'. Both words give credit to the wonderful but powerful God who created the universe and takes great delight in us.

He is worthy of our praise today! He had done so much for King David, and I have no doubt that each day David would take time to praise and thank God for all He had done. He was the One worthy of praise.

If you have not done so recently, spend time today, even for just a couple of minutes, thinking about God and praising Him for who He is, because He is great and He is awesome.

Remind yourself of who He is, and let Him know it today.

Father, you have done so much for me: you have stepped in when I have needed it; you have carried me forward when I was unable to go forward. Today, I praise you for who you are and what you have done for me. Amen.

CHOOSE HOPE

'Return to your fortress, O prisoners of hope; even now I announce that I will restore twice as much to you.' (Zechariah 9: 12)

God is all about restoration and He says, "I will restore twice as much to you." That is a powerful promise!

I came across this quote recently: 'Those people who carry the most hope, will be the people who have the most influence.' [18]

People are crying out for hope in the world today. If we choose to have hope in every circumstance that we find ourselves in, we won't walk with the chains of hopelessness and despair around our necks, but will instead wear a garland of hope. If we live and believe in God's word, it will come about in our lives, simply because it is written in His word.

So let's live in hope. Tie it around you; be a prisoner of hope today; watch and see how things will change within you, and with those around you. Increase your influence today!

Father, today I will live in hope in every area of my life. I will see your goodness in my life as I step out in hope. Amen.

STAND IN VICTORY

'So he said, "Do you know why I have come to you? Soon I will return to fight against the prince of Persia, and when I go, the prince of Greece will come."' (Daniel 10: 20)

In this verse, the angel gives us insight into the spiritual world around us. (What is fascinating is that the Greek empire didn't actually get established on earth for another 200 years!)

There are spiritual battles going on all around us and, as the scripture suggests, these can be current as well as in the future: battles for your life, your children's lives and even your children's children, and on and on.

The great news is that we have victory today because of what Jesus did on the cross! So we need to stand strong, walk in victory and in confidence, silence the lies, live in the truth of who we are, and believe that we can overcome the works of the enemy, because Jesus has won the victory! The battle has been won. You can claim it as yours today and enforce it in your life.

So, hold your head up high, and have confidence that angels are fighting with you and for you, as you live in the victory of the cross.

Jesus, thank you that you have won the greatest battle in history: death has been defeated. I choose today to walk in your victory and live in victory over the enemy. Amen.

IS IT TIME TO MAKE A CHANGE?

*'The Lord was with Jehoshaphat, because he walked in the earlier
ways of his father; he did not seek the Baals, but sought the God of
his father and walked in his commandments, and not according
to the ways of Israel. Therefore, the Lord established the kingdom
in his hand. All Judah brought tribute to Jehoshaphat, and he
had great riches and honour. His heart was courageous in the
ways of the Lord; and furthermore he removed the high places
and the sacred poles from Judah.' (2 Chronicles 17: 3-6, NRSV)*

King Jehoshaphat was one of the few kings of Judah who followed the
ways of the Lord and therefore God was with him and blessed him.

Will you do the same? There are three key things that Jehoshaphat did:

1. He walked closely with God and God was with him.

2. He sought God for guidance and was not reliant on other sources.

3. His heart was devoted to God's ways and so he removed the practices
    and influence of other gods from his life and, as a result, he was a very
    successful king.

Which of these three key things do you need to grow in? Which one do
you need to take more time focusing on? As you do, you will begin to see
more of God's increased presence and more of His favour and blessing
upon you in remarkable ways.

*Father, thank you that you blessed King Jehoshaphat, that his reign as
king was a success. May I learn to walk like him so that I too can see
your blessing and goodness in my life, and in the lives of my family and
friends. Amen.*

HIS PRESENCE IS KEY

"'I am telling you what I have seen in the Father's presence."' (John 8: 38a)

Jesus had the privilege of being in the Father's presence before He came to earth. But whilst on earth, it was clear from His lifestyle that He sought the presence of His Father, in order to hear from Him, rest in Him and experience the Father's love for him.

I have found it very useful to learn to stop a few times each day and be quiet and still both physically and in my thoughts, to sit and engage with the Father. I often tell Him how much I love Him or just ponder and rest in the knowledge that He loves me. When we do this, we too can enjoy and carry the Father's presence much more consistently, just as Jesus did.

I am more and more convinced that this is something that we need to engage in and seek for ourselves. Only then can we continue to live life in all its fullness whatever our circumstances. It is in His presence that we find true strength and true joy.

Father, I want to know you more, to sit with you and be in your presence so that I can know what is on your heart and mind, and see things from your perspective. Amen.

IT'S TIME FOR A BLESSING

'Instead, he took it aside to the house of Obed-edom the Gittite. The ark of the Lord remained in the house of Obed-edom the Gittite for three months, and the Lord blessed him and his entire household.' (2 Samuel 6: 10b-11)

The ark was the dwelling place of the Lord on earth. It seems that where God was, there was blessing. We don't know what the blessings were, but Obed-edom and his entire household were blessed. Something changed for them when God's presence was there. People noticed it, and that's why it is recorded in scripture.

Have you asked recently for God's presence merely to rest upon your entire household, your children and your spouse? God wants to bless us.

Test the scriptures - invite God's presence into your life and into your household, and watch how God will bless you and your entire household.

He is such a creative, generous, loving, all-powerful God.

Abba Father, your heart's desire is to bless people and for people to live life in all its fullness. Today, I invite you to dwell in my heart, home and at work, so that I too may receive all that you have for me today. Amen.

GOD IS SO GENEROUS

"'If you, then, though you are evil, know how to give good gifts to your children, how much more will your Father in heaven give good gifts to those who ask him!'" (Matthew 7: 11)

God has so much more goodness to reveal to us - He has so many wonderful gifts to bestow on us as well. Here in this one verse, Jesus uses a phrase that I love: 'how much more'.

God is a generous God and will always exceed our expectations! He has only good things to give to His children and there is no evil in Him. Jesus says, "Ask for good gifts from your Father." God is good, and when He gives us good things, our outlook and our situations change.

Have you asked God recently to reveal more of His goodness to you, or to give you a gift? There is nothing wrong with asking your Abba Father. Whatever He gives you, you can be sure it will be good and will make a huge difference.

Father, thank you that your heart is to bless, and your desire is to give good things to me. I ask today that I may see how much more you have for me. Amen.

IT'S TIME TO REMEMBER

'These things I remember as I pour out my soul: how I used to go with the multitude ... therefore I will remember you.' (Psalm 42: 4a; 6b)

As I read Psalm 42, the phrase, 'I remember' jumps out at me. The Psalmist actually uses it twice. The last time I read Psalm 42, I had not seen this phrase as I was focusing on how the writer is desperate for an encounter with God; his soul is thirsty for God; he needs refreshing; he needs God (vs. 1 and 2).

One of the best ways to experience refreshment, in whatever state you find yourself, is to take some time out to 'remember'. That's what the Psalmist is doing in these two verses: "I remember..."

As I read it again recently, I too started to remember things from my own life. I remembered when the Lord answered my prayer; I remembered that miracle that happened; I remembered the amazing provision of the Lord; I remembered that prophetic word; I remembered that truth in scripture: 'He will never leave me or forsake me'. Those 'remembrances' certainly refreshed my soul.

So today, remember what God has done for you, it will refresh you.

Father, thank you that you have done so much for me. May I look back and remember, and may I be refreshed by all those happy memories. Amen.

THE POWER IS REAL

'My message and my preaching were not with wise and persuasive words, but with a demonstration of the Spirit's power, so that your faith might not rest on men's wisdom, but on God's power.'
(1 Corinthians 2: 4-5)
'For the kingdom of God is not a matter of talk but of power.'
(1 Corinthians 4: 20)

Here are two challenging scriptures for us.

We seem to be in a season where people are hungry for more of God's supernatural power. There seems to be a buzz going round.

These words that Paul wrote in scripture are true and we see that a powerful encounter is stronger than words. I am more convinced than ever that the Spirit's power is 'the real deal' - the only thing powerful enough to change lives and bring us freedom. We need to be moving in that power on a daily basis. In some ways, the less we talk and the more we demonstrate the power of the Holy Spirit, the more chance we have of seeing the Spirit in action.

So today, ask the Spirit to use you to demonstrate His power. Don't be shy, take that step of faith.

Holy Spirit, thank you that you have not changed from what was written many years ago. I choose today to begin to walk in your power. Please show me how I can do this so that your kingdom can grow around me. Amen.

WALK IN THE GIFTS OF THE SPIRIT

'Now about spiritual gifts, brothers, I do not want you to be ignorant.'
(1 Corinthians 12: 1)

───────────────────────

As I read this verse, I ask myself, "Am I operating daily in the gifts of the Spirit?"

Paul was writing to a new church and he wanted to remind them that, if they didn't walk in these gifts of the Spirit and exercise them, then they would be no different to other human beings.

The church today cannot be ignorant of these gifts. They must be a normal part of our everyday lives as followers of Jesus. These gifts are not only for us, but for the benefit of others.

Let's be seeking the Lord, and asking to be filled each day with the Holy Spirit so that these gifts - that belong to Him - can be used on earth.

Holy Spirit, will you equip me today to walk in your gifts and not my own. I need your help to be different, so that others can see Jesus in me. Amen.

IT'S TIME TO SEE GOD MOVE

*'Now to him who is able to do immeasurably more
than all we ask or imagine, according to his power
that is at work within us.' (Ephesians 3: 20)*

This simple yet powerful verse gives us the opportunity to see God's Kingdom breaking into our lives, our families and communities. I believe that God is waiting for us to dream and imagine things where we would love to see breakthrough, and then to declare them out loud, 'to Him who is able to do more than I ask or imagine'.

Why not spend a few moments thinking of some areas in your life where you would love to see breakthrough. Write them down and then begin to believe and declare them.

Today will be the start for you to see breakthroughs in your life.

Father, thank you that nothing is impossible for you, no mountain too high, no valley too deep, you can do the impossible. I ask today for breakthroughs in areas of my life, in my family and in the communities that need it. Amen.

MAKE THOSE STEPS TOWARDS FORGIVENESS

"'Then his lord summoned him and said to him, 'You wicked slave! I forgave you all that debt because you pleaded with me. Should you not have had mercy on your fellow slave, as I had mercy on you?' And in anger his lord handed him over to be tortured until he would pay his entire debt. So my heavenly Father will also do to every one of you, if you do not forgive your brother or sister from your heart.'" (Matthew 18: 32-35, NRSV)

These verses are at the end of a story that Jesus was telling His disciples about the importance of forgiving people from the heart. Peter had asked Jesus, "How many times should I forgive my brother... up to 7 times?" Jesus replied, "No - up to 77 times!" (vs. 21-22). That is a lot of forgiving! Jesus is implying that our forgiveness should be limitless.

These verses show us why we need to keep forgiving: if we choose not to forgive or show mercy, as God has done for us, there will be consequences. But Jesus also reveals that we need to make every effort to forgive from our hearts, not just our mouths, which suggests how important this is to God.

Forgiveness is one of the key foundations to learning to live the free and joyful life that Jesus wants us all to live. If we decide not to forgive and instead live in unforgiveness, we will not be free and will live life with extra baggage which affects us and those around us.

I encourage you today to begin to take those brave steps and discover the power of forgiveness in your life. Engage with the emotions in your heart and know that Father God is waiting to reach out to you to show His mercy and grace, so that you can be free.

Father, thank you that I am forgiven through the blood of Jesus. Help me today to make those steps towards forgiveness of those who have hurt me. Amen.

LET'S GET ACTIVE

*'In the same way, faith by itself, if it is not accompanied
by action, is dead.' (James 2: 17)*

In this section of James' letter to the twelve scattered tribes of Israel, he is determined to make sure that faith is active in every believer - he wants to see faith in action.

As I read this, I find I need to ask myself this question: is my faith active? I don't want to strive to do things for the sake of it, but I do want to learn that following Jesus each day is not a passive lifestyle. It is not about just turning up to church on Sunday or going to a midweek group. It is so much more.

So how will you have active faith today? How can you make your faith alive and growing? I know for me I have had a few chances in recent times to exercise the gift of the prophetic and the gift of healing, and I have seen God move, but also I must confess that I have shied away from a few opportunities to bless people as well.

Be thinking about how you can activate your spiritual gifts each day. Ask God to give you opportunities to exercise your faith.

Holy Spirit, will you give me the courage to step out in faith to move in your gifts today. Amen.

CHANGE WILL HAPPEN

'Then will the eyes of the blind be opened and the ears of the deaf unstopped. Then will the lame leap like a deer, and the mute tongue shout for joy. Water will gush forth in the wilderness and streams in the desert. The burning sand will become a pool, the thirsty ground bubbling springs. In the haunts where jackals once lay, grass and reeds and papyrus will grow.' (Isaiah 35: 5-7)

I love these verses of scripture that the Lord opened my eyes to recently. In these few verses alone, we get a wonderful picture of hope, restoration, transformation and life. That's what we need to fix our eyes on and believe in!

These verses also remind us about the good news of Jesus Christ. The good news is that Jesus is the Saviour who has done, can do, does do and will do amazing life-changing things for you - surely, that is good news!

So today, I encourage you not to lose sight of the good news that Jesus can bring, but also know that whatever you face, there is hope, there is restoration, there is transformation and there is a better life waiting for you. Jesus is the Saviour of the world!

Jesus, thank you that you are my Saviour, you are the one who can transform my life. I will keep my eyes fixed on you and not on my problems. You give me hope that my life will be better. Amen.

HE IS GOOD AND TASTY!

'Taste and see that the Lord is good; blessed is the one who takes refuge in him.' (Psalm 34: 8)

Life can be busy, life can be rushed, life can be stressful, and many of us may feel that our lives need to improve. Is that true for you? I have found that one of the best ways to improve my life is to try to find more opportunities to 'taste and see that the Lord is good'. There is something so special about being with Him; He has never abandoned us; He has never shut Himself away; but sometimes we can forget to be with Him.

As we draw near to Him, He is as present and as active as ever, just waiting for us to join Him and work with Him.

Let today be the start of seeing and tasting God's goodness in your life and releasing it into the lives of others. Be active in asking God what He is up to; find out how you can join with Him in releasing His presence and His Kingdom. Be positive and make Him your place of refuge each day. He is longing to spend more time with you and bless you.

Father, you are good and you have some wonderful things to show me. I choose today to taste and see that you are good. I can't wait to find out what you have in store for me! Amen.

THINGS WILL CHANGE - DON'T LOSE HEART

'This is what the LORD Almighty says: "Once again men and women of ripe old age will sit in the streets of Jerusalem, each with cane in hand because of his age. The city streets will be filled with boys and girls playing there." ...This is what the LORD Almighty says: "I will save my people from the countries of the east and the west. I will bring them back to live in Jerusalem; they will be my people, and I will be faithful and righteous to them as their God."' (Zechariah 8: 4-5; 7-8)

Israel was in exile and the people had lost all hope; they were in despair; nothing looked good for them; their dreams had died and they were a shadow of what they used to be.

But God never abandons His family. In these verses, we get a glimpse of hope, and a vision of what God will do: He will save them, and He will restore the devastated streets of Jerusalem, so that the elderly can be together in peace and joy, and children can play again.

If you have lost hope or are feeling discouraged, and believing that there is nothing to look forward to or dream about, then take hold of the truths in these verses. Don't lose hope, and don't despair, but instead trust God to save us, His people. Let's work with Him to see families, communities and countries restored again so that we will see the elderly, as well as children, thriving again in our communities.

It will happen. God has not abandoned His people, so let's find positive ways today to join Him in bringing His Kingdom to life on earth.

Father, I know that you are with me despite difficulties. I ask that you will step in today and change what needs to be changed. Amen.

BE FILLED WITH HOPE

'Hope deferred makes the heart sick.' (Proverbs 13: 12a)
'I sought the Lord, and he answered me; he delivered
me from all my fears.' (Psalm 34: 4)

These two verses hold great truths for us to grab hold of and keep in the centre of our thinking and feelings today. For me, these verses have encouraged me not to let my heart sink and not to fall into the trap of negativity.

I wrote this in my journal recently: 'My neck and shoulders are getting worse; sleeping is now very difficult; speaking and hearing are getting harder; under the surface, I am getting angry as well as scared'.

These two verses have helped me not to give into fear, nor allow hopelessness to take over in my heart. Instead, I choose to live in hope and freedom that the Lord will step in, He will indeed give me light in these times and my heart will rejoice.

Therefore, may I encourage you to do the same: take these truths and the power they hold and live them out in your life today.

Father, I choose today to live in more hope than I have done for a while. I choose not to slip into hopelessness or fear, but instead I will seek you Lord. Amen.

MORE FRUIT

"'I am the true vine and my Father is the gardener. He cuts off every branch in me that bears no fruit, while every branch that does bear fruit He prunes so that it will be even more fruitful.'" (John 15: 1-2)

Wow, I have not seen this before: Jesus also needed cutting and pruning! Yet, He is the true vine and His Father is the gardener.

He was open and willing to allow His Father to cut away anything in Him that was not bearing any fruit in order for Him to be more fruitful. Amazing - if Jesus needed cutting and pruning, where does that leave us?

I was watching my neighbour's gardener the other day carefully cutting branches and pruning the bushes so that in a few months' time the garden will be blooming.

Our Father will be gentle and caring towards us and will cut away anything that stops us from being fruitful. He cuts away and He prunes... even in areas where we are fruitful, pruning is needed to help us become even more fruitful. We just have to allow Him.

These days, the biggest battle for me is in my mind and in my thought-life. I need to let God cut these unfruitful branches off so that I am in a position to be more fruitful in all seasons.

Where do you need to be cut and pruned by Father God today? A teachable disciple of Jesus is always fruitful.

Lord, today I want to be a fruitful, loving disciple of yours. Will you cut off anything in me that is not bearing fruit and prune the areas that are fruitful, so that I may be even more fruitful for you. Amen.

LET'S MAKE JESUS HAPPY

'At that time Jesus, full of joy through the Holy Spirit, said, "I praise you Father, Lord of heaven and earth."' (Luke 10: 21a)

Seventy-two disciples of Jesus had just come back from their second mission trip; they were excited and eager to share their stories as they had experienced how even the demons had submitted to the name of Jesus (v. 17). They had just witnessed the amazing power of the Kingdom of God on earth working through them. In response, Jesus was full of joy himself. The disciples - His friends, the ones He had chosen - were doing what He could do, and He praised His Father for allowing it to happen.

I remember when I arrived as a vicar at my first church. A group of people had just come back from a mission trip to Romania and they were full of stories of what Jesus had done through them. As they stepped off the coach, we gathered together and I released this truth of scripture over them. I felt immensely proud of them and I knew that Jesus was full of joy as we listened to their stories.

So today, how will you make Jesus full of joy? Think of ways in which you can release the fragrance of the Kingdom of God on earth. As you step out, enjoy knowing that Jesus is full of joy as you do so.

Jesus, I look forward to having a great day! Help me to be creative and step out to see your Kingdom grow in someone's life today, so that you rejoice and praise your Father, just as you did with your disciples. Amen.

NO SHORTCUTS

'And we rejoice in the hope of the glory of God. Not only so, but we also rejoice in our sufferings, because we know that suffering produces perseverance; perseverance, character; and character, hope. And hope does not disappoint us.' (Romans 5: 2b-5a)

Here in this verse, Paul shares with us a cycle that leads to hope.

Suffering is the doorway that leads to perseverance; perseverance is the doorway that leads to character; character is the doorway that leads to hope.

This promised hope is a supernatural hope, one that is not tied to an outcome, but a hope in Father God and His character, trusting that He will use everything we go through - every tear, every joy, every night spent in prayer - for His Glory, to strengthen and mature us. If we submit to this process, we will not be put to shame, we will not be disappointed.

However, so often there is an opposite cycle at work in our lives: suffering which can lead to disappointment; then disappointment which can lead to disillusionment; disillusionment which can lead to dissatisfaction; and dissatisfaction which can lead to distance and hopelessness. This cycle clearly works against the one which Paul says will bring us life. In the end, it can lead to us distancing ourselves from God, the very One who can help us.

Are there disappointments in any areas of your life: areas of suffering that you need to be honest with Father God about? Talk to Him. Have you allowed distance to creep in? Repent and return to Him. Then choose to trust in Him, choose to persevere, choose to worship Him today.

Father, thank you that your desire is to bless me with supernatural levels of hope in every area of my life. Help me today to engage with you, not to distance myself from you, trusting that as I persevere, you will build my character, giving birth to hope. Amen.

HE IS ENOUGH

'Philip said, "Lord, show us the Father and that will be enough for us."' (John 14: 8)

This year I am trying to read the bible slightly more slowly than I normally do, and what I have found is that I see new words or phrases that I have not noticed before.

In this verse, I have always thought, "Oh Philip, you missed the point, you missed out!" This was because I only focused on the first half of the verse. But no - Philip did get the point! He uses the phrase, 'that will be enough'. Philip knew the answer: the Father was 'enough' - that is it, nothing else, the Father is all he needed. He is enough.

I once heard that over 75% of young offenders in prison have not had a relationship with their earthly father. We all need God the Father: He is enough; He has unlimited provisions; He has got supernatural power; He is full of grace and mercy; He is compassionate and rich in love; He is enough. Philip got it and understood; that is all he needed to have.

Do you get it? How is your relationship with the Father? Is He enough for you or are you still needing other things or pursuing 'idols' that you think will help you?

Philip got it right, so let's all step deeper into a relationship with the Father today. He is enough.

Father, you are enough for me. Please help me walk in this great truth today, so that I can point people to you. You are enough, I don't need anything else but you. Amen.

GOD'S WORD IS THE BEST FOUNDATION FOR LIFE

'But his delight is in the law of the LORD, and on his law he meditates day and night. He is like a tree planted by streams of water, which yields its fruit in season and whose leaf does not wither. Whatever he does prospers.' (Psalm 1: 2-3)

This is a wonderful picture that the Psalmist uses to describe someone who spends time focusing and going deeper into God's Word. As they do so, they become like a tree bearing fruit in all seasons of life; its leaves not withering; a strong tree that has deep roots, drawing on the water in all seasons.

Are you bearing fruit that reflects Jesus today? The secret for this is to go deeper into God's Word.

Take time to meditate on God's Word and let the truth of God's word become your foundation for life. It is from these solid foundations that you can practise living out the truths of His Word in your life so that when you do this, you will be productive and bear fruit in all the seasons of life, fruit that others will enjoy and be blessed by.

Lord, thank you for your Word which is the source of life, the truth by which I need to live life. May my life be strong in every season that I face and may I bear fruit for others to enjoy. Amen.

MOVE ON!

'Then the Lord said to Moses, "Why are you crying out to me? Tell the Israelites to move on."' (Exodus 14: 15)

The Israeliites were on the run. They had just left Egypt and were travelling across the desert at high speed. They had been slaves for 400 years and were not used to fighting. They had the Egyptian army at their backs which was the biggest in the known world of the time, and there was panic in their ranks (vs. 10-12). But God's ways are so different to ours and His solutions are supernatural.

In the previous verse, speaking through Moses, God effectively said, "Be quiet, hold your peace, stop moaning, move forward and then watch, and I will do the fighting for you." What a victory it was when they walked through the Red Sea on dry land!

The challenge today is to believe that once we stop moaning, begin to move forward, the Lord will fight for us. Someone once said, "God can't steer a ship in harbour.'" In whatever situation you find yourself, the key is to make that choice to be at peace within, to be quiet, to acknowledge the Lord, move forward and then see Him fight for you. Don't let panic creep into your lives, don't try to fight the battle in your own strength, but play your part and then let God show up and sort it out.

How many of us fall here and end up fighting the battle ourselves, instead of letting God fight for us?

Abba Father, you have the solution to the situation that I am in. I will choose today to live in peace, move forward in faith and trust that you will then do the fighting for me. I will watch you step in. Thank you. Amen.

HE'S GOT A PLAN - STEP IN TO IT

"'I will send my terror ahead of you and throw into confusion every nation you encounter. I will make all your enemies turn their backs and run. I will send the hornet ahead of you to drive the Hivites, Canaanites and Hittites out of your way.'" (Exodus 23: 27-28)

Yesterday, we saw how God stepped in and did a supernatural miracle by destroying the Egyptian army and opening up a sea to walk across. All He asked the Israelities to do was to be at peace, then move forward while He fought for them. Today, we see another fighting strategy.

Again, we see here in these verses that God wants us to move forward: "I will send my terror ahead of you", implying that as the Israelites move forward, God will go before them. This is what faith is about. It has to be active and growing and, like any muscle, in order to grow stronger, it needs exercise. God wants us to keep moving forward and He will go ahead of us into every situation that we encounter today.

So if you need some 'land' to be taken, at work or any area of your life, ask God to send His power ahead of you, to clear the way to enable things to go smoothly as you move forward. The enemy may try to stir things up, but believe you will see him turn his back to you and flee as you resist him.

Almighty God, you are fighting for me today, the victory will be yours. I will trust you today to fight for me, to win the battle that I am in. Amen.

HE IS THERE

'"Father, if you are willing, take this cup from me; yet not my will, but yours be done." An angel from heaven appeared to him and strengthened him.' (Luke 22: 42-43)

In the midst of darkness and in the midst of sorrow and despair, Jesus was not left alone - an angel appeared and strengthened Him.

We are never alone, God is right there. Whatever situation you find yourself in today, whether sorrowful or joyful, God is there and wants to help.

So be looking out for Him or simply ask Him to draw near and wrap His arms around you. He loves it when we call upon Him.

Abba Father, thank you that one of your angels came to strengthen Jesus in His time of need. I ask today that you send an angel to me to strengthen me. Amen.

USE YOUR PROPHETIC GIFT

*'He told her, "Go, call your husband and come back." "I have no
husband," she replied. Jesus said to her, "You are right when
you say you have no husband. The fact is, you have had five
husbands, and the man you now have is not your husband.
What you have just said is quite true."' (John 4: 16-18)*

In this famous story where Jesus encounters a Samaritan woman and
changes her life forever, we see how the prophetic gift not only brought
salvation to someone, but also changed her community (v. 42). This
can be lived out in our lives today as we learn to exercise the gift
of prophecy to help people. Handled well, the prophetic gift can be
immensely powerful.

Prophecy has to be one of the most effective ways to reveal God's love to
people. As we minister to others, all we need to do is simply ask the Father
what is on His heart for this person and what to say to them. As we listen
and then share we will know whether or not it is from God, because it will
be strengthening, encouraging and comforting (see 1 Corinthians 14: 3).

So wherever you are today, why not ask God for a word for someone? It
might just open up the door to set them free. Prophetic words are very
powerful, as the Samaritan woman discovered.

*Father, you know everything about each one of us and what is going on
in our lives. Please use me today to be part of bringing freedom, joy and
hope to someone's life. Amen.*

DON'T BE STUCK IN YOUR THOUGHTS

'Samuel said, "Although you were once small in your own eyes, did you not become the head of the tribes of Israel? The LORD anointed you king over Israel."' (1 Samuel 15: 17)

The prophet Samuel gives an insight into what Saul was like before he was King: "you were once small in your own eyes". These words imply that he was struggling with issues, perhaps 'fear of man', inferiority or low self-esteem and he had never really dealt with these issues. We see from scripture that these traits were present throughout his reign and did not allow him to stand up and be the King he was called to be.

Are there areas in your life right now that you need to bring before the Lord and, with His help, deal with them? Do you struggle with fear of what others think? Or does inferiority play out in your mind? The Lord wants you to be free and move into your calling. Don't waste another day being stuck! The Lord loves you so much and He wants to help you move on.

Share your heart with Him today and see Him work for you.

Loving Father, you know me, you know what I struggle with and what causes me to lose sight of who I am. I ask today that you would help me move forward so that I can overcome and live in all the fullness you have for me. Amen.

SPEND SOME QUALITY TIME WITH JESUS

'"Come," he replied, "and you will see." So they went and saw where he was staying, and spent that day with him.' (John 1: 39a)

The two disciples whom Jesus invited to stay with Him, found that their lives were changed forever from that day forward. That day, those two disciples, who were in fact disciples of John the Baptist (see v. 35), dropped everything and went to be with Jesus for a whole day and never looked back.

When was the last time you spent a whole day with Jesus?

Rick Warren, pastor and author of best-selling book, The Purpose Driven Life, which has sold over 50 million copies, wrote this: 'Busyness is a great enemy of relationships'.[19]

When I was a full-time vicar working in a parish, I used to book a day retreat once a term to be on my own with Jesus. Hindsight is a wonderful thing - I should have done this once a month or more! However, we don't need to be leading a church or even in full-time Christian work to take retreat days. Taking time out to be with Jesus is crucial. However, in the busyness of life, it seems to be a real challenge for many of us - there is a battle over our time.

Why not have some time with Jesus today and see what He has to say to you? Or book a slot when you can have an extended time with Him away from your normal daily routine.

Let's be growing our relationship with Him. Time with the King changes everything.

Jesus, you are my best friend. I am going to spend today with you. I invite you to be with me and see how amazing you are! I know I am going to have a good day! Amen.

HOLD YOUR HEAD UP HIGH

'Those who look to him are radiant; their faces are never covered with shame.' (Psalm 34: 5)

Where do you look for help? Who or what are you pinning your hopes on?

This verse shows us that when we look to God, we get to experience radiance and light, rather than shame or embarrassment. The enemy and the voices in the world will always mock us when we choose to look to, and stand on the outrageous promises of God.

During our five year journey of infertility, this verse became a promise that my wife Michelle would regularly hold onto. Every month those mocking voices would come; voices that tried to make her feel ashamed for trusting and hoping in God. However, she learned to overcome their volume and power with this truth: that no child of God ever needs to be ashamed or embarrassed for trusting fully in His love and power, rather, as children of God, we can throw ourselves fully on Him, and we will be covered in radiance!

So today, whatever breakthrough you are believing for, whatever situation you are in, believing for the seemingly impossible to happen, you can hold your head up high. That sickness can be healed, that relationship can be restored, that provision can be released, that life can be turned around. As you look to God, know that He sees you as radiant and is so proud of your courage and faith.

Father God, you have all that I need. Today I will look to you, hope in you and feel your love and pride for me. Amen.

KEEP JESUS IN THE CENTRE

'Let us fix our eyes on Jesus, the author and perfecter of our faith.' (Hebrews 12: 2a)

This was the verse in scripture which, aged 18, I was asked to give my first ever talk on, and it was to an audience of young teenagers. I was a nervous wreck, but I will never forget what I learned that morning! Keeping your eyes on Jesus is the best thing to do.

He has walked the road of faith and He did it with perfection. He did not falter when they mocked him; He did not allow success to become His driving force; He did not give in to the criticism and words of others; He did not walk alone, but was constantly in touch with His Father and He walked in the power of the Holy Spirit. What an author of faith to follow and fix our eyes on!

When you use a magnifying glass, it is always the centre of the glass that is clearest. Is Jesus at the centre of your gaze today or are you allowing outside pressures to be in the centre which take your focus off Him? Let's put Him in the centre and He will help us with our faith journey.

Today, why not spend some time looking at Him, fixing the eyes of your heart on Jesus - it will transform your life.

Have a good day fixing your gaze on Jesus.

Jesus, thank you that you are the author and perfecter of my faith. I will keep my eyes fixed on you today and not allow the pressure of this world to distract me. Amen.

IT'S TIME FOR HEAVEN TO REJOICE

'I confess my iniquity; I am troubled by my sin.' (Psalm 38: 18)

The Psalmist breaks a wonderful pattern that so many of us get caught up in; he is prepared to recognise that he is not living a good life; that he is in sin and he admits it to God. He confesses it.

God loves our confession so much that He rejoices over us when we confess and repent of our sins. In fact, in Romans, it says, 'God's kindness leads us to repentance' (Romans 2: 4).

Confession and repentance of sin are wonderful things to do because by doing so, we are set free. Not only do we rediscover just how good Father God is, but we also discover the deep intimacy that we can have with Him.

So if you are troubled today by sin - in thought, in word, or deed - then I encourage you to embrace His kindness and return to Him. Know that God's desire is for more freedom and joy for you in your life, as you come into His presence.

Heaven rejoices when a sinner repents. So let heaven rejoice today!

Father, thank you that you are so kind, that when I repent and turn from my sin, you rejoice and shower me with your love. Amen.

SHOW HIS LOVE

'For I was hungry and you gave me something to eat, I was thirsty and you gave me something to drink. I was a stranger and you invited me in.' (Matthew 25: 35)

'The greatest disease in the West today is not Tuberculosis or leprosy; it is being unwanted, unloved and uncared for. We can cure physical diseases with medicine, but the only cure for loneliness, despair, and hopelessness is love. There are many in the world who are dying for a piece of bread but there are many more dying for a little love.'[20]

This famous quote by Mother Teresa challenges us to be more intentional each day in sharing Father's love to someone.

I spent a week consciously trying to do this and enjoyed seeing the results! If we all did this today, many people's lives would be powerfully impacted.

So be creative, give it a go, and share a little love.

Father, help me today to show your love to someone, to be there for someone who needs a listening ear or a comforting word. May I be full of your love so that I can give it to others. Amen.

LIES CAN MESS YOU UP

'The woman said to the serpent, "We may eat fruit from the trees in the garden, but God did say, 'You must not eat fruit from the tree that is in the middle of the garden, and you must not touch it, or you will die.'" "You will not certainly die," the serpent said to the woman. "For God knows that when you eat from it your eyes will be opened, and you will be like God, knowing good and evil."' (Genesis 3: 2-4)

Eve was lied to by the serpent: "You will not certainly die". He used this to lure her away from what God had said to her. Sin entered her life, broke her intimacy with God, and that was the beginning of the most extraordinary sequence of events in history: the Fall of humankind. But Jesus came to rescue, redeem and restore.

What lie are you listening to today? One summer, as I had time to reflect on the previous 18 months and prepare myself for a new term, a new season, and a new ministry, the Lord showed me a lie which had taken root in my thinking. It was a lie that I realised I knew about, but never really saw its full impact in the way I thought about my ministry and myself. It was a real revelation.

So today, I encourage you to ask the Lord if there is a lie that the enemy has sown - or might be trying to sow - that stops you from living a full and joyful life. The enemy is deceitful and cunning, so we need to be alert and prevent these lies from taking root and affecting us.

Father, you have so much more to show me and to give me so that I can fulfil all that you want me to do. I invite you, Holy Spirit, to show me where a lie or anything that I might be living under, might be stopping me from living life to its full potential. Amen.

LET PEACE BE PRESENT

'Let the peace of Christ rule in your heart.' (Colossians 3: 15a)

A more literal translation of the word 'rule' is 'be the referee'. It is wonderful to allow the peace of Christ to be the referee or governor of our hearts and to rule in every situation we find ourselves in.

I know a good friend, who has a long-term illness and whenever his symptoms get worse or his pain levels increase, he is able to still carry the peace of Jesus - it is such a powerful and inspiring thing to see and witness. Christ's peace is literally a strengthening and resourcing power helping my friend to keep going.

British evangelist and author Roy Hession wrote, 'Everything that disturbs the peace of God in our hearts is sin, no matter how small it is and no matter how little sin it may be, it removes the peace.'[21]

If you don't have peace in your heart, stop and ask, why not? Don't blame others, but instead examine what is going on within you. Take it to the Lord, confess it and ask Him for His peace to rule.

May you have a peaceful day.

Jesus, may your peace rule in my heart today. Amen.

GET GOD INVOLVED - JESUS DID

"'I know that His command leads to eternal life. So whatever I say is just what the Father has told me to say."' (John 12: 50)

Jesus was in direct communication with the Father every day, every hour, as well as communicating the Father's heart to those around Him. He knew what His Father was thinking and what His Father wanted to share and do. That's why He was so effective in His ministry, because He spent time with His Father.

Why not today follow Jesus' example and begin to ask God questions about the situations you find yourself in, or ask for a word of blessing for someone you are going to meet.

It is so much fun hearing God speak into every situation. He loves being involved.

Will you give Him the opportunity today?

Father, thank you that you showed Jesus what to do and what to say. Today, I choose to listen to you for advice and thoughts. Amen.

HE BELIEVES IN YOU

'As Jesus walked beside the Sea of Galilee, he saw Simon and his brother Andrew casting a net into the lake, for they were fishermen. "Come follow me," Jesus said.' (Mark 1: 16-17a)

From the outset of His ministry, Jesus thought differently to the culture around Him and in which He had grown up.

Usually for a person to follow a Rabbi, they would have to go and ask the Rabbi if they could follow them and become one of their disciples. In effect, this meant that they would be saying, "I want to be like you, Rabbi." The Rabbi would question them and then would say either yes or no.

Jesus turned the selection process on its head - He saw the potential in people. So when Jesus said to Andrew and Simon, "Come, follow me," what He was saying was that He believed that Andrew and Simon could be like Him and live like Him. Jesus believed in them.

Have you thought recently that Jesus believes in you, that He has faith that you can be like Him? He is calling you today to follow Him.

Jesus, you have chosen me to follow you because you believe in me. Help me today to follow you and be like you. Amen.

SHARE YOUR TEARS

'The whole crowd of the disciples began to praise God joyfully with a loud voice for all the miracles they had seen ... As He came near to the city, Jesus wept over it.' (Luke 19: 37b; 41)

The crowd were loving this situation: a chance to sing, dance and rejoice! However, despite all this, Jesus still wept. He knew what was coming - His own death and later the destruction of Jerusalem (v. 42), the Holy city of God, once so beautiful.

Today there is much to weep about: struggles in the world, impossible situations in our personal lives or circumstances that tear us apart and break our hearts. Jesus saw and knew the fate of this great city and He knew the task that lay ahead of Him. He saw the situation, and the seeming impossibility of it and He wept.

It is good to share your emotions with Father God, but we must be like Jesus - yes, weep - but keep trusting that God has the answers. Remember He raised Jesus from the dead and His power is still available for us today.

Jesus, thank you that you continue on the path that your Father had for you despite its challenges and what lay ahead. Help me today to be honest with the Father, so that I may trust Him that all will be well. Amen.

HE KNOWS YOU SO WELL

'O Lord, you have searched me and you know me. You know when I sit and when I rise; you perceive my thoughts from afar ... Search me, O God, and know my heart; test me and know my anxious thoughts. See if there is any offensive way in me and lead me in the way everlasting.' (Psalm 139: 1-2; 23-24)

God knows us better than anyone else, as these verses in Psalm 139 say.

Whatever season we are in right now, one of the most important things to do, is to check out how well we are doing in our relationship with the Father. We need to believe that God is with us, to continually re-align ourselves with Him and be willing to change into His likeness. Let Him change you so that you can be more free through encountering the love of Father God - more open to His presence, transformed through His grace-filled power - more able to serve and love your family and the community around you.

As you navigate this season, may you be free from fear and full of faith, because Father God is with you. He is right by your side. He knows you so well.

Father, you know me through and through. I choose today to change, to re-align myself with you, so that I will not be plagued by anxious thoughts or have any offensive way in me. Amen.

JESUS IS PRAYING FOR YOU

'Jesus... is at the right hand of God and is also intercding for us.' (Romans 8: 34b)

This is a wonderful picture to hold in your mind and heart today: Jesus is alive and is seated next to His Father - our Father - and He is interceding for you today.

Wow! That is so good to know! I am on Jesus' heart, His mind and His lips. The One who taught us how to pray is praying for us. What a comfort this is! Jesus is not detached or removed from our lives or troubles, but rather is intimately involved in the everyday details of our lives.

In light of this, a good question to ask today could be this: "Jesus, what are you praying for me today?" The answer might surprise you!

Jesus, thank you that you are alive and you are in heaven with your Father and you are interceding for me today. I appreciate your prayers for me. Amen.

NO MORE FEAR

'There is no fear in love. But perfect love drives out all fear, because fear has to do with punishment. The one who fears is not made perfect in love.' (1 John 4: 18)

Fear stops us from living in freedom and love. Fear is a barrier between us and God, and between us and our family and friends.

I have discovered more and more that fear can be one of our greatest enemies. It seems to be there, ready to pounce and devour us! I am not sure that we can ever make fear disappear from our lives. Fear can be an appropriate reaction to danger. Fear itself is not a sin, but can lead to sin and can take us away from God. But if we have a heart that is full of love, when fear tries to jump at us, we are ready to rest in the truth of the Father's perfect love.

Why not today ask for a deeper revelation of God's love? His 'perfect love drives out all fear'.

Enjoy a fear-free day!

Father, your love is perfect and is so big that I can't even imagine what it is like, but today, I want to experience your perfect love in a new and refreshing way so that fear is not the master of my heart. Amen.

IT'S TIME TO REVEAL JESUS

'We always carry around in our body the death of Jesus, so that the life of Jesus may also be revealed in our body. For we who are alive are always being given over to death for Jesus' sake, so that His life may be revealed in our mortal body.' (2 Corinthians 4: 10-11)

Today, we have a wonderful opportunity to allow Jesus' life to be revealed in our mortal bodies by allowing His characteristics, His thoughts, His actions and His voice to be heard and seen by others. All we have to do is allow Him to grow in us.

So why not give Him permission today to be present in all areas of your life: your body, your mind, your heart, your soul and your strength? Then others will see Jesus revealed in you. You will be different, you will carry Jesus in you.

Give Jesus permission to be alive and active in you today.

Jesus, you are so real and alive in my life. I choose today to live for you more than I have ever done. May you be present in all I do. Amen.

ACTIONS SPEAK LOUDER THAN WORDS

'Dear children, let us not love with words or tongue but with actions and in truth.' (1 John 3: 18)

Actions truly speak louder than words.

Why not show someone today how much you love them by doing something for someone to bless them? Remember that every day, even small actions speak louder than words.

Why not make today a fun day and do something differently from your normal way of life! Bless someone with actions: a phone call, a cup of coffee, or help someone, even in a small way.

Ask the Lord how you can love someone today without using words.

Father, you have called me to show love to all those I meet and those I live with. Please show me today how I might do something for someone that will bless them and really make them feel loved. Amen.

CHOOSE YOUR WORDS CAREFULLY

*'Gracious words are like a honeycomb, sweetness to the
soul and health to the body.' (Proverbs 16: 24, ESV)*

A true disciple follows and imitates Jesus. Jesus always used words
carefully, so the way we talk is very significant.

I recently spent a day with a good friend, whom I have known for over
25 years. At the end of the day, I felt so full from hearing positive and
encouraging words spoken over me that it made me feel so much better
about myself!

We need to choose our words carefully because words spoken wrongly
can have enormous power to tear down and curse. According to Proverbs
18: 21, 'The tongue has the power of life and death.' And we don't know
who might be listening to our words! If someone hears good words being
spoken about them, it will bless them and give them life as well.

So may your words today build up and encourage people so they grow
stronger in body and soul. It might just be the turning point they need in
life.

*Jesus, you spoke words that touched people's hearts and set them free
and gave them hope. May the words I speak today do the same. Amen.*

FIGHT IN THE RIGHT PLACE

'For our struggle is not against flesh and blood, but against the rulers, against the authorities against the powers of this dark world and against the spiritual forces of evil in the heavenly realms.' (Ephesians 6: 12)

We so often forget this truth: our battle is not against flesh and blood.

One of the enemy's schemes is for us to fight amongst ourselves. He will try to take our focus off the real battle, which is a spiritual battle, and get us to concentrate on other battles that normally end up causing havoc among families, churches, and communities - that is just what the enemy wants! We must be aware of this and learn to move against it.

How do we do that? There are many ways but what I have learned over the years is to keep our focus on Jesus. We can simply ask him, "Lord, what is going on here?" As we remember that our battle is not against flesh and blood, we can discern the schemes of the enemy and see what the enemy is up to.

Whatever we are facing, whether a health problem, a work issue or a family crisis, we must first recognise that the battle is in the heavenly realms. We can put on the whole armour of God, take up the sword of the Spirit, which is the word of God (see Ephesians 6), for 'the weapons we fight with are not the weapons of the world' (2 Corinthians 10: 4). We have all the weapons we need to fight this battle. The enemy is defeated and we must learn to walk in the confidence of this truth. At Jesus' name, the enemy must submit. We fight from a place of victory.

So, let's begin to discern what is happening in the spiritual realm around us and focus our prayers there.

Jesus, you have won the greatest battle over the enemy. Help me to know how to fight with you so that your Kingdom may prevail. Amen.

IS THERE AN IDOL IN YOUR LIFE?

'But their idols are silver and gold, made by human hands. They have mouths, but cannot speak, eyes, but cannot see. They have ears, but cannot hear, noses, but cannot smell. They have hands, but cannot feel, feet, but cannot walk, nor can they utter a sound with their throats.' (Psalm 115: 4-7)

There are quite a few 'cannots' in these verses! Even now, in the present day, people worship and are drawn to idols that are man-made, such as celebrity, popularity, status, image, and wealth. These idols cannot meet our deepest needs or satisfy us in the long term. They cannot speak words of comfort to us or heal our bodies - they are not much good really!

In contrast, Father God is ever-seeing, ever-speaking, ever-hearing and always ready to embrace us.

Is there an idol that you worship? A good test is to see what preoccupies your mind or heart more than God.

So today, let's check that our hearts and minds are right and that our worship is for Him and Him alone.

Father, you are full of mercy and grace. You are alive and real. Please forgive me if there is any idol that I have put up in my life that I worship and draw strength from. I want to worship you today. Amen.

STAND UP AND BE COUNTED

"'If anyone is ashamed of me and my words in this adulterous and sinful generation, the Son of Man will be ashamed of him when He comes in His Father's glory with the holy angels."' (Mark 8: 38)

Here are some challenging words from Jesus today: He will be ashamed of us if we do not stand up and be different in the generation that we are living in.

We can be confident, however, that if we are obedient to Jesus' word and stand tall, then He will not be ashamed of us, He will welcome us with open arms.

I remember a season in my life as a young adult, when I was beginning to get serious in my walk with Jesus, I was pressured by a friend to drink up my pint of beer and to get drunk like everyone else. I refused and my friend shrugged his shoulders, and walked off slightly confused. That decision back then to stand up and be different radically changed my life.

Let's stand strong in confidence today and be a shining light to our friends and work colleagues. They need to see Jesus in us.

Jesus, you will come in your Father's glory to judge this world. I choose today to stand up and be counted for your name. As I walk with you today, please give me the strength to follow you. Amen.

HE IS THE GOD OF THE IMPOSSIBLE

*'All of this took place to fulfil what had been spoken by the
Lord through the prophet, "Look, the virgin shall conceive
and bear a son, and they shall name him Emmanuel,"
which means, "God is with us."' (Matthew 1: 22-23)*

He is the God of the impossible! 2000 years ago, a young teenage girl found favour with God and an impossible thing happened. A virgin became pregnant, bore a son, and He was given a name that means 'God is with us'. He is still with us today and He is still doing the impossible.

I was at a meeting recently where we were encouraged to look back over the year and share a highlight with one another. The testimonies that were shared spoke of God doing the impossible amongst us. We heard stories of people being healed of cancer, teenagers being set free from anxiety, addictions being broken, financial blessings, and miracles of healing outside a mosque in Africa... all speaking of lives being changed dramatically.

I encourage you today to believe even more for the impossible in your own lives and in the lives of others. He is still with us and is still doing the impossible.

No wonder we still celebrate the Christmas story every year, as it is an impossible story to forget and one that changed the world and our lives forever!

Thank you, Father, for what you have done over the years in my life and in the life of my family and ministry. You are the God of the impossible. I look forward to seeing more of the impossible. Amen.

THE ANGEL GABRIEL ON THE MOVE (PART 1)

'The angel answered, "I am Gabriel. I stand in the presence of God, and I have been sent to speak to you and to tell you this good news."' (Luke 1: 19)

The Christmas story begins with a supernatural visit of the angel Gabriel with a message which is good news! We will see more of the good news over the next few days, but today, let's look at where Gabriel had come from: he had been standing in the presence of God.

I have a desire to spend more time in the presence of God, not only to hear God speaking, but also to be filled with joy and love, as well as freedom from worry, stress and much more. Being in God's presence is the place to be!

Some of us may well be very busy over the next ten days with lots of celebrating with family and friends. However, in the fun and rush of these days, don't miss out on being in God's presence. Being in His presence and enjoying Him will give you the ability and strength to enjoy each day as it comes. You may even hear a message of good news from Father God! Gabriel did, and he shared it.

Abba Father, thank you that I can be in your presence, that I can be with you and know you intimately. As we enter this season of celebrating the good news of the announcement of the birth of Jesus your son, I choose today to make time and space in my day to be with you. Amen.

THE ANGEL GABRIEL ON THE MOVE (PART 2)

'The angel went to Mary and said, "Greetings, you who are highly favoured! The Lord is with you."' (Luke 1: 28)

There are two wonderful truths here in this verse of scripture. The first is this: "the Lord is with you". This is a powerful truth: the Lord is with you right now.

Why not turn and acknowledge Him and speak to Him, and ask Him if there is anything He would like you to do for Him today. Also thank Him that you do not have to face today on your own.

Secondly, what a wonderful greeting from the angel: "you who are highly favoured". It has always surprised me that the Lord would say that to a teenager. We don't know anything about Mary before now, but this one phrase from the Lord speaks volumes about how He sees His children. We are precious to Him and, as it says in Psalm 17, we are 'the apple of His eye' (v. 8).

So take some time to allow these words to soak in and go deep into your heart. It speaks about how God sees you. Yes, you are His child and the apple of His eye.

It is a very powerful word that the Lord wants you to believe today.

Father, I am blown away that these words spoken to Mary by the angel Gabriel are true for me today! Help me believe them and live them out. Amen.

THE ANGEL GABRIEL ON THE MOVE (PART 3)

'In the sixth month... God sent the angel Gabriel to Nazareth...
The angel answered, "The Holy Spirit will come upon you, and the
power of the Most High will overshadow you."' (Luke 1: 26; 35)

"The Holy Spirit will come upon you, and the power of the Most High will overshadow you". As a result of these words, an incredible miracle took place: a virgin gave birth to a child! It happened because of the power and presence of the Holy Spirit.

Nothing is impossible for the Holy Spirit, even today. Do you need a miracle in your life? Do you need help in a certain area of your life? Is there a thought-pattern that you need victory over?

Take these words for yourself today and ask for the Holy Spirit to overshadow you with His power and help you through your day, and through any situation. Be overshadowed by the Spirit today, and see what happens.

Holy Spirit, I invite you to overshadow me today, to be present in my life so that I may enjoy all that you can do for me. Nothing is impossible for you. Amen.

THE BEST PRESENT EVER

*'But after he had considered this, an angel of the Lord appeared
to him in a dream and said, "Joseph, son of David, do not
be afraid to take Mary home as your wife, because what is
conceived in her is from the Holy Spirit. She will give birth to
a son and you are to give Him the name Jesus, because He
will save his people from their sins."' (Matthew 1: 20-21)*

Here we have another angel, but this time in a dream, telling Joseph what to do and even the name of the baby and what He was destined to do.

This is no ordinary baby. In fact, He has made more impact on the earth than anyone else in history, since the day He was born. Jesus was born for one purpose only: to eradicate sin and to reconcile us back to Father, so that we can enjoy the life that God has for us - a life in relationship with the Father.

We are all sinners in need of saving and in need of help. Jesus was born to save us from our sins.

So this Christmas, in all the busyness around us, let us remember why He was born - it was such good news! As you celebrate Christmas, perhaps with family and friends, take a moment to remember that Jesus was born to save us, He was God's rescue plan for the whole world.

What a wonderful present that is!

Jesus, you have saved me from my sins. I thank you for this wonderful present you have given me. Help me to make the most of it every day so that my walk with your Father and my Father is made even more special. Amen.

THE GOOD NEWS

'But the angel said to them, "Do not be afraid. I bring you good news of great joy that will be for all the people. Today in the town of David a Saviour has been born to you; he is Christ the Lord."' (Luke 2: 10-11)

The shepherds were the least respected in the communities of their day, normally away from the villages and towns for long periods of time.

It is so fascinating that God consistently goes against the thinking and rhetoric of the culture of the day, turning things on their head. Here, the angel appeared, not to those who were clever or to the elite, but on this night, he sent the angel to the poor and marginalised with this good news. On this night, the shepherds would become known, they would be the ones to spread the good news around the town of Bethlehem. The good news that they heard was that the Messiah had been born that very night. This was news that the whole of Israel had been waiting for! It was good news to hear; it was life-changing for the shepherds and for the whole world.

As we draw near to Christmas, let's remember the good news of great joy and in our own way, let's share this good news with friends and family that Jesus is born and that He is the Saviour of the world!

Father, thank you that the shepherds spread the good news of great joy. Help me today to join in with them and tell people about the good news that Jesus is the Saviour of the world. Amen.

CAN YOU DO THE SAME?

'When Elizabeth heard Mary's greeting, the child leaped in her womb. And Elizabeth was filled with the Holy Spirit and exclaimed with a loud cry, "Blessed are you among women, and blessed is the fruit of your womb. And why has this happened to me, that the mother of my Lord comes to me? For as soon as I heard the sound of your greeting, the child in my womb leaped for joy. And blessed is she who believed that there would be a fulfilment of what was spoken to her by the Lord."' (Luke 1: 41-45, NRSV)

The first person ever to recognise Jesus was John The Baptist who, as a baby, leaped in his mother's womb. What an impact the baby Jesus was already having!

As the baby John leaped, his mother Elizabeth was filled with the Holy Spirit and she began to speak prophetic words of encouragement over Mary, affirming her. No doubt Mary was still processing the impact of the angel Gabriel's visit, so hearing these words of Elizabeth must have been a huge encouragement and blessing for her.

There are a couple of things for us to learn from these wonderful verses. Firstly, as well as letting people see Jesus in us, (He is still having an impact today), we must also do what Elizabeth did. We must affirm and bless those we meet, speaking words of life over them and into their situations.

Therefore, I encourage you today to be filled with the Spirit and be asking Him how you can be a blessing and affirm people, either at work, or with your family and friends. It will make such a difference in their lives.

Holy Spirit, will you speak to me today as I want to bless and encourage people whom I encounter and spend time with. Amen.

NO NEED TO BE AFRAID

'Then an angel of the Lord appeared to him, standing at the right side
of the altar of incense... But the angel said to him: "Do not be afraid."'
(Luke 1: 11; 13a)
In the sixth month... God sent the angel Gabriel to Nazareth... The angel
went to her and said, "Greetings, you who are highly favoured... Do not
be afraid."' (Luke 1:26a; 28a; 30b)
'An angel of the Lord appeared to them... The angel said to
them, "Do not be afraid. I bring good news."' (Luke 2: 9a; 10a)

The Christmas story continues to amaze me every year!

In these three passages in Luke's gospel, when each person is visited
by an angel and receives the message from God about the coming of His
Son, the angel tells them not to be afraid. Why is that? Because their
lives would be changed forever, and they would never be the same again.
Zechariah became speechless; Mary became pregnant; the shepherds
spread the good news everywhere. These words, 'don't be afraid' would
have encouraged them, not only in the moment of their encounter with
the angels, but later in their lives as well, as they lived out the plans and
purpose God had for them in a hostile world.

It is the same for us today as we walk and live out our faith. We must not
be afraid to share the good news and to give testimony of God working in
our lives.

*Jesus, your birth and your coming into the world as Saviour is something
that people need to hear and receive. Give me the courage today to
share this news with the people I am with as the opportunity arises.
Amen.*

IT'S CHRISTMAS DAY!

'The people walking in darkness have seen a great light; ... For to us a child is born, to us a son is given, and the government will be on his shoulders. And he will be called Wonderful Counsellor, Mighty God, Everlasting Father, Prince of Peace.' (Isaiah 9: 2a; 6)

This famous verse that is read every year, all around the world at carol services or on Christmas Day gives us such a powerful image of who Jesus is and what He can offer to people. As these verses are read, not only does it remind us of who Jesus is, but also it sows seeds into the hearts of those who hear God's word, maybe for the first time in the year.

Which one of these titles of Jesus speaks to you today? Which one do you need to engage with? Do you need some wisdom from the Wonderful Counsellor? Or a miracle from Mighty God? Or an embrace from the Everlasting Father? Or some peace from the Prince of Peace?

Don't miss out, but engage with Jesus today and make the most of who He is and what He can do for you.

Have a wonderful Christmas Day!

Jesus, you are amazing! You are everything I need today. Amen.

KEEP BELIEVING

'"I am the Lord's servant," Mary answered. "May it be to me as you have said." Then the angel left her.' (Luke 1: 38)

Mary is a great example of faith. An angel of the Lord spoke to her about an amazing supernatural miracle that was about to take place and Mary believed it. We must remember that Mary was just a teenager, but she was open to what the Lord had for her. She stepped out in faith and was willing to say, "Yes, here I am," and the miracle happened and Jesus was conceived.

In all the celebrations of the last few days, is there a miracle you are still waiting for? A promise you are still hoping for? Do not lose heart... believe in it. God will not disappoint you. He is working right now to accomplish all that has been promised. He is a good Father and He knows what you need.

So as we come to the end of the Christmas season, hold onto your faith, keep hope alive and you will see His divine intervention. You will be blessed, you will see it come true.

Father, today I will believe in you for more, I will not lose heart and I will not fall away. May my faith muscles grow and be ready to receive all that you have for me. Amen.

GOD IS SOWING A SEED TODAY

'"Listen! A farmer went out to sow his seed. As he was scattering the seed ... He also said, "This is what the kingdom of God is like. A man scatters seed on the ground."' (Mark 4: 3-4a; 26)

For many people, their concept of God is built around a God who is outside of everything, a God who is somewhere else, a God who made the world then stands back at a distance and views from a vantage point. Actually, God is all around us, working amongst us, scattering seeds - that is what Jesus is implying in this well-known parable.

God is active and involved in everyday life. He is sowing seeds, and we must learn to work with Him, whether we are at home, at work, at rest or at play.

Are we in tune with Him and prepared to help sow His seeds, see them flourish, so that His Kingdom grows on earth?

Work with Him today and see the joys of His Kingdom, not only by making sure the seeds God has given you are taking root, but also by believing that God has already sown seeds in the lives of the people you meet today.

Today, I choose to help the Kingdom of God grow. Father, will you show me where I can help your seeds flourish and grow in my life, in the lives of others and in the world around me. Amen.

TELL GOD ABOUT HIS LOVE

'It is good to praise the LORD and make music to your name, O Most High, to proclaim your love in the morning and your faithfulness at night.' (Psalm 92: 1-2)

Here in this Psalm, we find a powerful pattern to start the day with. To proclaim God's love, to think about this amazing love in the morning will transform you. To be in touch with the vastness and depth of God's love will be something that empowers you. To be free to approach the day, knowing the truth that the Lord Most High loves you and accepts you for who you are, will stir your heart. In response, tell Him how much you love Him and how much He means to you.

Finally, at night, as the end of the day draws near, it is always good to thank God for His faithfulness, not only for the day but also while you sleep.

In recent years I have adopted a habit of saying a simple prayer as I close my eyes:

We bless the Lord who gives us council in the night

To give us dreams; To give us visions;

To refresh us; to strengthen us

And may your Holy angels dwell with us and guard us in peace.[22]

Abba Father, I will proclaim your love for me today and I will live knowing that your love for me is so vast. I love you, Father. Thank you for your faithfulness to me in the day and in the night. Amen.

CONFIDENCE IN THE GOODNESS OF GOD

'I am still confident of this: I will see the goodness of the Lord in the land of the living.' (Psalm 27: 13)

I want to relate my testimony to this verse today. For 32 years, I have lived with the long-term effects of aggressive radiotherapy. This treatment helped me survive the rare nasopharyngeal cancer with which I was diagnosed when I was 18. Still, it decimated my neck and facial muscles and nerves and affected my ability to hear, speak and eat.

During my last annual check-up, my consultant reflected that if he had just met me and read my medical history for the first time, he would expect to meet a very sick man. He believes that at 50, I am not who my medical records say I am. He considers my quality of life to be exponentially superior to my prognosis.

I celebrate his professional opinion: I am not what my medical records say I am. Instead, I enjoy a good quality of life established in the firm foundation of His Word, praying saints, rich hope, and abundant grace. I am living proof that God's goodness is seen in the land of the living!

Today, ask God to remind you about a testimony of His goodness in your life. Give Him thanks that He has been faithful to His word.

Lord, may I believe that this day, this week, this year, I will witness your goodness in my life, in my family, and in the community in which I live. Amen.

PURSUE FORGIVENESS

'Be kind and compassionate to one another, forgiving each other, just as in Christ God forgave you.' (Ephesians 4: 32)

As we focus on the word 'forgiveness' in this verse, we turn our attention to one of the most important keys to living life well.

Forgiveness is the very foundation of God's Kingdom and the very nature of God Himself. His throne room is full of grace and mercy towards us. If He is prepared to forgive us for the things we get wrong, then in response we must seek to forgive others. By forgiving others, we allow God to heal us from any hurts, and the love of God can begin to flow out of our lives towards others.

I remember once leading a woman in prayer to forgive a person who had hurt her 17 years earlier. The next day her husband said to me, "What have you done to my wife? She's changed!" (In a good way!)

If we choose to remain in unforgiveness, it can create bondage and its fruits can be bitterness, anger and rage. If we live in that place, we will struggle to be kind and tenderhearted towards one another. We must pursue forgiveness. It is at the heart of God's Kingdom, and at the centre of God's thinking.

Is there someone today that you need to forgive? If so, begin the process of letting go and asking God to help you make those steps towards forgiveness. Remember how much you have been forgiven and as you forgive, you will be set free.

Father, thank you that Jesus Christ died for my sins and that I am forgiven. I choose today to begin to make the right steps towards living in forgiveness towards others so that I can know the joys of living freely in your love. Amen.

FINISH WELL

'Later, knowing that all was now completed, and so that Scripture would be fulfilled, Jesus said, "I am thirsty." A jar of wine vinegar was there, so they soaked a sponge in it, put the sponge on a stalk of the hyssop plant, and lifted it to Jesus' lips. When he had received the drink, Jesus said, "It is finished." With that, he bowed his head and gave up his spirit.' (John 19: 28-30)

"It is finished". These three words are probably the most powerful ever spoken. Every time I read the narrative about the crucifixion, it is these three words that seem to stir in me. When Jesus said these three words, "it is finished", He was declaring that He had now completed His Father's work: the curse of Adam has been broken, the sins of humanity are forgiven, the enemy is defeated in every area, the supernatural work of the Holy Spirit has been released and, most importantly, a relationship with Abba Father has been made possible. Jesus had to die. He had to finish His work well in order that you and I could enjoy these things. It was all done. Then He bowed His head in submission and committed His soul and spirit into His Father's hands, believing that His Father would raise Him up. Wow, what an amazing person Jesus is, obedient until death! He finished well.

As we come to the close of the year, can I encourage you to reflect on these three words and on this great moment in history. Realise again how much Jesus has done for you and for humankind by dying on the cross. Remember that we too are called to 'finish well' the work that God has called us to. Let's not give up, but press in and see God work through us.

Jesus, thank you that you are my role model. May I continue into this New Year on the path that you have for me and may I finish well and fulfil the mission you have given me to do whilst I am on earth. Amen.

BIBLIOGRAPHY

---

1. Smith Wigglesworth Devotional - (Whitaker House, 1999), page 541.

2. Oswald Chambers, My Utmost For His Highest (Discovery House Publishers, 1996), 20 September.

3. Corrie Ten Boom, https://libquotes.com/corrie-ten-boom/quote/lby7y9c .

4. Hudson Taylor, (Men of Faith), The autobiography of a man who brought the gospel to China (Bethany House Publishers, 1987), page 32.

5. Mark Stibbe, The Father You've Been Waiting For (Authentic Media Limited, 2005), page 13.

6. Dutch Sheets, Intercessory Prayer (Regal Books, 1996), page 139.

7. Henri J. M. Nouwen, The Return of the Prodigal Son: A Meditation on the Fathers, Brothers and Sons (New York: Doubleday, 1992), pages 66-67.

8. Niki Hardy, Breathe Again: How to Live Well When Life Falls Apart, (Revell, 2019), page 149.

9. Oswald Chambers, My Utmost For His Highest (Discovery House Publishers, 1996), 1 October.

10. Viktor E Frankl, Man's Search for Meaning: An introduction to Logotherapy (New York: Simon and Simon, 1959) page 82.

11. Mark Stibbe, Every day with the Father (Monarch Books, 2011), page 256.

12. Steve Thompson, You May All Prophesy (Morning Star Publications, 2000) page 16.

13. Philip Yancey, What's So Amazing About Grace, (Grand Rapids, MI: Zondervan, 1997) page 45.

14. S. Payne Best, The Venlo Incident (Hutchison & Co, 1950, p. 200), cited in Eric Metaxas: Pastor, Martyr, Prophet, Spy (Thomas Nelson, 2010), page. 528.

continued on next page

BIBLIOGRAPHY (CONTINUED)

15. C. S. Lewis, The Screwtape Letters (originally 1942; this edition: Harper Collins, 1996) page 5.

16. Steve Backlund, Igniting Hope, 2021, page 18.

17. Brennan Manning Live At Woodcrest on YouTube.

18. Steve Backlund, Igniting Hope, 2021, page 77.

19. Rick Warren, The Purpose Driven Life: What on earth am I here for (Zondervan, 2002), page 125.

20. Mother Teresa, compiled by Lucinda Vardey, Mother Teresa, A Simple Path (Rider, 1995), page 83.

21. Roy Hession, The Calvary Road, (CLC Ministries, 2002), page 31.

22. Adapted from the Daily Prayer Book from Ffald Y Brenin, pages 8-10.

Printed in Poland
by Amazon Fulfillment
Poland Sp. z o.o., Wrocław
04 August 2023

b017b5fe-85e6-4541-a049-ec5209d8e6f6R01